From the reviews . . .

"If you're looking for an under-the-pillow book to provide exotic dreams, here it is."
The Charlotte Observer

"(the guide) can direct you to more than 150 charming historic inns and guest houses with amenities and data on their surroundings."
Los Angeles Times

"The author vividly describes the history, architecture, grounds, services, decor, furnishings, meals and more for each, making it easy to choose between the varied offerings."
Dallas Morning News

"Want to get away from it all? . . . Maybe you'd prefer the quieter pleasures of *The Caribbean Bed & Breakfast Book*."
The Philadelphia Inquirer

"The more than 150 charming accommodations . . . were selected for their distinctive hospitality."
The Toledo Blade

"Looking for a different kind of Caribbean vacation? Take a look at Kathy Strong's *Caribbean Bed & Breakfast Book*."
Businesswoman

To our Brent David whose spirit of adventure makes traveling a special joy.

Special appreciation to Don Yeackle of Rice Travel, Kirk Stephens of American Airlines and Sam Dillon of Pink Fancy.

Copyright ©1985 by Fast & McMillan Publishers, Inc.
Second Printing, 1986.

All rights reserved. No part of this book may be reproduced without permission from the publisher, except by a reviewer who may quote brief passages in a review; nor may any part of this book be reproduced, stored in a retrieval system or transmitted in any form or by any means, electronic, mechanical, photocopying, recording or other, without permission from the publisher.

Library of Congress Cataloging in Publication Data
Strong, Kathy, 1950—
    The Caribbean Bed & Breakfast Book

    Includes index.
    1. Bed and breakfast accommodations—Caribbean Area—Directories.
I. Title.   II. Title: Caribbean Bed and Breakfast book.
TX910.C25577   1985   647'.94729   85-71254
ISBN 0-88742-054-0 (pbk.)

A few of the illustrations and photographs in this book have been reproduced with permission of the establishment or representative. Special credit and appreciation are given to the following: Hotel Frangipani, Bequia; Hotel Splendid, Haiti; El Canario Inn, Puerto Rico; Pasanggrahan Royal Guest House, St. Maarten; Grand Hotel Oloffson, Haiti; Mary's Boon, St. Maarten (Sontheimer-Hazlett Ltd.)

Cover design by Talmage Moose
Maps and photographs by Robert Strong
Typography by Raven Type.

Printed in the United States of America.
The East Woods Press
Fast & McMillan Publishers, Inc.
429 East Boulevard
Charlotte, N.C. 28203
(704) 334-0897

the Caribbean Bed & Breakfast Book

Kathy Strong

The East Woods Press
Charlotte, North Carolina

About The Author

Kathy Strong's *California Bed & Breakfast Book* has proven a popular guide to the more than 300 bed & breakfast establishments in that state. Now Ms. Strong has compiled a thorough and enticing guide to those intimate bed & breakfasts, charming historic inns and plantations and unique, small hostelries of the Caribbean. The owner and originator of a nine-guestroom inn in a turn-of-the-century house in California, Ms. Strong combines her personal knowledge of the industry with her enjoyment of visiting intimate, unique and hospitable lodgings such as those listed in this book.

Contents

Introduction 7

Part One:
Exploring the Caribbean
1. The Caribbean: A Tourist Destination 11
   When to Travel to the Caribbean 11
   How to Get There 12
   By Plane 12
   Cruises and Yachts 12

2. The Caribbean's Inns and Guest Houses: Variety, History and
   Hospitality 15
   Architecture and Period 15
   Size and Type 16
   Furnishings and Accessories 16
   Settings 17
   The Extras 17
   Bed & Breakfast and Other Meals 18

3. Reservations and Other Concerns 19
   Making Your Reservation 19
   Special Concerns 21
   Water 21
   Shared Baths 21
   Air Conditioning 21
   Medical Concerns 21
   Clothing 22

Part Two:
The Caribbean Bed & Breakfast Book Directory 25
4. How to Use the Caribbean Bed & Breakfast Book
   Directory 25
5. Turks and Caicos Islands 29
6. Cayman Islands 35
7. Jamaica 41
8. Haiti 53
9. Dominican Republic 67
10. Puerto Rico 71

11. U.S. Virgin Islands 87
    St. Thomas
    St. Croix
    St. John

12. British Virgin Islands 119
    Tortola
    Virgin Gorda

13. British Leeward Islands 133
    Antigua
    St. Kitts and Nevis
    Montserrat
    Anguilla

14. Dutch Windward Islands 161
    Saba
    St. Maarten
    St. Eustatius

15. French West Indies 175
    Martinique
    Guadeloupe
    St. Barthelemy
    St. Martin

16. British Windward Islands 195
    St. Vincent & The Grenadines
    Grenada
    St. Lucia
    Dominica

17. Barbados 225
18. Trinidad and Tobago 239
    Trinidad
    Tobago

19. Netherlands Antilles 251
    Aruba
    Curacao
    Bonaire

20. Reservation Representatives 263

Index 265

Introduction

The Caribbean offers exotic beauty, sun-inspired recreation and, perhaps above all, unparalleled diversity. In one relatively small geographic area lie several small groupings of islands referred to as the Caribbean, each group containing individual qualities that range from powdered-sugar beaches dissolving into crystal-clear turquoise waters to licorice and cotton candy-pink sands washed by deep-blue tides. The traveler will find old-world Danish villages and Las Vegas-type hotel and casino strips, as well as prim white colonial mansions and pastel-splashed Mediterranean bungalows clinging to mountain sides. These islands delight the traveler with volcanic peaks, waterfall-laden rain forests, jungles draped in purple bougainvillaea, hibiscus and flamboyant, as well as flat, arid cactus-sprouting desert and rolling hill pastures bathed in endless sunny days. But the diversity does not stop here.

The Caribbean is composed of many cultures, evolved from five centuries of rich history and reflected in the varied languages, clothing, arts, religion, customs, architecture and food. The traveler here can choose one or several of these multi-heritaged civilizations to experience, with the added promise that no more than 30 minutes away is a new world to explore.

For those adventurers who seek the genuine Caribbean—its people, its food, its way of life—there is no better way to visit these islands than by staying in those special, intimate spots that offer local hospitality and perhaps a slice of history. These are the inns and guest houses that are set apart from the plastic and neon, the spots that try hard not to hide their heritage or surroundings, but instead invite the guest to sample their hospitality with personal, friendly service and to enjoy an intimate and individual stay. These special inns accomplish these goals in many ways which often include unique furnishings such as island antiques and artwork, local foods prepared lovingly by the innkeeper, complimentary breakfasts and many extra services not found in larger hotels.

The traveler to the Caribbean may choose from stays in

historic inns such as a 15th-century great house surrounded by acres of tropical gardens, a gingerbread-decorated Victorian overlooking a story book village or a converted sugar warehouse with cobblestone walkways, to name just a few. Or the visitor wanting a special stay might opt for a gracious inn or guest house built of locally quarried lava stone or white coral, an ancestral home filled with antiques, a working banana plantation decorated in rattan and Casablanca-style fans or a simple, yet congenial, private residence with guestrooms.

Whether it be a historic inn, small hotel or guest house, these individual offerings, both simple and elaborate, are all the same in several important ways. They are for the traveler seeking authentic, unique stays often overlooked by travel agents and feature innkeepers willing to share their knowledge of the area and their special form of hospitality. So go ahead, picture yourself sipping rum while sitting on a fragrant veranda, diving into a sparkling mountain spring-fed pool, sleeping in a massive four-poster in a former governor's mansion, eating stuffed breadfruit and mangoes fresh from the innkeeper's garden, all in the slow, intimate pace afforded by these special bed & breakfast inns and guest houses of the Caribbean.

Part One:

Exploring the Caribbean

The Caribbean: A Tourist Destination

The Caribbean is surely one of the most popular travel destinations of the world, and the tourist offices there are eager to help the visitor discover its many attractions and beauty. But what exactly constitutes the Caribbean? In this publication and in many others presently dealing with this area, the Caribbean "tourist" islands are those generally referred to as the "West Indies." Therefore, terms such as "West Indian guest house" and "West Indian charm" are used almost interchangeably with "Caribbean." The West Indies are the islands that border the Caribbean Sea on both the east and north. These islands surrounded by warm, calm waters begin with Cuba and curve boomerang-style down to Trinidad and Tobago. The Netherlands Antilles of the Caribbean are a reasonable jump away off the coast of Venezuela.

When to Travel to the Caribbean

One of the most agreeable details of planning a trip to the Caribbean is not having to worry about *when* you go. The traveler can choose almost any time of the year and still experience the idyllic warm days, tepid waters and refreshing trade winds. Not many travel destinations can promise such a perfect situation with year-round temperatures averaging about 80 degrees!

Since climate is not a major criterion for selecting a trip time, you may want to consider instead the factors of crowds and costs. If you want to avoid crowds in the stores, restaurants and on transportation and have the innkeeper's keener attention as well as save up to 50 or 60 percent on room costs, then the Caribbean's generous off-season is for you. During this mid-April through mid-December period the traveler can be more spontaneous in general and possibly save additional money on

Caribbean Bed & Breakfast

flights and/or cruises. Not only does the off-season traveler save money and hassles, but he or she also has a better chance of getting reservations in the small inn or guest house of preference.

How to Get There

By Plane: Direct flights into the Caribbean from major United States and world cities go to all of the larger islands and many of the smaller ones; the number of flights is steadily increasing to meet the expanding tourist demands in this area. Flying to the Caribbean is certainly the fastest way to get anywhere there, even when connecting flights are necessary to more out-of-the-way spots. The traveler will discover that flying is more ideally suited to visiting a particular island or a group of islands, but can become more complicated when trying to island-hop extensively. Island-hopping is possible with the aid of local airliners or small boats that ferry between islands, but it is something to be attempted without a rigid timetable and with a spirit of adventure. The commuter airliners that travel between islands can be an experience in themselves. You may find them surprisingly prompt, but often very small and informal. In order to gain entry to each of the islands in the Caribbean you must have a return or on-going ticket from that same island. Thus too casual an itinerary won't work. Also, boat or ferry tickets often do not fulfill the requirement of an out-going ticket which may force you to purchase an airline ticket you do not need in order to satisfy entry requirements. These unused tickets may be returned for refund at a later date. Some of the major airlines offer savings during off-season from certain cities. This can change with each new schedule, so it is advisable to have your travel agent check on any special discounts and the restrictions that may accompany them. Also have your travel agent check into reasonable charter flights as well as stop-over flights on regularly scheduled airlines that may allow you to see two islands for the price of one. One other thing to remember about flying is that on some of the islands airport car rental agencies may close early. Be prepared to take a taxi and pick up your car in the morning if necessary.

Cruises and Yachts: Traveling via water has been a tradition in the Caribbean since the days of Columbus; the traveler may choose from a wide range of boating possiblities

A Tourist Destination

from "barefoot" sailing to opulent "Love Boat" cruising. The more adventurous traveler might select a Windjammer with a fully trained crew or charter a boat that matches his or her level of expertise, with or without aid of a crew.

Of course, the luxury cruise lines offer a vast array of choices, including smaller or larger vessels and a choice of as few as two island stops in a week to as many as a dozen in a two-week period. The number of ports offered will give you an idea of the thrust of your trip—whether it is more ship-oriented or geared toward in-port sightseeing. If the traveler wants to combine the experience of luxury cruising with a stay in the various Caribbean inns and guest houses, then a travel agent is the best bet for arranging a "land and sea" package. Note that cruising, like flying, to the Caribbean seems to be more competitive at present with an influx of more ships with more berths to fill; watch the ads carefully for discounts, especially when round-trip airfare is included.

Whether traveling by land or sea, do try to book your transportation as far ahead as possible; during on-season it is a must.

2

The Caribbean's Inns and Guest Houses: Variety, History and Hospitality

Just as the islands of the Caribbean vary so do each island's special offerings—its intimate inns and guest houses. Several centuries of colorful history since the first Europeans sailed into the Caribbean have yielded an abundance of preserved historical sites. The traveler here will also enjoy the contrasts: the modern among the very old and the creative and the unique combinations of the various cultural influences and periods.

Architecture and Period

The inns and guest houses of the Caribbean are often prime architectural examples of well preserved history, having been converted through the years to overnight lodging establishments as well as restaurants and mini-resorts. Many times this conversion has taken place with great sensitivity to the inn's original use, its history kept intact for current generations to enjoy and experience. This sometimes translates into less modern amenities: shared baths, lack of air conditioning, less sophisticated plumbing systems, etc., but many of these historically preserved establishments have successfully blended the modern amenities with the past without sacrificing too much of the structure's original identity. The inns and guest houses in this publication include both types, all worth the experience. You have the rare opportunity to stay overnight in a 150-year-old shipwright's home turned guest house, in a former Spanish consul's residence, in a 1780-built Danish townhouse, a 1650 plantation house, in cottages and suites built around the ruins of a 300-year-old sugar mill or in a 1788 dockyard storage warehouse constructed of giant ship beams and thick brick walls. Or you may want to stay in an English-style country house, in a romantic 1780 governor's mansion with twin gables, in a 200-year-old coffee plantation home, in a gingerbread-decked Victorian or on a working banana plantation situated on 16 tropical acres.

For those seeking more modern facilities, the Caribbean islands also offer many family-run guest houses and homes with traditional West Indian ambience. Choose from a two-story residential-style villa with upper and lower verandas, a newly built bungalow or a simple white stucco block home, to name just a few examples.

Size and Type

The inns and guest houses of the Caribbean range from simple to quite elaborate architecturally, and they also vary in size. However, they tend to be smaller and more intimate than comparable U.S. lodgings, and this accounts for the personal level of service they all offer. A small, family-run guest house may offer as few as 2 guestrooms, while some of the larger inns have nearly 100 units. But most of the establishments in this guide offer fewer than 20 rooms for guests, a quantity that lends itself well to the personal touches the inn-goer is seeking.

Furnishings and Accessories

The furnishings and accessories found in the guestrooms and common areas of these inns and guest houses range from design magazine showpieces to quite literally sparse; this variety is often reflected in the rates. Depending upon your traveling budget, needs and preferences, you can choose from a wide selection of interesting, exciting and culture-reflecting motifs. The two things that almost all these establishments have in common are uniqueness of decor, with every room and every inn a new experience, and an emphasis on comfort and cleanliness, even in the most modest.

Four-poster beds are also common in many of these intimate spots, especially those historical in nature; some are ornately hand-carved. Century-old French colonial beds, Victorian wicker, island and New England antiques, as well as handmade built-in furnishings grace many of these inns and set off interior

Inns and Guest Houses

architectural detailings such as thick, stone walls, cathedral-beamed ceilings, wood-paneling and mahogany spiraling staircases. The floor coverings range from hand-painted tiles to flagstone, as well as very modern wall-to-wall carpeting.

Colors and fabrics in these often spacious, airy rooms are frequently coordinated and can be in colorful island fabrics or even chintz. Tropical print wallcoverings are common, as well as use of local art and tapestries. Special guestroom detailing might include a hand-quilted bedspread or French doors or a balcony leading out to a flower- and fruit-filled courtyard.

Settings

These Caribbean islands encompass mountains, beaches, forests, deserts, urban centers and rolling countryside, all of which serve as settings for these intimate hostelries. The traveler will discover charming spots on tree-lined residential streets, in the heart of town, in the center of an operating cattle ranch, on a 700-acre estate that is also a bird and wildlife sanctuary, amid a rain-forested coffee plantation and on a multitude of ocean- and beach-embracing sites.

The Extras

Factors other than furnishings and accessories commonly go into making your stay at these inns and guest houses warm and hospitable. These extra services performed by the innkeepers, as well as additional facilities, set these spots apart from the average hotel or motel.

Most of the inns and guest houses herein provide their guests with a common area for reading, socializing or enjoying often complimentary afternoon tea or evening drinks. This common area might be a living room, drawing room, library or veranda, but is usually stocked with reading material and comfortable furniture and sometimes music, television or an honor bar. Outside, terraces offer spectacular views, sunbathing decks are designed for privacy, and patios and courtyards are the locales of meals and poolside lounging.

The recreation facilities go from a simple pool to mini-resort status. Among these inns and guest houses you will discover almost every kind of sport facilities available in the Caribbean. Many have their own tennis courts or offer courts nearby; almost all have a swimming pool whether it be a fresh water, salt water, mountain spring-fed, free-form or traditional pool. You'll find virtually every water sport offered on a loan or rental basis, including scuba and boating, with many spots possessing their own docks in case you arrive with a yacht of your own. Add to this horseback riding and breathtaking walks or hikes through tropical gardens, acreage and plantations.

Guests at these special inns and guest houses are often offered use of the kitchen for storing groceries or even cooking. The innkeepers assist in many ways from arranging sightseeing trips, providing free transportation to the beach, turning down the beds at night and even polishing guests' shoes at the end of the day. Staff members at one historical inn even dress in old-fashioned attire.

Bed & Breakfast and Other Meals

Most of the establishments in this guide may be referred to as bed & breakfasts, fitting into the North American and European definitions of the concept very well. That is, they offer a personalized stay combined with complimentary breakfast fare. Others here would fit into this category except that the breakfast is an additional charge, and a few inns offer no breakfast at all. However, most inns and guest houses herein do offer the morning meal in some form, and you'll be pleased at the variety you will find. The guest might enjoy breakfast on an outside veranda or private patio overlooking the ocean or surrounded by tropical gardens, in a gracious dining room with a table set in fine china or in a homey parlour with homebaked breads and fruit fresh from the garden.

Lunches and dinners, when offered, are sometimes included in the rate and very often you'll be glad. Indeed, some of these establishments are renowned for their cuisine, another personal statement by the innkeeper. Rates fluctuate from modest to gourmet as do the dishes offered. Very European in nature, some of the inns in this guide consist of a few rooms above a highly revered eating establishment. Many local dishes are found on the menus including a lot of fish and fresh vegetables, as well as some memorable French cuisine.

3

Reservations and Other Concerns
Making Your Reservation

Reserving a room in your special inn or guest house need not be difficult just because you are many miles away in a different part of the world. All of the listings in this guide provide a mailing address, phone number and, when available, toll-free phone numbers and/or a United States reservation representative. (Complete listings are in the back of this guide.) A reservation is a must in on-season and is a good idea in off-season because of the limited number of accommodations in many of these establishments. If you are to arrive on an island in the late evening, make every attempt to have a secured reservation in advance. There is nothing more frustrating than to begin searching for an overnight accommodation when you are tired and unfamiliar with your surroundings. This guide will give you an idea of distance from a particular establishment to the airport and/or public transportation when possible. Always book with a U.S. reservation agent, when provided, for speed and efficiency. If you are booking directly with the Caribbean innkeeper, allow for delayed mail each way and don't be surprised if a confirmation takes up to a month or more. Also, you may find that your innkeeper's response is less formal and more personal than you may be used to. If you choose to phone your selected inn for a reservation, you will find that the method of calling individual islands varies, even from area to area within the island itself. All of the islands in this guidebook provide phone service, and, by dialing 1 plus the area code 809 followed by the establishment's phone number, you may now dial directly to many of the islands. Some of the islands can be reached by dialing the international access code (011) plus the area codes 596, 590, 509 or 599 and then the local phone number. However, it is not possible to dial directly from some areas in

Caribbean Bed & Breakfast

the U.S. with an international access code; in those instances the operator will complete your call. Some of the establishments in this book (those displaying only a local phone number) require operator assistance.

To confirm a reservation you are usually required to send a deposit, normally the charge for the first night's stay or longer for on-season. When sending the deposit or asking for information, be sure to request the establishment's brochure, rate card, post card and even menus when applicable. Do not be afraid to ask for advice or assistance, such as special dinner reservations or car rental information, etc. This is one of the delightful benefits of staying in a small, intimate spot. Also, remember to notify your inn of your time of arrival, especially if it will be late, so that they will be prepared for your "homecoming."

When making your travel plans be sure to consult with your travel agent about time changes. The Caribbean islands in this guidebook have two separate time zones which equal Eastern Standard Time and Atlantic Standard Time, one hour later than Eastern Standard Time. However, only a few of the islands (Turks and Caicos, Cayman Islands, Jamaica and Haiti) employ Daylight Savings Time (May through late October). During those months, the islands on Eastern Standard Time become an hour earlier than EST, and the islands on Atlantic Standard Time are in harmony with Eastern Daylight Time.

One word about staying at these inns and guest houses with children. Many are ideally suited for family situations; others are not due to the intimacy of the inn or the fragile furnishings. Be sure to notify your innkeeper or the booking agent if reservations include a child to avoid any inconvenience or embarrassment. When meals are included in the stay, check to see if you must pay for a third person, fourth person, etc. to compensate for additional meals. Having traveled the Caribbean with a three-year-old child, I can attest that the Caribbean people are generally very loving toward small children and considerate of their needs, and your trip can be very rewarding family-style.

By the time you have gotten to know more about your selected inn and innkeeper and made your reservation, don't be surprised to be greeted like part of the family upon arrival. One innkeeper relates that it is difficult to charge her guests for the evening drinks they share because they are more like company than paying customers!

Reservations and Other Concerns

Special Concerns

Water: Most of the drinking water in the Caribbean has been chemically treated and is safe to drink, but it is different nonetheless. If you have an oversensitive system, you may want to try the water in small doses at first or request bottled water instead. Though surrounded by miles and miles of water these islands do have a fresh water scarcity problem; a conscientious traveler here will use water carefully. Not only is water at a premium, but hot water is very precious—in fact, sometimes not offered at all. But this deficiency is less important than you might think. When the constant temperature ranges from 75 to 95 degrees, a cool shower could be quite welcome!

Shared Baths: Those very familiar with guest house and bed & breakfast travel in the United States and Europe have this topic well in hand; they know it isn't a problem. But for those of you who are hesitant about sharing a bath, you may choose from many establishments in this guide that offer private facilities or you might like to be adventurous and give the bath "down-the-hall" a try. What you'll discover is that there is rarely any inconvenience involved with the usual small ratio of sharing, and that a high degree of privacy and concern is practiced by fellow travelers. If this factor gets in the way, you may lose the opportunity to experience some very charming little inns and guest houses as well as historic abodes that have chosen not to alter the plumbing for the sake of architectural preservation and authenticity.

Air Conditioning: A combination of ceiling fans and air conditioning is provided in these establishments; some offer both, others just one or the other. Because the refreshing trade winds often provide ample natural ventilation, you may find that a ceiling fan is quite adequate, if not preferable. Although air conditioning sounds like a bonus, many of the units in the Caribbean are noisy and distracting and can create an unhealthy temperature fluctuation from outside to inside.

Medical Concerns: Although sophisticated medical care is available in the larger cities of the Caribbean, it is wise to travel with a medical history and ample current medications if you are under a doctor's care. The most common traveler's maladies are sunburn and sunstroke. Common sense should keep these potential problems under control, but be sure to drink plenty of liquids, wear light but protective clothing and gradually increase exposure time in the sun.

Caribbean Bed & Breakfast

Clothing: Packing for the Caribbean means taking light and comfortable clothing suited to the warm, tropical weather. For your stay at an intimate inn or guest house, plan for informality and very casual dress, which is in tune with the relaxed lifestyle you'll experience there. For meals at nicer restaurants, plan on a casual elegance in clothing which can mean jackets for men; above all, pack as little as possible to make your trip all-around carefree. For the shared bath, take along a light robe and a make-up tote for carrying the essentials "down-the-hall." Every island in the Caribbean agrees that beach attire should not be worn in town or on city streets. You will see it done, but out of respect for the local people's feelings take along and wear appropriate beach cover-ups.

Part Two:

The Caribbean Bed & Breakfast Directory

4

How to Use the Caribbean Bed & Breakfast Directory

Caribbean Bed & Breakfast

The **Caribbean Bed & Breakfast Book** is divided into basic island groups with descriptions of the islands contained in each grouping. These descriptions will give you an overview of each island and help you select the type of Caribbean vacation you have in mind. Such information as the island's geography, points of interest, history, culture, currency, languages and other practical hints will be included there.

Individual Listings: Each inn or guest house listing in the Directory is followed by a block of information that will give you basic data about that particular establishment. This "key" information is designed to give you the opportunity to select or omit a particular spot based upon the following facts:

Type of establishment:
1. Inn—Inn or small hotel
2. Historic Inn—Inn with historical significance or restored vintage
3. Guest House—A West Indian term that can mean a private residence with guest quarters or a small hotel
4. Plantation—A former or present plantation

Number of Guestrooms: This is the total number of units available and may include cottages as well as suites.

Rates: Rates are based upon double occupancy in the following fashion: on-season/off-season. These rates are exclusive of room tax as well as service tax, which is common in the Caribbean. Also, be warned that rates are constantly changing and current rates should be obtained from any particular establishment before a reservation is secured. Be aware that one or more meals may be included in the rate (see "Meals" below) which could make an establishment classified as "expensive" comparably priced with one that is "moderate" but includes no meals, etc. The rate categories are broken down in the following manner:
1. Inexpensive—Less than $50
2. Moderate—$50–$95
3. Expensive—$95–$150
4. Deluxe—$150 and up

Meals: Whether or not meals are included in the rate is indicated by the following:
1. EP—European Plan or without meals included.
2. CP—Continental Plan or with breakfast included.

This will signal many of the "bed & breakfast" establishments included in this guide.

Bed & Breakfast Directory

3. MAP—Modified American Plan or breakfast and dinner included.
4. AP—American Plan or all meals included.

Credit Cards: Indicates what credit cards are accepted, if any: American Express (AE); MasterCard (MC); VISA (VI); Diners Club (DC).

Children: This refers to children under the age of 16 generally or as stated. Sometimes children are only allowed during off-season which will also be indicated.

Smoking: Most of the establishments in this guide do allow smoking in general, but a few have limitations or do not allow smoking at all.

The remainder of the description will give you an idea of the establishment's special character: its architecture, history, furnishings, recreational offerings, location, facilities, food, grounds, entertainment and perhaps a glimpse at its hospitable innkeepers. While some descriptions are longer than others, this does not necessarily mean that your stay will be correspondingly more or less memorable. It simply means that more information was available for some listings than for others. The "Also on the Island" listings at the end of each section include those establishments that I was unable to research thoroughly but seem worthy of inclusion and/or those establishments that provide alternative accommodations to an island's offerings, i.e. a resort listing on an island that mainly offers historic inns, etc. The **Caribbean Bed & Breakfast Book** strives to be a comprehensive guide to inns and guest houses in the Caribbean and suggests that you use the information provided as a basic guideline. It is highly recommended that you personally contact each establishment (or its agent) you are considering for more detailed information to help in your ultimate selection.

Whether your Caribbean dream vacation involves a 16th-century plantation, a family-run residence or a palatial governor's mansion with gourmet cuisine, you are sure to experience a unique stay underscored with hospitality and comfort.

Turks and Caicos Islands

Caribbean Bed & Breakfast

The Turks and Caicos Islands consist of eight main islands and numerous small cays (small islets formed chiefly of coral or sand) within a 166-square-mile area and are surrounded by a continuous coral reef. Situated halfway between Miami and Puerto Rico, these protected and private islands are home to about 8,000 residents including Turks and Caicos islanders, English, Americans, Canadians and Haitians. English is the principal language, but many islanders also speak Creole.

Arawak Indians may have first inhabited these islands. Their discovery by Europeans is generally attributed to Ponce de Leon in 1512, although Columbus may have landed on East Caicos around 1492. Today, Turks and Caicos stand as one of the few remaining Crown Colonies, headed by a Governor appointed by Queen Elizabeth II.

Known best for their 230 miles of pure white and amber beaches as well as clear, uncrowded waters, Turks and Caicos offer an array of water sports and private, sandy retreats. The reef-surrounded islands and their calm, unpolluted waters offer skin diving, scuba, sailing and excellent fishing.

Sightseeing expeditions will lead the visitor through rare tropical bird sanctuaries, national parks and plantation and mining ruins. The nights here come alive with small, informal gatherings rather than nightclub life, soft calypso sounds and intimate inns and restaurants serving fresh foods from the sea.

Continuous trade-wind breezes and constant sunshine make Turks and Caicos a year-round vacation destination with temperatures averaging 77 to 83 degrees. Dress is informal and light, although protection from the tropic sun is suggested, as well as a light wrap for breezy evenings. The electrical current is compatible with North American appliances.

Getting to the islands is easy from the United States with many regular, direct flights, as well as a local airline, Cayman Airways, that departs regularly from Miami to Turks and Caicos. Bahamasair and National Airways provide convenient island-hopping service after your arrival. Taxis are available at most of the airports, but car rentals are handled by local businesses only. If you do drive here, remember to drive on the left side of the road.

A passport, birth certificate or voter registration card is an acceptable form of identification; a nominal departure tax is payable upon leaving the islands. Each U.S. resident is eligible for $100 duty-free exemption, not including up to $10 a day in gifts mailed home. The U.S. dollar is legal tender, and full

Turks and Caicos Islands

international banking is available in the major towns. Credit card use is sparse in Turks and Caicos, but the visitor will find traveler's checks welcome almost everywhere.

To underscore the reclusive qualities of these islands, there is no television or daily newspaper, although a radio station and other publications offer contact with the outside world.

> For more detailed information on Turks and Caicos contact:
> Turks and Caicos Tourist Board
> 6403 N.W. 36th St., Ste. 103
> Miami, Florida 33166
> (305) 871-4207

Salt Raker Inn
P.O. Box 1
Grand Turk
Turks and Caicos
(809) 946-2260/946-2558

Historic inn; 9 units; Moderate EP year-round; AE,VI,MC; No children; Smoking ok.

Location: On beach; Near town; ½ mi. to airport.

Doug and Angela Gordon have owned and managed this former shipwright's home built in the 1800's for over 13 years, creating a haven for guests who want historical ambience, very personal service and modern conveniences. Angela relates that her goal in this homey and charming inn is "to resurrect the art of conversation," and the pair accomplish this among their varied and international collection of guests that keep returning.

The home itself, surrounded by trees and gardens, was built by a Bermudian family and features Bermuda-style architecture.

Caribbean Bed & Breakfast

It is in a prime location 25 steps from the beach and a pleasant stroll from town. The 150-year-old home contains the indoor dining room, the kitchen, the cozy guest library with lots of books and comfortable seating and three spacious guest rooms. The recently renovated interior features Haitian paintings and carvings, family photographs and original paintings on the walls.

The guest accommodations include rooms and suites. The suites feature living rooms, refrigerators and large screened verandas. All of the guestrooms, located in the house and nearby the house, offer private baths and comfortable furnishings, attractive bedspreads and draperies and pieces of the Gordons' own art collection. All accommodations boast wall-to-wall carpeting, some offer air conditioning and wet-bars, and each one has a homey feel.

The outdoor dining area, decorated with beachcombing mementos and floats, is surrounded by the inn's garden filled with bougainvillaea, hibiscus and flame trees. The inn serves all three meals, and the adjacent bar provides beachside drinks, including an impressive selection of German and U.S. beers. Like the inn itself, the food is homestyle with all homemade breads, simple but good food and plenty on the table. Dinners feature freshly caught seafood.

The usually crystal-clear sea water is just steps away from the inn and provides current-free, safe swimming. Five-hundred yards from the shore is the "Wall of Turk," where divers delight in viewing sponges, corals and wildlife to a depth of 5,000 feet. The Salt Raker, like many of the resorts in this area, offers special diver packages.

Admiral's Arms Inn
South Caicos
Turks and Caicos
(809) 946-3223

Historic inn; 15 units; Moderate EP year-round;
AE; Children ok; Smoking ok.

Location: Near sea; Near town; Near airport.

This 1890 plantation house surrounded by gardens sits primly on a cliff surveying the harbor and small fishing village below. The house was originally the family home of the Stubbs, who had the salt concession for the islands, and an old salt fort built by early Bermudian traders also graces the grounds. Old cannons that surround the property once guarded the salt fort from marauding pirates.

New owners, the Kollars, have been hard at work refurbishing the inn, now in business over 20 years, that is a favorite of divers. The old home is fronted by local stone and coral and an attractive archway entry. The house itself holds the dining room, kitchen, lounge and guestrooms, and more guestrooms are located in an addition. The furnishings are simple and pleasant, and the petite guest accommodations offer some nice sea views.

The harbor below the inn offers no swimming, but good diving spots are nearby. Guests at the inn may also enjoy the saltwater pool on the premises with terrace sunbathing. Special dive packages that include equipment use are available.

The restaurant and bar at the Admiral's Arms are popular and specialize in island favorites, especially freshly caught lobster.

Also on the Islands

Turks Head Inn
Grand Turk
Turks and Caicos
(809) 946-2466

This one-time governor's mansion was built by a Bermudian shipwright in the late 1860's. The two-story home with gingerbread-adorned verandas has an old-fashioned garden with graceful trees and pleasant terrace. The finely constructed home sits on over 200 feet of ocean frontage and offers a thatched patio bar and popular restaurant. The homey guestrooms are pleasant, and a few feature carved four-poster beds with canopies. The inn offers eight guestrooms and rents the Drift Wood cottage next door as well. Rates are moderate year-round.

Cayman Islands

LITTLE CAYMAN

CAYMAN BRAC

GRAND CAYMAN

N

Caribbean Bed & Breakfast

Approximately 500 miles south of Miami are the three islands that compose the Cayman Islands: Grand Cayman, Little Cayman and Cayman Brac. These islands formed of calcareous rock are quite flat, in contrast to many other islands of the Caribbean that tend to be mountainous or volcanic. Grand Cayman is the largest of the islands, measuring 7 miles by 28 miles.

The islands were discovered by chance in 1503 by Christopher Columbus during his fourth voyage into the West Indies. Eighteenth-century pirate activities are legendary in these islands; "Pirates Week," a colorful festival held in late October, commemorates this swashbuckling history. The early settlers in the Cayman Islands "farmed" turtles; hence the national symbol of these islands combines the two points of history with a peg leg "turtle-pirate."

Over half of the 18,000 population is of mixed origin and the language, although basically English, is a mixture as well. An American Southern drawl is combined with the English slur and a Scottish lilt, and "v's" are pronouced as "w's" in this interesting dialect. The Cayman Islands dollar is the legal tender.

Daily scheduled flights from the United States into Grand Cayman are available, with Cayman Airways providing inter-island air service. Proof of citizenship in the form of passport, birth certificate or voter registration is adequate, and a nominal departure tax is collected upon leaving the islands. Taxis with government-regulated rates as well as scheduled bus service and rental cars are available on the islands. Remember to drive on the left side of the road.

Summer or winter temperatures vary between 75 and 80 degrees in the Cayman Islands; light, casual and comfortable clothing is appropriate everywhere. North American electrical current enables you to use your small appliances such as dryers. The Cayman Islands are on Eastern Standard Time all year, so that during Daylight Savings Time in the Eastern U.S. the islands will be one hour earlier than Eastern Daylight Time.

Interested visitors can check out a giant turtle farm, Cayman Brac's limestone bluffs that are honeycombed with former pirate treasure caverns or Little Cayman's migratory bird sanctuary. But the endless sugar-colored beaches and the clear, coral- and fish-filled sea complete with underwater shipwrecks are the main tourist attractions on these islands. Divers here delight in the brilliantly painted reefs, the up to 200-foot

Cayman Islands

visibility, as well as the famous 1798 "Wreck of Ten Sails" at Gun Bay in Grand Cayman.

The nightlife of the islands is restricted to small clubs and intimate pubs and restaurants where food specialties include turtle steaks and turtle soup, of course.

For more detailed information on the Cayman Islands contact:
Cayman Islands Department of Tourism
420 Lexington Ave., Suite 2312
New York, New York 10170
(212) 682-5582
or
3440 Wilshire Blvd., Suite 1202
Los Angeles, CA 90010
(213) 738-1968

Erma Eldemire's Guest House
P.O. Box 482
Grand Cayman
Cayman Islands
British West Indies
(809) 949-5387

Guest house; 5 units; Inexpensive/Inexpensive EP; No credit cards; Children ok; Smoking ok.

Location: ½ mi. to beach; 1 mi. to town; 3 mi. to airport.

This charming little guest house with four guestrooms and one furnished apartment is owned and operated by Mrs. Erma Eldemire, the hospitable former owner of Casa Bertmar (now South Cove). Mrs. Eldemire and her late husband Wellesley helped to build the popular dive resort's reputation for friendliness, and Erma continues the tradition these days at her own little guest house just across the street.

The guest house is within walking distance of excellent dive sites and a short way from Seven Mile Beach. The Cove, a sugar-white beach with crystal-clear water, is just a stroll from the guest house.

Erma's casual and homey guest house has a pleasant guest lounge with fresh plants and rattan seating, but offers no

Caribbean Bed & Breakfast

restaurant. However, guests may have breakfast in the morning with some advance notice for an additional charge. Several restaurants are about 1/2 mile away.

The four guestrooms have ceiling fan cooling and pleasant but simple accommodations, along with private bathrooms. The one bedroom apartment can sleep six and boasts a fully equipped kitchen.

South Cove
P.O. Box 637
Grand Cayman
Cayman Islands
British West Indies
(809) 949-2514

Guest house; 22 units; Expensive AP year-round;
AE,MC,VI; Children ok; Smoking ok.

Location: 200 yds. to beach; 1 mi. to town; 2 mi. to airport.

This extended guest house is the former Casa Bertmar and, although now under the ownership of the somewhat larger Spanish Cove management, is still a small, friendly spot frequented by the diving crowd. The hotel, a few yards from the sea, has a good following that seeks its informality, camaraderie and proximity to excellent diving sites.

The good, local seafood specialties, with all three meals included in the rate, are another draw to the guest house. Guestrooms, located in a long, wooden structure are very basic, but do boast air conditioning.

The congenial spot offers an aquasport center, short boat trips, a lively bar and special "dive" packages for aficionados.

Tortuga Club
P.O. Box 496
Grand Cayman
Cayman Islands
British West Indies
(809) 947-7551

Cayman Islands

Inn; 14 units; Deluxe/Expensive MAP;
AE,MC,VI; Children ok; Smoking ok.

Location: On beach; 30 mi. to town; 25 mi. to airport.

This casual inn embraced by a coconut grove is a bit distant from town, but near some of the best scuba and snorkeling sites on the island. The inn has a peaceful, secluded quality that fits well with its informal, beach-life surroundings. Tortuga Club sits on a quiet stretch of reef-protected sea, and hammocks draped about invite relaxation.

The informal grounds include an open-air lobby and bar, a dining room of natural stone and wood beams and a stretch of one-story guestroom units that are nestled among the coconut trees and along the sand. Meals, with both breakfast and dinner included in the stay, are served in the sea-view dining room with local mahogany tables and chairs. Delicious specialties from the sea include conch pie, lobster and turtle steak. Tortuga, meaning turtle, is in fact a theme in the decor that features various turtle shell accents.

The guestrooms are fairly simple, but spacious and airy with glass doors that open onto terraces with views of the sea through palm-frond frames.

Besides the excellent scuba activities, the inn offers a tennis court, a scuba shop, a freshwater pool and transportation for stays of three days or longer with advance notice.

Montego Bay
Sandy Bay

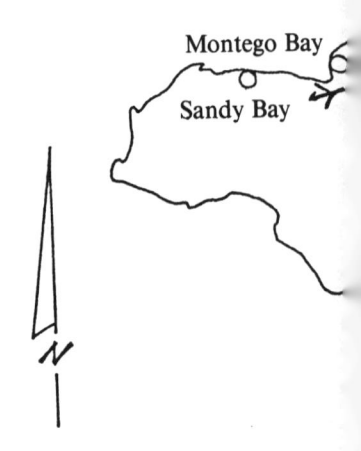

N

7

Jamaica

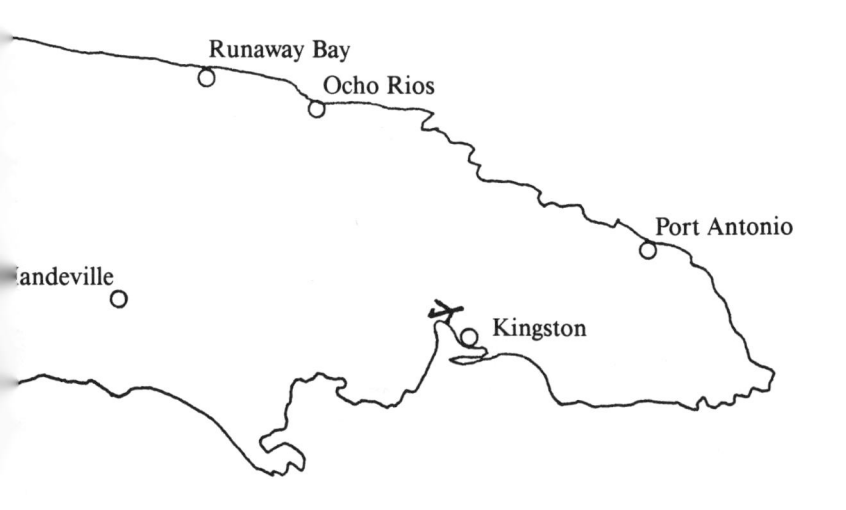

Caribbean Bed & Breakfast

Jamaica is the third largest of the Caribbean islands. Its 4,400 square miles consist of lush green scenery, sugar-white beaches met by clear blue water and a 7,400-foot mountain ridge. The 2.5 million inhabitants are mainly of African or Afro-European descent; the country's motto, "Out of Many, One People," refers to the island's many ancestors from China, India, Britain, Spain, Portugal, Germany and the Middle East.

Formerly a Crown Colony of Great Britain, Jamaica has been an independent country since 1962, with a government similar to that of Great Britain. Jamaica's official language is the Queen's English, but Jamaicans have adopted their own variations influenced by the many nationalities there as well as the days of slavery on the island. The Jamaican dollar (J$) must be used while in the country and cannot be taken in or out of Jamaica. The rate of exchange fluctuates constantly, so check for current rates. Currency receipts for all money exchanged must be presented when leaving the country. Most major credit cards are accepted in Jamaica, and most lodging establishments use standard American electrical voltage. A converter can be requested at most that do not. Jamaica time is equal to eastern U.S. time all year. When the East practices Daylight Saving Time, Jamaica does as well.

The visitor enters Jamaica from one of two international airports, most commonly at Montego Bay. U.S. citizens are required only to have proof of citizenship for entry and when leaving to pay a nominal departure tax. On the island there are many choices for getting around. Taxis, called contract carriages, have predetermined rates from area to area. Also, limousines, air-conditioned coaches and local buses connect towns. Kingston and Montego are linked by a train, the Jamaica Railway Service, which departs twice daily on an interesting 4 1/2-hour excursion. Rental cars and mopeds are plentiful, but remember to drive on the left. For speed, Jamaica offers an intra-island airplane service that connects the major resort areas.

Soft, balmy tropical breezes combine with year-round warm temperatures in Jamaica. Winter averages high-70 degree to mid-80 degree temperatures; summer goes up to 90 degrees with cooler temperatures in the Blue Mountains. Some brief daily showers are common between October and early November and May through early June.

Should you want to really experience Jamaican life, the Tourist Board offers a program called "Meet the People" that has operated since the sixties. This program introduces the visitor

Jamaica

to local residents with similar interests and hobbies, often resulting in an invitation to their homes.

Kingston with a population of 700,000 is the capital of Jamaica and the center of culture, industry, finance and government. As the most cosmopolitan city in the country, it contains a mixture of old and new structures with excellent dining and nightlife until dawn. Visitors here might explore the Devon House, a 19th-century mansion housing Jamaican crafts; Spanish Town, a colorful square surrounded by Georgian architecture; Port Royal, the former headquarters of Captain Morgan and his buccaneers; and the Hope Botanical Garden, famous for its orchid collection and Sunday afternoon band concerts.

Montego Bay, Jamaica's second largest city, dates back to 1494. Here the visitor will see great houses and plantations of the past or swim in the crystal-clear, mineral spring-fed water of Doctor's Cove Beach. An evening torch-lit canoe ride goes up the Great River, and a train ride goes through thick mountain forests to the Ipswich Coves with their eerie underworld limestone formations.

Ocho Rios was once a sleepy fishing village, but today is full of modern resorts. Open jitneys take visitors on tours to working plantations of banana, sugar cane, coconut and breadfruit. Runaway Caves is reached by a boat ride that goes 120 feet below the earth and a climb up Dunn's River Falls leads to cool pools. The visitor here will find Noel Coward's former home as well as Harmony Hall, a gingerbread-decked Victorian filled with up-and-coming artists' works.

Port Antonio whose twin harbors welcome cruise ships offers rafting expeditions, cascading falls, an ultra-marine blue lagoon and caves and caverns.

Negril has seven miles of white beach with crystalline water and all the activities that go with it. Mandeville and the south coast of Jamaica provide cool tropical mountains with spas, horseback riding, golf, bird sanctuaries, fascinating great houses and a true Lover's Leap.

For additional information on Jamaica contact:
Jamaica Tourist Board
866 Second Avenue, 10th floor
New York, New York 10017
(212) 688-7650
or

Caribbean Bed & Breakfast
>3440 Wilshire Blvd., Ste. 1207
>Los Angeles, CA 90010
>(213) 384-1123

Charela Inn
P.O. Box 33
Negril Beach
Jamaica
West Indies
(809) 957-4277

Inn; 14 units; Expensive-Del./Expensive MAP; AE,VI,MC; Quiet children ok; Smoking ok.

Location: On beach; 1½ mi. to town; 2 mi. to local airport.

 This beachfront hacienda is located about midway along beautiful Negril Beach, hidden behind coconut palms and surrounded by gardens rich in hibiscus, orchids and jasmine. The 1975-built inn has an elegant, Spanish villa feel with curved arches and a central fountain, yet because of its recent construction offers all the modern amenities. Owners Daniel and Sylvie Grizzle have operated the inn for the past five years and, along with a cheerful staff, have earned a reputation for ultra-personal service and delicious homemade cuisine.
 A lounge with bar in the main house is available to guests and is furnished in wicker with voile draperies and marble tile floors. Guestrooms in the house and in a new wing feature both suites and bedrooms, all with full private baths, wall-to-wall carpeting and either a balcony or a covered patio. Guest accommodations offer both air conditioning and ceiling fans and either queen size beds or two double beds. The attractively appointed guestrooms are decorated in a combination of tropical prints and colonial furnishings and, at this writing, are being refurbished with new drapes, bedspreads, carpets and mattresses. Charela's newest suites consist of one large bedroom with queen size bed, a small bedroom with two single beds and a full bathroom; all boast a lovely view of the sea.
 A new dining room built late in 1983 has open arches with hanging flower boxes, a flower garden and a central open-air fountain and views of the sea. The elegant setting with high-backed chairs, fine linens and candlelight makes for romantic

gourmet dinners that include five courses of French or Jamaican cuisine. A good selection of French wines is available to complement the special meals. A full English breakfast is served under umbrellas on the patio each morning, and lunches include salads, hamburgers and house specialties.

Scuba, snorkeling, boating and fishing are all available within walking distance of the Charela, and the staff at this friendly inn is always pleased to suggest or arrange any other activities.

Eaton Hall Great House
P.O. Box 112
Runaway Bay
Jamaica
West Indies
(809) 973-3503/973-3404

Historic inn; 36 units; Deluxe/Deluxe AP;
No credit cards; No children; Smoking ok.

Location: Near beach; 20 mi. to town; 50 mi. to airport.

This restored plantation great house became a hotel in 1973 when over $2 million was invested in its meticulous renovation and the addition of bedroom wings that carry out the same 18th-century feel. The pace of the elegant resort is quiet due to the absence of children, ample facilities for a handful of guests and gracious interiors and service. As a "mini" Club Med type of resort, Eaton Hall includes all meals, wine, beer and cocktails, entertainment and gratuities in what first looks like a steep tab. All considered, the inn is comparably priced with other quality establishments.

The gracious white mansion with wrought-iron-scrolled trim and French doors is located in a residential neighborhood with spectacular views of the ocean. The grassy grounds include two swimming pools, a tennis court and a private beach below with snorkeling equipment available.

In the lobby, traditional high-back chairs with handsome print coverings encircle an inviting fireplace with mahogany mantel. A wooden-beamed ceiling, polished Jamaican hardwood floors and mahogany antiques and reproductions all add to the

Caribbean Bed & Breakfast

elegant feel of another era. Guestrooms at Eaton Hall are located in the great house as well as in attached wings; all are furnished in attractive mahogany reproductions reminiscent of the 18th century and feature private baths, telephones, attractive fabrics, Oriental rugs and paintings. Some of the units open onto the arched portico of the mansion, and many of the units boast private balconies that face the ocean.

The Jamaican and French cuisine is served graciously in the Regency-style dining room or on the pool terrace. The formal dining room with high-backed chairs serves elegant meals with wine included. The shady dining terrace that adjoins overlooks a large swimming pool and offers dramatic ocean views with a background serenade of waves pounding on the rocks below.

This relaxing resort gets a little more active during the week when a traditional barbecue with combo entertainment is held. Otherwise, a piano bar is the night's main activity besides a game of backgammon, checkers or chess or a quiet stroll through the impressive gardens.

Hotel Astra
P.O. Box 60
62 Ward Avenue
Mandeville
Jamaica
West Indies
(809) 962-3265

Inn; 22 units; Inexpensive-Mod. EP year-round;
Credit cards accepted; Children ok; Smoking ok.

Location: 1 mi. to town; 40 mi. to beach; 70 mi. to airport.

Owner and manager Diana McIntyre-Pike gives a very personal touch to her family's home-turned-inn. The main building of the inn was a nursing home for about five years, and in 1970 the McIntyres converted it to a hotel, adding more rooms, a bar, swimming pool and sauna. Diana takes pride in the family abode and its surroundings in a non-resort area just outside Mandeville, which she claims is the cleanest town in Jamaica.

The spacious grounds with interesting flowers and plants have a quiet, countryside feel. A guest lounge with red

Jamaica

carpeting has wicker decor, and the adjoining Zodiac Room restaurant decorated in mirrors serves excellent meals made from family recipes. Breakfast, lunch and dinner are available to guests buffet style or with table service. A popular event is the Friday night barbecue held around the pool which provides some entertainment and attracts locals as well as visitors. Another restaurant is located near the swimming pool, and the Revival Room of the Astra serves snacks and an assortment of drinks to revive its guests, including a homemade liqueur.

Each of the 20 guestrooms and 2 suites at Hotel Astra is decorated individually, but all contain private baths, telephones and radios. Guestrooms are located in the main house and in adjoining wings at this most hospitable inn.

Terra Nova Hotel
17 Waterloo Road
Kingston 10
Jamaica
West Indies
(809) 926-2211

Inn; 35 units; Moderate EP year-round;
Credit cards accepted; Children ok; Smoking ok.

Location: Near town; 14 mi. to beach; 17 mi. to airport.

This white colonial mansion with broad arches, graceful balustrades and romantic night-time lighting sits in a quiet, secluded residential section close to town. The mansion was built as an elegant residence in 1921 and converted to a small hotel in 1959. In October of 1984 the entire inn on five acres of well-manicured grounds was refurbished and stands as one of the most intimate and charming small hostelries on the island.

Terra Nova offers guests an attractive lounge with carefully selected period furnishings and a crystal chandelier. Several meeting rooms with similar decor are available for private groups, making the hotel a popular choice for business travelers who enjoy hotel-type services in more intimate surroundings. The El Dorado dining room of the inn boasts

Caribbean Bed & Breakfast

attractive deep coral walls, Hepplewhite chairs, mahogany tables set in fine linens and arched windows overlooking the garden. Both lunches and dinners are served in these elegant surroundings. Breakfast is served on the outside terrace with lovely views of town, greenery and the mountains. The inn offers light flute and guitar music twice weekly.

The guestrooms at Terra Nova contain all the modern amenities, including central air conditioning, telephone, television and bath. The contemporarily furnished rooms are color-coordinated in shades of gray, white and peach and from the balconies you can see the Blue Mountains in the distance.

Nestled behind the villa, among the shade trees, brilliant poinsettias and well-tended gardens, is the swimming pool. Golf, water sports and other recreation are available nearby, and Kingston's convention center and main shopping are just a few minutes away. The congenial owner and manager of Terra Nova is Michael Bryne.

Tryall Golf and Beach Club
Sandy Bay Post Office
Hanover Parish
Jamaica
West Indies
(809) 952-5110/952-5111
Rep: Tryall Golf and Beach Club, Va.

Plantation; 44 units; Deluxe/Deluxe MAP;
VI,AE,MC; Children ok; Smoking ok.

Location: On beach; 12 mi. to town; 15 mi. to airport.

This tastefully restored and decorated great house at the core of this resort was built in 1834 and stood in the heart of a rich 2,200-acre sugar plantation. The former plantation, now rich in bougainvillaea, towering palms and flowering trees, has been transformed into a gracious historic inn with full resort offerings and a spectacular location on a sugar-white curve of beach. All of this luxury that includes lodging, breakfast and dinner costs a bit more, but is one of the better bargains in the

Jamaica

hotel's short off-season periods of November 1 through December 14 and April 15 through May 15. The hotel itself is closed May 15 through November 1, although other resort offerings remain open year-round. Off-season great house guests sometimes get a bonus of unlimited greens fees and tennis court time.

The Tryall Great House, surrounded by immaculately manicured lawns and flowering plants, has a country manor feel on the inside created by designer color schemes, overstuffed furnishings in coordinated chintz fabrics, French doors and small-paned windows with views of the sea and plantation countryside. This decor combines both the tropical and elegant with the use of fresh, white walls, striking colors and nice touches such as fresh flowers and potted palms.

Guests at Tryall enjoy a sitting room and lounge in the great house as well as the equally intimate and gracious dining room with beamed ceilings, tropical planters, pink and coral linens, comfortable seating and French doors that lead to the terrace with breathtaking views of the sea. Gourmet dinners include entrees of lemon veal, lamb chops with mint sauce, Jamaican seafood platter and medallions of beef. Lunch may be enjoyed by the sea at the Beach Cafe, and a full breakfast with extensive selections is served in the dining room or al fresco on the inspiring terrace. After 6:30 p.m. gentlemen generally wear sports jackets with or without ties and ladies wear cocktail attire. Music and dancing are evening pastimes at the great house.

The 44 guestrooms of the great house are all individually decorated and air conditioned and offer various views of the dramatic scenery. All of the guest accommodations have private baths, telephone, patio or balcony and attractively coordinated decor with an airy, tropical feel. The spacious rooms mostly offer sitting areas, fresh white walls, framed prints and tasteful and comfortable furnishings.

For recreation there are six all-weather tennis courts (two lighted for night use), an excellent diving and sailing ocean with beach, a large swimming pool with swim-up bar directly in back of the great house and the pride of the establishment; a championship 18-hole, 6,800-yard golf course. In fact, Tryall uses a water wheel as its logo because of the plantation's original water wheel that has been restored and now stands as the backdrop to the course's sixth tee. The restored 200-year-old wheel that once supplied the power for the mill now provides water for the green, flowing fairways of the golf club.

Caribbean Bed & Breakfast

Tryall Golf and Beach Club is overseen by expert general manager Josef Berger.

Note:
As previously mentioned, the hotel great house is closed May 15 through November 1, but the Tryall also offers luxurious villas in secluded areas around the grounds that are available year-round. These villas offer private pools and full staffs.

Also on the Island

De Montevin Lodge Hotel
21 Fort George Street
P.O. Box 85
Port Antonio
Jamaica
West Indies
(809) 993-2604

This late-1800's Victorian with detailed trim is family run and offers hospitality and reasonable rates near town. The 15 guestrooms are simply furnished but tidy and include both private bath and shared bath offerings. The budget-minded rates include breakfast. A comfortable lounge with television and a small bar is available for guests as well as a porch and side patio. Good Jamaican dinners are offered.

Orchid Hill Guest House
98 Main Street
P.O. Box 366
Ocho Rios
Jamaica
West Indies
(809) 974-2926

Mrs. Jean Shell owns and runs the Orchid Hill, a pleasant two-story guest house with a relaxed, family feel. The convenient lodging is within walking distance of the beach, the bus and town, and the informal grounds host local birds and animals. Inside, the villa offers ten guestrooms, all but two

Jamaica

with private baths, and a spacious lounge and bar. The reasonable rates attract many guests on moderate travel budgets.

Richmond Hill Inn
P.O. Box 362
Montego Bay
Jamaica
West Indies
(809) 952-3859/952-5432

This 18th-century great house was once the winter home of the Dewars of the Dewars Whiskey fame. The historic inn owned and managed by Mrs. Stefanie Chin has been in operation for over 20 years, offering a homey atmosphere in its scenic location overlooking the city of Montego Bay and the coastline. Perhaps better known as a top-rated restaurant serving international cuisine, the inn also offers 20 guestrooms around the well-kept grounds. Guest accommodations boast some antique furnishings and private baths, as well as television and radio. Children, smoking and credit cards are allowed, and rates double occupancy are in the moderate range. A swimming pool with statuary invites guests; a beach is one mile away.

8

Haiti

Caribbean Bed & Breakfast

Haiti is located in the western portion of the island of Hispaniola, the second largest of all the Caribbean islands, and occupies 10,714 square miles. Haiti shares a border with its friendly neighbor, the Dominican Republic. The two countries are surrounded by the sparkling Caribbean Sea, and the topography includes dramatic mountains with mahogany and pine forests. Haiti's landscape also includes wide-open plains, tropical vegetation and broad beaches of either white or unusual black sands. The average temperature of 79 to 90 degrees, with slightly cooler mountain temperatures, allows for a tropical feel year-round.

Haiti is a blend of cultures and contrasts, of a heritage steeped in both African and French influences. It offers charming French homes as well as thatched huts, Roman Catholicism as well as voodoo and treats the visitor with its own art and bright, native colors everywhere.

Haiti became the first black republic in the world in 1804. Its over six million population is reflected in the crowded yet colorful city areas. Haiti also retains the lowest per capita income level in the Western Hemisphere, but according to a recent United Nations survey, has one of the lowest crime rates in the world. French is the official language, but Creole is spoken everywhere. Both English and Spanish are spoken widely as well. The currency is the "gourde." Haiti is on Eastern Standard Time all year, which makes it one hour earlier during Eastern Daylight Time.

Regularly scheduled airliners from North America travel to Haiti, and some of the major cruise lines include Haiti as a port. Entry requirements for U.S. and Canadian citizens are proof of citizenship (passport, birth certificate or voter's registration); a departure tax is collected.

Major car rental companies are represented on the island and many of the roads are good. However, remember that most gas stations close at night and also watch carefully for animals in the road. Reasonable taxis with government-controlled rates as well as tour cars that are rented with driver by the hour, day or half-day are available. Be sure to negotiate a fixed price in advance when hiring a car with driver. Public cars are signaled by red ribbons. Camionette buses and "tap-taps" also are good ways to get around the island if you are adventurous. Tap-taps are the way most Haitians travel; they look like moving "art galleries," brightly hand-painted with pictures and Creole sayings.

Haiti

Haiti's art and culture is its personal and unique draw for the tourist. The brilliant colors and natural, primitive paintings are an integral part of Haiti and many of its artists, both renowned and unknown, hail from Haiti's "Centre d 'Art." The mysterious ritual, music and dance of the African voodoo is actually a spiritual, religious practice of the Haitians, and it offers a fascinating glimpse of Africa to the visitors who attend one of these ceremonies.

Port-au-Prince, the capital of Haiti, is decorated in 19th-century gingerbread structures, created by Haitian architects who visited Paris. One preserved example now open to the public is the Defly Mansion. A colorful downtown market, The Iron Market, is held in Port-au-Prince and native foods, art and crafts can be purchased at bartered prices. The Cathedral of St. Trinity, filled with native paintings by Haitian masters, is worth visiting as is the Museum of Haitian Art, open 8 a.m. to 12 p.m. weekdays.

The nightlife is plentiful with an emphasis on the island's legalized gambling structure. Full casinos operate in Port-au-Prince and nearby Petionville, and slot machines may be found in many of the hotels.

A spectacular mountain ride takes the visitor to the New Orleans-looking town of Cap-Haitian, 3,000 feet up with views of the Caribbean Sea from all angles. A few miles south of town are the ruins of Sans Souci Palace, in its day a rival of Versailles in elegance. Towering over Sans Souci is the amazing 100,000-square-foot Citadelle, often called the eighth wonder of the world. Built in 1804 as a fortress "in the sky," it affords breathtaking views and can be reached by jeep or horseback.

The south shore of Haiti is characterized by the 17th-century French colonial homes in the slow-paced coffee town of Jacmel. Two hours from here on horseback is a spectacular mountain pool called Bassin Bleu.

The French cuisine of Haiti is considered among the best in the Caribbean and has its touch of local spice. From simple cafes to gourmet, master-chef-presented feasts, the international fare is worth sampling. Creole specialties include grilot (grilled pork with hot sauce), cashew chicken, homemade "mamba" peanut butter and strong Haitian coffee.

For additional information on Haiti contact:

Caribbean Bed & Breakfast

Haiti National Office of Tourism
1270 Avenue of the Americas
New York, New York 10020
(212) 757-3517

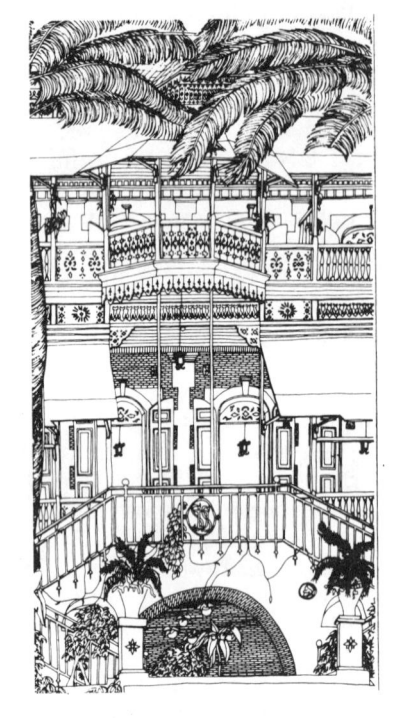

Grand Hotel Oloffson
P.O. Box 1720
Port-au-Prince
Haiti
West Indies
(011-509) 2-0139/2-5810
Rep: American International

Historic inn; 22 units; Moderate-Exp. CP year-round; VI,MC,AE,DC; Children ok; Smoking ok.

Location: Residential; 5 mi. to town; 50 mi. to airport.

This 1880-built mansion draped in gingerbread, turrets, ornately scrolled balconies and cupolas is a thriving legend among hotels, an overstatement of 19th-century adornment with an abundance of character and personality. It was built as a home for the first Haitian president, President "Sam," and became a hotel in 1935 after a stint as a military hospital. The hotel has long attracted celebrities: writers, artists, politicians,

Haiti

actors and society; after ex-Connecticut resident Al Seitz bought the hotel in 1960, its growing clientele included the famous and the ordinary, all gathered at the Oloffson to soak in the inspiring and relaxing ambience. In fact, Al Seitz and the Oloffson became the central figures in the movie *The Comedians*. Al passed away three years ago, but his warm and charming wife, Sue, carries on the tradition of the Grand Hotel.

A dramatic circular driveway through informal bougainvillaea gardens leads to the front of the house and its double staircases that connect with one of the two wide and fragile verandas filled with peacock wicker chairs for lounging and sipping. The lobby area is reached through French doors and is decorated, like the rest of the house, in a conglomerate of wicker, calico prints, wall hangings, peacock chairs, antiques, a bar, lots of paintings, an old piano, ceiling fans, bamboo and "whatever." Mrs. Seitz has added some newer, refined touches, but the overall effect is still a hodgepodge that seems to fit the one-of-a-kind exterior jumble.

The guestrooms number 22 in all and are located in the old mansion upstairs or in cottages scattered around the pretty garden. The guestrooms in the mansion are the most interesting; they come in all shapes and sizes with very personalized decor. Suites, named after celebrities who have stayed at the inn, include the turret-enclosed "John Gielgud" with wrap-around balcony, the "Anne Bancroft" or the "Marlon Brando" cottage. All of the rooms feature air conditioning and private baths and are furnished in a combination of antiques, wicker, bright handwoven Haitian cottons, original local art and fresh flowers. Books are everywhere, from best sellers to classics--some presumably supplied directly from the author. Balconies and terraces are found in many of the units, and four-poster beds grace four guest accommodations.

This bed & breakfast serves a full American fare, featuring French toast, on the veranda or even in bed. Lunch is a mixture of French, creole and American offerings and is served on the same relaxing veranda or poolside. Dinners feature five courses of delicious cuisine selected daily and not repeated for at least ten days. The evening feast with two daily specials is offered on the veranda or in the inn's mountainside restaurant. The special drink of the house is the rum punch which flows endlessly.

The rambling Victorian offers its guests a swimming pool, a boutique with historical memorabilia, backgammon by the pool and

Caribbean Bed & Breakfast

a small orchestra every night. It is very close to major art galleries and museums. The Grand Hotel Oloffson also rents a stone villa on a private beachfront. The house, which accommodates up to six people, is fully equipped and staffed by three housemen.

Hotel Mont Joli
P.O. Box 12
Cap Haitien
Haiti
West Indies
(011-509) 3-20300
Rep: Robert Reid Associates

Inn; 45 units; Moderate MAP year-round; AE,MC,VI,DC; Children ok; Smoking ok.

Location: Residential; 1½ mi. to beach; 3 mi. to airport.

This former private home offers spectacular views in its tranquil hilltop setting above the town and bay. Surrounded by lush tropical greenery and flowers, the white Haitian structure with open verandas is immaculately maintained. The family home of Walter and Marie Bussenius, the main building has grown over the years to first a 17-room inn, then 32 rooms and now 45 tasteful accommodations. The Busseniuses are the gracious owners and innkeepers of the family abode and keep the personal service and hospitality intact despite the inn's increased size.

There is a lovely inner garden at the Mont Joli, but all of the buildings are on a promontory with ocean and mountain views; an inviting kidney-shaped swimming pool is tucked within the foliage. The entry of the small hotel is a wide, open patio with tropical surroundings, and guests may also relax in one of five inter-connecting lounges with mahogany paneling and attractive Haitian art and fabrics. Good creole, French and American specialties are served on the dining terrace by the pool, and a local combo provides nightly music. Both breakfast and dinner are included in the stay here, and lunch is offered a la carte. Two bars serve drinks.

The guestrooms at the Mont Joli are located in the main house, in a newer wing and in the most recent addition of

Haiti

cottages that are nestled in the rear gardens. All of the guestrooms are air conditioned and offer private baths, radios, telephones and pleasant and attractive furnishings. Many of the guest accommodations boast terraces offering romantic hilltop views, and the older rooms in the home are furnished charmingly in antiques, including turn-of-the-century French colonial beds and mahogany chests and chairs.

The family provides free transportation to the beach a short hop away and will assist in your local sightseeing, providing a useful visitor's guide and map that they have put together for their guests.

Hotel Roi Christophe
P.O. Box 34
Cap Haitien
Haiti
West Indies
(011-509) 3-20414
Rep: Robert Reid Associates

Historic inn; 20 units; Moderate MAP year-round;
AE,VI,DC,MC; Children ok; Smoking ok.

Location: In town; 1 mi. to beach; 3 mi. to airport.

Situated in the heart of Cap Haitien, but entwined in beautiful tropical greenery and gardens, is this 1724 former governor's palace. The white stucco mansion with graceful arched windows, columns and overflowing vines is now owned by the Bussenius family who extend the same hospitality and top service to the Roi Christophe as they are known for at the Mont Joli.

The two-story home with peaceful, mature gardens has a large swimming pool, a plantation-type front veranda and mini-casino. The mansion boasts arched doorways, interior courtyards and beamed ceilings. The lounge is decorated elegantly in period antiques and chandeliers and an abundance of leafy, potted plants.

The guestrooms at the historic inn once used by General Leclerc and Pauline Bonaparte are all unique; some are more elegant than others. The most charming rooms are decorated in

Caribbean Bed & Breakfast

antiques and have terraces, but all of the rooms are comfortable, and boast private baths.

The dining room of the inn has a fine reputation for Haitian and French specialties. The high-vaulted ceilings and thick walls of the 18th-century room add an intimate elegance to the meals and superb service, and both breakfast and dinner are included in the stay at this charming inn. A poolside bar refreshes sunbathers, and the inn offers a private stretch of beach just one mile away.

Le Picardie
P.O. Box 15099
Petionville
Haiti
West Indies
(011-509) 7-1822
Rep: Jane Condon Corporation

Inn; 11 units; Moderate/Moderate MAP;
AE,VI; Children ok; Smoking ok.

Location: 2 mi. to town; 40 mi. to beach; 10 mi. to airport.

This 1940-built private home with distinctive, curved portico and local stonework is better known as a gourmet restaurant. Nestled high in the green hills of this residential area, the Picardie enjoys impressive views of Port-au-Prince, the sea and the mountains. Its four acres of lush vegetation include a modest pool and six cottages that offer guest accommodations in addition to the five guestrooms within the main house.

Mrs. Manousso is the owner and manager of the 25-year-old business. Guests are treated to comfortable and modest interiors which include a central lounge. The guestrooms and cottages are decorated in French provincial-style furnishings that are rather basic, but have telephones, private baths and some balconies and terraces. The cottages boast kitchenettes with refrigerators.

The exquisite French-creole cuisine of Le Picardie is served along with views of the city and sea. Specialties such as Kenscoff snails, onion soup, charcoal lobster flambe and homemade ice cream are offered, and a full American breakfast is also a part of the stay here. Lunch is offered al la carte.

Haiti

Prince Hotel
P.O. Box 2151
Port-au-Prince
Haiti
West Indies
(011-509) 2-2765/5-2764
Rep: Robert Reid Associates

Inn; 33 units; Inexpensive-Mod./Inexpensive-Mod. CP; AE,VI,DC; Children ok; Smoking ok.

Location: In town; 15 mi. to beach; 5 mi. to airport.

This mansion-turned-inn is a few minutes from downtown Port-au-Prince in a hilly residential area that grants views of the town and harbor. The charming, French colonial-style inn was adapted to its present use by owner Raymond Chancy and has been a quiet retreat for guests for the last 11 years or so.

Imported antiques can be found in the lounge and in some of the guestrooms of the inn, adding a European ambience. Guestrooms all boast private baths, telephones and air conditioning. Mahogany furnishings, some antiques, Haitian paintings and prints, armoires, dressing tables and old-fashioned wallcoverings can be found in many of the rooms; some are more ornate than others. A few of the accommodations have terraces with romantic views.

The dining room of the Prince specializes in creole dishes. The "Colonial" boasts high-back chairs, bright Haitian paintings and antique memorabilia mounted on the walls, making for pleasant dining surroundings. All three meals are offered at the inn, and the continental plan includes a generous breakfast.

Guests at the Prince mingle at the pool with a pretty view of the terrace or at the adjoining "Jungle Bar" in this informal and friendly spot.

Hotel Splendid
P.O. Box 1214
Port-au-Prince
Haiti
West Indies
(011-509) 1-50116
Rep: Reservations Systems Incorporated

Caribbean Bed & Breakfast

Hotel Splendid

Historic inn; 40 units; Moderate EP year-round; AE,VI,MC; Children ok; Smoking ok.

Location: 1 mi. to town; 25 mi. to beach; 4 mi. to airport.

This turn-of-the-century, palatial mansion was built by a Danish entrepreneur to accommodate his elegant lifestyle. The Mediterranean- and Victorian-blended architecture captures an old-world charm that is matched by the excellent, personal service and modern comforts that have been tastefully added to the 1905-built structure. The elaborate white mansion with red awnings and trim and gingerbreaded balustrades is under the directorship of owner Wolfgang Wagner, who with manager Marie Pia Alexis, keeps things running smoothly and professionally.

The inn is one of the country's oldest hostelries and is within walking distance of the cutural centers of the city. Although convenient to town, Splendid is located in a tranquil residential area in the center of the Gingerbread district of Port-au-Prince and surrounded by lush tropical gardens that create an oasis of old-fashioned elegance.

Guests are greeted by a black- and white-tiled veranda lined in handmade Haitian rockers and potted ferns. The gracious entry with polished wooden floors leads to a sweeping central staircase with ornately carved bannisters and overhead ceiling medallion; the inn's adjoining parlor combines tasteful antiques with tropical touches.

Hotel Splendid offers guests two dining rooms, one the well-respected La Bougainvillee Restaurant serving gourmet French cuisine with live classical music every night.

Guestrooms at Splendid are located in the mansion as well as in newer buildings that give the feeling of a courtyard around the pool. The decor is more contemporary than the public rooms of the house, but not less attractive. The rooms, all with private baths, radios, air conditioning and telephones, boast freshly painted white walls with lively Haitian art, coordinating bedspreads and draperies, leafy plants and terraces, balconies or patios. The most charming units are those upstairs in the mansion itself.

A swimming pool is nestled in the inner court of the hotel and sports a wooden bridge that stretches from side to side. The pool terrace is an ideal spot for breakfast or an afternoon of lounging.

Villa Creole
P.O. Box 126
Port-au-Prince
Haiti
West Indies
(011-509) 7-1570/7-1571
Rep: International Travel & Resorts

Inn; 70 units; Moderate-Exp./Moderate CP;
AE,MC,VI; Children ok; Smoking ok.

Location: Near town; 15 mi. to beach; 4 mi. to airport.

This hilltop hotel was Dr. Assad's private mansion in the 40's and early 50's. The main house now contains the reception area, lobby, bar, lounge and a few of the guestrooms of the expanded inn that includes several buildings added gradually over the years. The restored white stucco mansion with graceful arches, sweeping drive and brick walks retains a quiet, intimate elegance despite its increased offerings.

Caribbean Bed & Breakfast

Guestrooms at the Villa Creole vary, each one furnished uniquely in walnut, mahogany or carved "taverneau" (golden oak) pieces. The spacious rooms have thick Haitian cotton bedspreads, private baths, television, radio, telephones and some balconies. Color themes vary from room to room, but most of the guest accommodations feature impressive Haitian artwork. In fact, the villa boasts one of the country's most impressive Haitian art collections.

The Villa Belle Restaurant with bar has spacious high ceilings and rattan furnishings and overlooks the garden. Charcoaled specialties are offered at the Monday night barbecue, and on Thursdays a creole buffet serves lobster, red snapper, conch and shrimp. Haitian troubadours blend merengue beats nightly, and music for dancing is provided on Mondays and Thursdays.

A large inviting pool is umbrella shaped and surrounded by gardens and shade trees. A leisurely day at the Villa Creole begins with a full American-style breakfast under the picturesque almond tree here. The inn also has two all-weather tennis courts for its pampered guests.

Also on the Island

Le Manoir Alexandre
P.O. Box 916
Jacmel
Haiti
West Indies
ph: 8-2711

This former private home filled with family pieces and tasteful decor offers an intimate six guestrooms in varying shapes and sizes. The attractive, tiered home overlooks the bay and its own impressive gardens with giant palms. Guests dine on creole and French cuisine served family-style on the top-floor veranda with splendid views of the sea and mountains in the distance. Most of the guestrooms, which are modestly furnished but immaculate, share baths. This budget choice offers inexpensive to moderate rates on the MAP.

Haiti

Santos Guest House
20 Rue Garoute
Port-au-Prince
Haiti
West Indies
(011-509) 5-4417/5-2102

This 30-room guest house on three acres in a residential area of town was built in 1920 as the residence of the U.S. ambassador. Later it became the home of a senator, then went on to its present use for over 20 years as a "home away from home" at very moderate prices. The modest units all share baths and have twin beds. On the MAP guests are served a breakfast of fruit and eggs or pancakes and an American-style homecooked dinner. Your hosts are S.A. Santos and Mrs. Marie Therese Santos.

9

The Dominican Republic

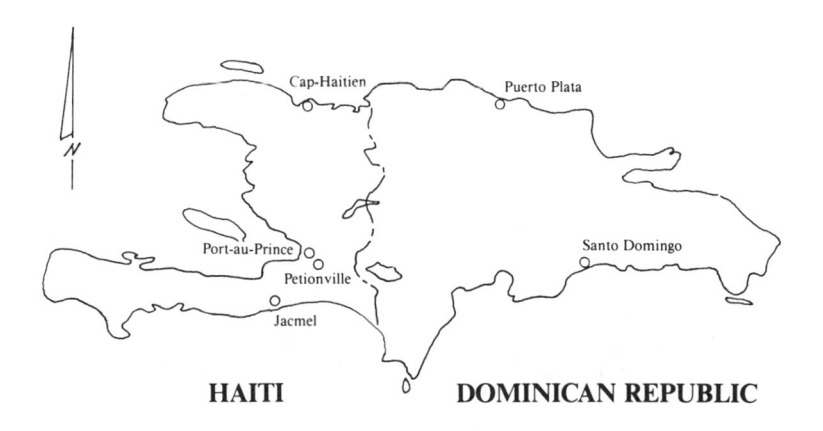

Caribbean Bed & Breakfast

Only 54 miles from Puerto Rico, sharing the island of Hispaniola with Haiti, is the Dominican Republic. Situated on the eastern half of the island, this still unspoiled Caribbean nation contains the highest peak in the West Indies, Pico Duarte, with an elevation of 10,417 feet. The interior of the island is lush and produces rich sugar cane; the coastline is characterized by miles and miles of beautiful, coral beaches. Considered a new entry into the Caribbean tourism market due to past political unrest, the Dominican Republic is making up for lost time with some ultra-new resorts, many under Gulf+Western ownership.

The language of the Dominican Republic is Spanish, but English is becoming more common. Likewise, the peso is the currency although many establishments will accept the U.S. dollar. It is wise to have any money exchanges handled at a bank or exchange house to be sure you are receiving the proper exchange rate. United States and Canadian citizens are required to provide proof of citizenship with a passport, voter's registration card or birth certificate and to buy a tourist card upon entering the country. A nominal departure tax is collected in pesos upon leaving the Dominican Republic.

The Dominican Republic is on Atlantic Standard Time (one hour earlier than Eastern Standard Time) except during Daylight Savings season when the time on the island and in the Eastern U.S. are the same. The electrical current is compatible with U.S. appliances.

Getting around the Dominican Republic can be achieved in several ways, but it is not always easy. Taxis are available at major hotels and the airport, but are not metered. If you are able to conquer language differences, be sure to decide on cost before hiring your taxi. Taxis may also be rented for sightseeing excursions but at a much greater cost than a bus tour. Regularly scheduled buses get you around the city of Santo Domingo for very reasonable rates. Car rentals, available in Santo Domingo and Puerto Plata, are relatively inexpensive and include Budget and Hertz. Driving is on the right side of the road.

The capital of the Dominican Republic, Santo Domingo, is currently undergoing major restoration, its streets brimming with the country's colorful history as well as modern additions. Museums that are restored examples of former palaces, 16th-century homes and monasteries have been opened to the public as "living" history lessons. The Alcazar was a palace built for

Dominican Republic

Columbus' son and is full of precious antiques, tapestries and art. The National Pantheon was a 1714 Jesuit monastery as well as a warehouse for tobacco; the Museo de las Casas Reales was the Governor's residence and is decorated in colonial artifacts.

Entertainment abounds both day and night in Santo Domingo. A large park, the Plaza de la Cultura, contains the National Theater which puts on local concerts and ballets. Horseracing, tennis, golf and champion deep-sea fishing are available, but the nicer beaches, rated high for scuba and snorkeling, are a distance out of town. Nightlife in Santo Domingo includes many discos, gambling casinos and Las Vegas-type acts with local talent.

Shoppers in the Dominican Republic will enjoy the handcrafted items found in the colorful market places, small shops and more modern shopping complexes. Among the attractive bargains are various jewelery items fashioned out of the national gem, amber, and macrame and mahogany items.

Puerto Plata, meaning "port of silver," was named for the ships that stopped here full of treasures from the New World. Today it is a busy cruise ship stop and is a mixture of modern and old-world charm. Cobblestone streets and outlying sugar cane fields are mixed with industry and signs of growth.

The visitor to the Dominican Republic will also find one of the largest sugar mills in the world, coral reefs and shipwrecks as well as undersea gardens, a 15th-century artists' colony and a secluded island off the coast for sunbathing and snorkeling.

For more detailed information contact:
Dominican Tourist Information Center
485 Madison Avenue
New York, New York 10022
(212) 826-0750

Hostal Nicolas de Ovando
53 Calle las Damas
Santo Domingo
Dominican Republic
(809) 687-7181

Historic inn; 55 units; Inexpensive-Mod. EP; AE,DC,VI,MC; Children ok; Smoking ok.

Location: In town; 20 mi. to airport.

Caribbean Bed & Breakfast

Historic in every way, this large-scale inn is the namesake of the 16th-century governor of Hispaniola, is created from two lovingly restored 15th-century mansions and sits in the heart of the historic district of Old Town. History lies on every side of the inn, and within the weathered walls of the hotel, there is a palace fit for a prestigious resident, in this case its many overnight guests.

The common rooms of the inn are bedecked in colonial-era antiques, ceremonial tapestries and bronzed mirrors. The classic courtyards give views of the Ozama River and are peaceful retreats complete with bubbling fountains, umbrella-covered tables and the original arches of the mansions. A swimming pool with pleasant sunning terrace and adjoining bar makes up for the lack of nearby beach facilities. A good restaurant, Extremadura, is a part of the hotel and serves all three meals amid its antique Spanish decor highlighted by a high beamed ceiling and gilded chandeliers.

The guestrooms at the Nicolas de Ovando carry out the antique feel with many colonial-era reproduction beds and imported hardwood furnishings. The rooms are all air conditioned and boast private baths with attractive hand-painted tile.

Also on the Island

Hotel Castilla
34 John F. Kennedy
Puerto Plata
Dominican Republic
(809) 586-2559

This 19th-century wooden structure sits on a busy corner in the heart of the city. The inn with balcony and shuttered windows offers a street-level restaurant and bar and 16 guestrooms upstairs. The restaurant with nautical decor is notable for its American cuisine and is popular with the sailing and cruising set who stop for some homecooking and a "bed" for the night. Most of the modest guestrooms share baths, but are clean and comfortable. The guestrooms have overhead fan cooling. The Castilla is an alternative for those on a tight budget.

10

Puerto Rico

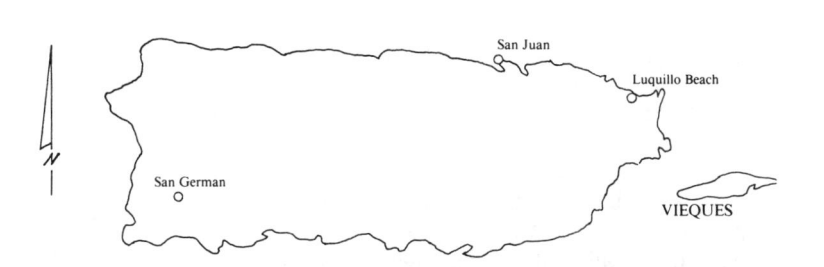

Caribbean Bed & Breakfast

The Puerto Rico Tourism Office invites the tourist to "follow the footsteps of the early Spanish conquistadores from the cobblestones of (the) historic city of San Juan to the luxurious vegetation of (the) tropical forests to the beautiful white sand beaches ..." Add to this a bustling strip of casinos and nightlife-filled hotels, and it sums up the varied offerings of the Caribbean's number one tourist destination, Puerto Rico.

San Juan, the capital of the 100-mile-long by 35-mile-wide island, is a mixture of old and new. Historic Old San Juan's narrow streets are lined with 16th- and 17th-century buildings and lead to El Morro, a four-century-old fortress, and a central plaza surrounded by charming boutiques and sidewalk cafes. In abrupt contrast is the city's Condado strip packed with high-rise hotel casinos, international restaurants and fast-food familiars, night clubs with lavish spectacles and live music.

But outside of San Juan, Puerto Rico offers visitors a lush tropical rain forest, El Yunque, with orchids, waterfalls and rare birds, a crescent-shaped, coconut tree-lined beach called Luquillo and a magical Phosphorescent Beach. Across the island is Ponce, the second largest city in Puerto Rico, with its ancient black and red firehouse, now a Tourism Information Office.

Getting to and from Puerto Rico is easy since it boasts the most extensive air service in the Caribbean with daily flights from all major North American cities. No passports or visas are required for U.S. citizens, and the currency is the U.S. dollar. Major banks are located in San Juan, and credit cards are widely accepted. English is spoken extensively here as well. Puerto Rico is on Atlantic Standard Time (one hour ahead of Eastern Standard Time) but does not recognize Daylight Savings Time. Therefore, in Daylight Savings season Puerto Rico's clocks are in harmony with those in Eastern U.S. states.

Local transportation is plentiful with metered taxis, "publicos," on frequent schedules between towns, several rental car agencies, sightseeing buses and regularly scheduled bus service around town. Publicos or public cars charge per person for destination requested and are in the habit of picking up passengers along the way. It is wise to be aware that this form of transportation can be economical but at times may take longer than anticipated. An old-fashioned trolley shuttles between the public parking lots and the narrow streets of Old San Juan.

Sports on the island include all the beach and ocean

Puerto Rico

offerings: snorkeling, scuba, surfing and fishing, although some beaches are better suited in terms of clarity of water and general beauty. Tennis, horseback riding on mountain trails, a race track, El Comandante, and ten 18-hole golf courses make recreational opportunities pretty much unlimited.

Puerto Rico offers its own brand of personal inn; a few are mentioned in this guide. The "parador" is a simple inn found in the countryside and is government-sponsored. Also, the out-islands of San Juan, Culebra and Vieques provide some charming guest house accommodations.

For more detailed information on Puerto Rico contact:
Government of Puerto Rico Tourism Company Office
1290 Avenue of the Americas
New York, New York 10104
(212) 541-6630
or
3575 W. Cahuenga Blvd.
Los Angeles, CA 90068
(213) 874-5991

Arcade Inn
#8 Taft Street
San Juan
Puerto Rico 00911
(809) 725-0668/728-7524

Guest house; 19 units; Inexpensive/Inexpensive EP; No credit cards; Children ok; Smoking ok.

Location: Condado; 75 ft. to beach; 3 mi. to airport.

This hospitable inn can be found on a Condado area sidestreet populated by various multiple housing developments. The three-story, Spanish-style house stands out as an intimate retreat for guests just a few feet from the beach. Resident owners Aurelio and Renee Cinque have made this a popular guest

Caribbean Bed & Breakfast

house for the past 16 years, as they personally see to guests from the moment they arrive to the time they depart. The only other staff in attendance consists of housekeeping personnel who keep the simple quarters spotless.

The white residence with olive green trim has attractive arches and scallops, and the guest enters through a neat patio area with potted plants and concrete tables and chairs on the side of the house. Arched, iron-grill doors lead to the office in this front structure and the guestrooms contained within. An annex building in the back of the property provides efficiency units and cabana-style rooms.

Guest accommodations at the guest house are all very pleasant, especially those with views of the ocean; each unit is a little different in size and shape. The main house offers several rooms with balconies, and some of the rear units have private patios. All of the guest accommodations have cheerful curtains and bedspreads, private shower-baths with pretty tilework and nicely waxed floors.

Adjacent to the rear structure is the patio bar that serves breakfast, sandwiches and drinks all day in a relaxed outdoor setting. The continental breakfast of juice, coffee, toast and jelly and the full American-style morning meal are very reasonably priced. Picnic lunches are also available if ordered in advance. Guests may keep their own supply of cold drinks or fruit in the guest refrigerator in this area.

The Cinques enjoy playing host to their many return guests who come from all over the world. Mr. Cinque speaks five languages which enables him to easily convey that "his home is your home."

Arcos Blancos
10 Carrion Court
San Juan
Puerto Rico 00911
(809) 728-6725/728-6755

Guest house; 37 units; Moderate/Inexpensive-Mod. MAP; VI,MC (via Western Union only); No children; Smoking ok.

Location: Ocean Park; 103 ft. to beach; 4 mi. to airport.

Three early-1900's mansions make up this guest house that

caters to the gay community. The integrated former residences are just 100 feet from the Condado beach and shops in the Ocean Park residential area. Hosts Peter Bessi and Ray Falcon are responsible for the personalized service and well-kept guestrooms at the guest house.

The mansions are surrounded by lush tropical gardens, and a palm-shaded pool is a refreshing focal point. The attractive Garden Restaurant, with bridge entrance and hanging plants, has a soothing tropical atmosphere and serves the complimentary continental breakfast and sandwich or cold platter lunches. A complimentary pina colada or Planters Punch greets the guest in the bar upon arrival.

A Spanish arch serves as entrance to the guest house; the old colonial lounge has handsome, open arches, a small library and television. The guestrooms at Arcos Blancos vary in size and are all color coordinated. All accommodations at the modestly priced inn feature air conditioning, overhead fans and private baths.

El Canario Inn
1317 Ashford Avenue
San Juan
Puerto Rico 00907
(809) 722-3861/724-2793

Inn; 25 units; Moderate/Inexpensive CP;
AE,VI,MC; Children ok; Smoking ok.

Location: Condado; 1 block to beach; 4 mi. to airport.

This informal b&b inn is a small oasis of individuality nestled among the high-rises and casinos of the Condado. The 1923-built, Spanish-style structure with tile roof and heavy wrought iron was originally a doctor's residence. Several small buildings in the rear have been combined with the former residence to make up El Canario, located within a block of all

Caribbean Bed & Breakfast

the Condado action. For added convenience the city bus passes directly in front of the inn.

The guest enters the b&b through a small guest lounge with color television and comfortable seating. A round-the-clock reception desk is here, manned by the friendly staff and owner-manager Keith Olson. Some of the inn's guestrooms are located on the three floors of this building. Guests will also find a small communal kitchen with guest refrigerator in this building on their way out to the attractive side patio.

The brick patio of the inn is protected from the busy Ashford Avenue noises by a tall wall and relaxing tropical vegetation. Guests at El Canario seem to gravitate to this inviting spot both day and night. In the morning a serve-yourself, complimentary breakfast is offered on the patio. A toaster flanked by various breads, butter and jams is provided along with lots of coffee or milk. Guests help themselves and take a seat at one of the large covered patio tables for some friendly socializing in addition to the morning fare. No other meals are offered at the inn, but you are within easy walking distance of a number of good restaurants. A treat for the children is the Chuck E. Cheese Pizza Parlour with games, rides, animated shows and playground right next door.

Just past the side patio area are convenient cold drink and ice machines and then the picturesque stone-decorated pool. This is the afternoon gathering spot for the congenial guests at El Canario as they chat, sunbathe and swim in the small, but pretty pool with fountain, waterfall and handy built-in drink table. The other small buildings that hold guestrooms at the inn are situated near the pool; some of those contain efficiency units. A convenient guest laundromat is also in this vicinity.

The guestrooms at El Canario are very basic and often petite. The walls are freshly painted white splashed with some local artwork, and bamboo curtains grace the windows. The asphalt tile floors are adequate, but the bright floral or geometric print bedspreads liven up the rooms. A compact, tiled shower-bath and air conditioning are found in all the guestrooms. Either director's chairs or rattan seating is provided as well as ample closet and dresser clothes storage. The quieter accommodations are located in the rear buildings of the inn.

Although the accommodations are not luxurious at El Canario, no one seems to care. In fact, the heavy repeat clientele at this informal inn attests to its popularity as a congenial spot where the guest can be totally involved in the fast pace of the Condado or just relax in this friendly hideaway that is also kind to the budget.

La Condesa Inn
Calle Cacique #2071
San Juan
Puerto Rico 00911
(809) 727-3698/727-3900

Inn; 18 units; Inexpensive/Inexpensive CP;
Credit cards accepted; Children ok
off-season only; Smoking ok.

Location: Ocean Park; 100 ft. to beach; 4 mi. to airport.

La Condesa Inn is hidden away on a residential street just a mile from the shops and restaurants of the Condado. The inn, composed of two 1954-built homes (one formerly a Spanish consul's residence), is locked behind a large wall. Only guests have keys to the gate for optimum privacy and security, giving it a home-like feel. The exteriors of the two structures are attractive with pretty orangish-rust awnings and balconies.

Within the walls of the inn the guest will discover instant tranquility provided by waterfalls, goldfish ponds and planters filled with tropical plants. This patio area with covered dining and bar is the site of the complimentary morning meal served from 8 to 10 a.m. each day. Guests relax at quaint ice cream tables and chairs placed around the terra-cotta floors and enjoy the continental fare. Breakfast may be upgraded for a minimal additional charge to a full breakfast with bacon or ham, eggs, French toast or omelettes. Lunch, with a large variety of sandwiches, is served here between noon and 3 p.m. Dinner is not presently offered, but the "Two Gates Patio Bar" stays in operation, beginning with your complimentary cocktail upon arrival.

Adjacent to the patio is a spacious swimming pool molded in a scalloped design. The privacy wall that protects sunbathers from the street serves as a scenic diversion with four mini-waterfalls cascading down the stone-embedded concrete. This touch adds to the many tranquil aspects of the inn. Serenity and privacy are also provided in the courtyard/patio layout of the guestrooms themselves. A combination of individual, striped awnings over guestroom doors, tiny patios dotted with neat potted plants and quiet courtyards between building areas creates a quiet, private feel.

The guestrooms at La Condesa Inn all contain private baths with tub/showers and attractive ceramic tile floors. Each guestroom is individually decorated, but each features such detailing as pretty bedspreads and shower curtains, cleverly used mirrors that enlarge the more modestly sized rooms, large closets, cheerful wallcoverings and radios. A few of the units boast television and kitchens; most offer pleasant balconies or patios. All of the guestrooms at the inn are immaculately kept.

La Condesa Inn remains a well-kept secret in many ways. A majority of the inn's guests are repeat clientele or have been referred by word of mouth. The service, under the careful eye of owner Luis Cintron for the last 13 years, is friendly and accommodating.

El Convento
100 Cristo Street
P.O. Box 1048
San Juan
Puerto Rico 00902
(809) 723-9020
(800) 468-2779

Puerto Rico

Historic inn; 100 units; Moderate-Exp./Moderate-Exp. EP; Credit cards accepted; Children ok; Smoking ok.

Location: Old San Juan; 3 mi. to beach; 8 mi. to airport.

This Gran Hotel El Convento is one of Old San Juan's proud historical landmarks. Owned by the government of Puerto Rico, the hotel, steeped in centuries of rich history, is itself a restored treasure. The original 1600 convent was closed in disrepair in 1903 as a nun's retreat and reopened as a special historical inn many years later after careful restoration that incorporated most of the original architecture, tile and beams.

The pinkish-brown, Spanish building with tall white columns and black iron railings is situated in the heart of the historic city, fronted by the quaint cobblestone streets of town. Guests enter through the massive wooden doors to a lobby decorated in Mediterranean-style antiques, giant wall tapestries and black and white marble flooring. The hotel complex, surrounding an attractive courtyard area, is a melding of arches, hand-painted tiles, chandeliers, antiques and carved wooden beams.

The guestrooms of the hotel number 100, disqualifying it for an "intimate inn" classification, but each guestroom has an identity of its own in keeping with the 17th-century Spanish heritage of the building. All guestrooms have the modern amenities of color television, private modern baths, radios and air conditioning, but many are decorated in elegant four posters with canopies, velveteen seating and various antique pieces.

Dining at the hotel is on the delightful atrium patio in the courtyard with breakfast bar or in the more formal dining hall. A small but attractive pool is located in the central courtyard as well.

The hotel offers free transportation to the Condado Beach, and entertainment is provided nightly with flamenco shows twice a week.

Doncella 109
Calle Doncella 109
San Juan
Puerto Rico 00913
(809) 726-1630

Guest·house; 5 units; Moderate/Inexpensive CP;

Caribbean Bed & Breakfast

No credit cards; No children; Smoking ok.

Location: Punta Las Marias; 3 blks. to beach; 5 mi. to airport.

A white concrete fence and tropical shrubbery that borders on overgrown hides this little guest house from passers-by in this otherwise residential district. The former private home with distinctive striped awning became a guest house some 17 years ago when former owners and originators Paula Glendale, Bill Snelson and Marji Weaver personalized the non-touristy location into a small and elegant guest house for those who wanted to escape the large hotels.

New owners Linda Glenn and Charlotte Norris have the same goal in mind, and, other than not serving evening meals, the guest house functions very similarly today.

Once you've located the cozy house with blue wooden gates and tiles that spell out "109," you've got it made. Inside the house is an attactive decorating theme carried out in blue, green and white with an interesting mixture of island wicker and rattan and warm antiques. The guestrooms are decorated individually in the same theme. Three have private baths, and two rooms share a bath.

The morning meal at the guest house consists of local fruits and fresh breads served with coffee or tea. A luncheon menu includes sandwiches and salads; drinks are available at the attractive bar.

A refreshing in-ground pool at Doncella 109 is surrounded by tropical gardens and banana and mango trees. Even though you are just a few minutes away from the busy Condado, this hidden little inn provides a delightful oasis.

Hosteria del Mar
5 Cervantes Street
San Juan
Puerto Rico 00907
(809) 724-8203

Puerto Rico

Guest house; 17 units; Inexpensive-Mod./Inexpensive-Mod. EP; VI,MC,AE; Children ok; Smoking ok.

Location: Condado; On beach/few steps; 4 mi. to airport.

Hosteria del Mar is tucked away on one of the quieter side streets in the Condado area. In fact the two turn-of-the-century homes that compose the inn with restaurant were originally private homes when the Condado was an elegant residential area. Owners Elsie Herger and Mercedes Mulet have spent the last six years adapting the facilities for guests, but have kept the basic architecture and rambling gardens that surround intact.

The inn's street-fronting structure is what the guest first views. The Spanish-style, white building with green trim and wooden shutters has a distinctive red and white awning; trees line the street in front. Guests enter through the covered sunporch-veranda with comfortable seating. A small connecting guest parlor has wicker rockers and couch and a white beamed ceiling. Arched entries lead to the upstairs guestrooms and also to the guest house's restaurant.

The restaurant has a comfortable waiting area with twin pink couches and an antique buffet. Diners enjoy mainly vegetarian specialties at rattan tables. Or they may pass through the French doors to an outdoor patio dining area. All three meals are offered here to guests and visitors, but drinks are limited to the fruit juice variety.

The upstairs guestrooms in this building are of simple decor, but offer an airy feelng. A hall bathroom is shared by two units and the others here have private baths. A quaint windowseat is built into the upstairs landing.

A path lined with untamed gardens and grassy areas leads to the other guest facility of Hosteria del Mar. This large white stucco and wood structure has an impressive and spacious veranda with black and white tile floor that reaches out to the Atlantic a few steps away. The guest parlor here is more than spacious and its simplicity is attractive. Wooden floors, matching mauve couches, wicker chairs, propped-open French doors, a piano and white, wood-beamed ceilings give the area a gracious and airy feel. Guestrooms in this annex are up a pretty white-bannistered staircase. A combination of old and new furnishings fill the modest rooms, some with king size beds, and a few with kitchenettes. About half of the guestrooms at the inn have private baths.

Caribbean Bed & Breakfast

Innkeepers Herger and Mulet are still busy with the renovation of the guest house, and tidying is still underway. It is refreshing that the structures have been left intact and offer a great deal in a budget category in this splendid location overlooking the Atlantic. Future plans include a pool.

Parador Martorell
Ocean Drive 6-A
P.O. Box 384
Luquillo Beach
Puerto Rico 00673
(809) 889-2710
(800) 223-6530

Inn; 7 units; Inexpensive CP/Inexpensive EP;
No credit cards; Children ok; Smoking ok.

Location: ½ blk. to beach; Near town; 17 mi. to airport.

On the verge of 20 years in business, Parador Martorell is distinguished as the pioneer of the government parador program, Paradores Puertoriquenos. The paradores are akin to country inns that have been set up with the encouragement of the government to foster tourism in other parts of the island to let the visitor know that Puerto Rico has a lot more to offer than San Juan itself.

This parador opened in 1966 and was designed personally by the owner-manager Irma Martorell, a former social worker who before becoming an innkeeper worked in that field in Washington, D.C., and in her native Puerto Rico. Ms. Martorell's training in social work prepared her well for her second career of innkeeping, which at this inn is focused on personal attention to guests.

The modern two-story structure features a ground-floor patio garden/guest lounge where the complimentary breakfast buffet with local and international dishes is served during on-season. This pleasant patio is surrounded by tropical foliage, palms and lemon and orange trees. The seven guestrooms at the inn all have shared baths, except one, and are decorated in colorful posters and paintings by local artists. Double- and twin-bedded rooms are available as well as some with terraces or balconies.

Puerto Rico

Outside of the intimacy of the inn, one of the most appealing aspects is its location just a few minutes by car from pretty Luquillo Beach, which is just half a block away. The Parador Martorell will provide free beach towels for sunning, and scuba and snorkeling arrangements can be made. Also, the inn is very convenient to El Yunque, the Rain Forest and the ferry to the outer islands. The parador is about an hour's ride from Old San Juan and 45 minutes from the airport. As you might guess, this stop is most convenient when you're renting a car, or you might opt to spend all your time at the parador, which is within easy walking distance of town or the beach.

Tres Palmas
2212 Park Boulevard
San Juan
Puerto Rico 00913
(809) 727-4617/727-5434

Guest house; 7 units; Inexpensive-Mod./Inexpensive CP; MC,VI,AE,DC; Children on approval; Smoking ok.

Location: 1 mi. to Condado; Across from beach; 2 mi to airport.

This impeccably neat, gray Spanish-style house with tile roof is locked behind a wrought-iron gate. The petite hacienda beckons a small group of guests who delight in its intimacy as

Caribbean Bed & Breakfast

well as its outstanding, unobstructed views of the Atlantic just across the roadway. Within the gates is an attractive gravel garden with potted tropical specimens and a small pond with bridge. The front porch area, a popular lounging and breakfasting spot for guests, looks over this tidy little front garden to the ocean activity just beyond.

Directly inside the inn is the smartly furnished guest lounge with navy blue and rust chintz couches and chairs, color television and a medley of good-looking contemporary and antique furnishings. The tile floor in black, gray and rust shades blends harmoniously with the light gray walls of the comfortable room. The small reception desk is here with hosts Paul and Bud at guests' beck and call. The service at this b&b is special due to the personal attention of its two innkeepers, as you can confirm by glancing through any one of the seven volumes of thank-you correspondence from past guests. In fact, Bud and Paul claim that 60 percent of their business is repeat.

The complimentary breakfast at Tres Palmas is really more than a continental breakfast and changes almost daily. The morning meal, served as each guest arrives for breakfast, consists of Danish or muffins, choice of juices, fresh pineapple and papaya (always) and fresh brewed coffee which is kept in a large silver urn for guest refills at will. Guests may breakfast on the front patio as mentioned or on a quiet side patio with umbrella tables.

Lounging at Tres Palmas is encouraged in every way. A small "mini-pool" that looks more like a jacuzzi has been fitted into the only pool space available on the property. It is intimate, but relaxing nonetheless. Hidden on the roof of the house, at the top of rather steep spiral stairs, is a spacious sundeck with a spectacular view over the palms of the Atlantic's horizon. This attractive escape is furnished with umbrella tables, shaded lounges and lounges open completely to the sun. Potted plants and cactus add a pretty touch, but can't compete with the views. Paul points out that this is an ideal, protected spot to sun when the wind begins to blow.

The guestrooms at Tres Palmas are very pleasantly modest. Little touches such as attractive wallcoverings, mirrors over the beds and modern, private baths (except two rooms that share one bath) make the accommodations a very good value. All of the guestrooms at the b&b boast air conditioning, clock radios and separate outside entrances.

Puerto Rico

Also on the Island

Parador Oasis
72 Luna Street
P.O. Box 144
San German
Puerto Rico 00753
(809) 892-1175/892-9580
(800) 223-6530

One of the handful of island paradores, the Oasis is a sublime historical addition, located in the oldest community on Puerto Rico, San German. The small town of San German retains its Spanish-colonial charm with two picturesque plazas, the beautiful Porta Coeli Church (a 1606 monastery) with 18th-century art and the 200-year-old Oasis. The hotel was originally a family mansion, later a winery and then most recently a parador. The Spanish-style home offering 22 guestrooms is draped in lattice work, balconies and arches. Its serene environment includes an interior patio, gardens, fountains and walkways. The veranda, the setting for fine local cuisine, has traditional Spanish tiles and high-backed rocking chairs.

Vieques Island (Out Island)

La Casa del Frances
P.O. Box 458
Vieques Island
Puerto Rico 00765
(809) 741-3751
(800) 223-6530

Historic inn; 22 units; Moderate/Moderate EP;
No credit cards; Children ok; Smoking ok.

Location: 7 min. walk to beach; Countryside; 5 mi. to airport.

The island of Vieques, a part of Puerto Rico, can be reached via a ferry boat ride from Fajardo or by small aircraft from the Isla Grande Airport. The air trip will be much more

Caribbean Bed & Breakfast

comfortable for those who are troubled by a fairly frisky sea crossing. Vieques, like this charming parador, offers uncrowded, tropical countryside and long stretches of white sand lined with palms. Though it takes a little bit of effort to get there, La Casa del Frances offers those seeking a quiet getaway a bit of history mixed with personal attention.

La Casa del Frances is a turn-of-the-century plantation house that was recently honored with an historical landmark designation by the government of Puerto Rico. La Casa, situated on a knoll top, boasts beautiful architecture of the era marked by 17-foot-high ceilings and wide verandas. The guestrooms tend to be spacious with the same high ceilings, simple but cheerful decor, shutters, old-fashioned fans and French doors; all feature private baths. Guest accommodations in the mansion surround an airy two-story atrium.

The outdoor dining room at the inn has a lovely view of the tropical grounds and the inviting swimming pool. All three meals are offered here at reasonable prices.

Sun Bay Beach, a popular, palm-fringed stretch, is within walking distance of the inn; the tiny fishing village of Esperanza is also a short walk away. Arrangements can be made there for fishing trips, night cruises on Phosphorescent Bay (an inspiring phenomenon) and snorkeling or scuba.

11

U.S. Virgin Islands

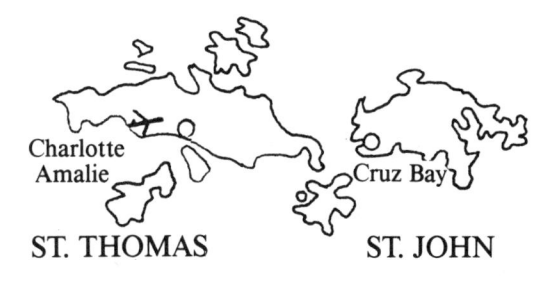

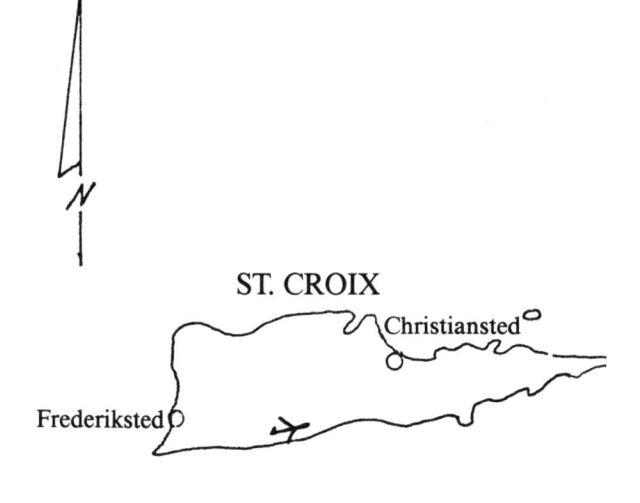

Caribbean Bed & Breakfast

In all there are some 50 islands that make up the U.S. Virgin Islands, some no bigger than large rock formations protruding from the incredibly clear aqua sea. The main islands are St. Croix, the largest, St. John and St. Thomas, the latter two just 35 miles from St. Croix and 3 miles apart from each other. These islands, lying between the Atlantic Ocean and the Caribbean Sea, were discovered in 1493 by Columbus who named them the "Virgins" due to their unspoiled beauty. A history which includes almost 200 years of Danish rule and a rich, pirate-inviting trade has left intriguing marks on these islands for the visitor to discover.

In 1917 the United States purchased these islands and, as a U.S. unincorporated Territory, all residents born here are U.S. citizens. Visitors are not required to have passports, but identification such as a voter's registration card or birth certificate is required. The language spoken is English and the currency is, of course, the U.S. dollar. Traveler's checks and credit cards are honored in these islands extensively, but not personal checks. The U.S. Virgin Islands are on Atlantic Standard Time (one hour ahead of Eastern Standard Time) except during Daylight Savings Time when U.S. Virgin Island time and Eastern Daylight Time are the same.

Another benefit of being a part of the United States is shopping in the Virgin Islands, sometimes referred to as the "shopping mecca of the Caribbean." With no customs duties on tourism-related products, U.S. residents are allowed a duty-free limit of $800 per person (twice the allowed amount of any other island) and may mail home to friends an unlimited number of gifts each worth $100 or less.

The U.S. Virgin Islands can be easily reached by airplane from all major cities in North America; the islands are connected to other islands and each other by several small commuter lines. Also, all the major cruise lines operate cruises here year-round, with St. Thomas holding rank as the number one cruise port in the Caribbean. Island-hopping is also easily accomplished via ferry and seaplane shuttles; a high-speed ferry connects the U.S. Virgins to Tortola and Virgin Gorda in the British Virgin Islands.

Transportation on the islands includes bus service on all but St. John where jeep and taxi are the mode. Taxis on all three islands are fare-regulated by destination rather than mileage and, as on Puerto Rico publicos, the driver is apt to

U.S. Virgin Islands

pick up passengers along the way and make stops you had not anticipated. Car rentals and mopeds are available, but remember to keep on the left side, a carry-over from Danish rule.

The weather in the Virgin Islands is always comfortable; winter averages 77 degrees and summer 82 degrees with easterly trade winds.

Beaches on all three islands boast powdery white sand, and the right-of-access to any beach is protected by law. The turquoise, clear sea water is popular for all water sports including boardsailing (surfboard with sail), catamarans, yachting, diving and sportsfishing. The U.S. Virgin Islands is one of the most popular dive areas in the world, and excellent fishing is revealed in the many world records set in these waters. Tennis, golf, horseback riding and exploring are also tops on the recreation list.

While the nightlife in St. Croix and St. Thomas is not as lively as San Juan's Condado, many small clubs and fine restaurants provide the flavor of the islands with limbo dancers and calypso singers. The tranquil island of St. John offers no real nightlife, just quiet beauty.

For additional information on the U.S. Virgin Islands contact:
U.S. Virgin Islands Division of Tourism Office
1270 Avenue of the Americas
New York, New York 10020
(212) 582-4520
or
3450 Wilshire Blvd.
Los Angeles, CA 90010
(213) 739-0138

St. Thomas

The capital of the U.S. Virgin islands, St. Thomas, is 32 miles square and is a combination of ship docks, shopping, pastel-washed, red-tiled homes clinging to green hillsides and spectacular ocean and island vistas.

Two ocean-offerings not to be missed are in St. Thomas. Magens Bay was called by *National Geographic* "one of the ten most beautiful beaches in the world," and the small admission fee is certainly worthwhile. The calm, clear water and powdery sand of Magens Bay make it an idyllic spot for snorkeling, swimming, sunning or renting a windsurfer or raft. Also, Coral World, an

Caribbean Bed & Breakfast

underwater observation tower and marine park open to the sea, gives the visitor a chance to observe rare rainbow-colored fish and unusual coral formations. The park is one of two such offerings in the world.

St. Thomas' capital, Charlotte Amalie, is filled with interesting architecture and literally hundreds of small shops and restaurants that cater to the steady influx of cruise line passengers and other tourists. Lunch time becomes a circus in the small, crowded streets as the "food barkers" vie for attention. The narrow, hillside roads of the town can prove confusing, but give dramatic views of the picturesque, boat-filled bay below.

St. Thomas is not short on historic sites, many within Charlotte Amalie, including the pastel green Legislature Building completed in 1879 and the seat of the Virgin Islands legislature; the 1671 Fort Christian, the oldest standing structure on the island; 99 Steps, a reminder of the 1700's Danish builders of the city; Market Square, the slave market of the 1600's; the 1867 Government House; and Frenchtown, a gallic colony with winding streets and inhabited by descendants of the original Bretons and Normans.

The United States' influence on St. Thomas is apparent in the fast food chains and modern shopping centers cropping up around the island. Whether this is viewed as a detriment to island scenery or a nice blend of the familiar and the exotic, it is hard to dispute the natural beauty of St. Thomas.

Carnival, a colorful festival filled with festive dances, parades and excitement, is celebrated after Easter each year. Mocko Jumbi, an elevated "spirit" on 17-foot-tall stilts, is the traditional symbol of the festival.

Bluebeard's Castle
P.O. Box 7480
St. Thomas
U.S. Virgin Islands 00801
(809) 774-1600
(800) 524-6599

Historic inn; 100 units; Expensive-Del./ Expensive EP; AE,DC,MC,VI; Children ok; Smoking ok.

Location: In town; 3 mi. to beach; 3 mi. to airport.

U.S. Virgin Islands

When you first enter the town of Charlotte Amalie, your eye is immediately drawn to a complex of white buildings with bright red roofs on a prominent hilltop, holding court over the busy harbor and town. Submerged in tropical greenery is Bluebeard's Castle, a historical monument that has grown into one of the best-known resorts in the Caribbean.

A favorite of sightseers to St. Thomas, the hotel features 20 acres of well-manicured gardens, pools, tennis courts and assorted restaurants and duty-free shops. But not to overlook its historic significance, the tourist will also find the 17th-century castle tower intact with its distinctive blue shutters, as well as cannons in the old fortress wall.

Although it's hardly intimate, having grown by leaps and bounds since the 1930's, Bluebeard's Castle can boast attractive accommodations, a spectacular view and in-town location as well as attentive, professional service, all the while keeping alive some of the flavor of its original 17th-century pirate days.

The guestrooms at the hotel are modern and pleasantly furnished with ceramic tile floors, coordinating tropical prints, television, rattan furnishings and view terraces. All of the rooms are air conditioned; spacious suites feature comfortable living room areas.

Bunkers' Hill View Guest House
9 Commandant Gade
St. Thomas
U.S. Virgin Islands 00801
(809) 774-8056

Guest house; 21 units; Inexpensive-Mod./ Inexpensive-Mod. CP; No credit cards; Children ok; Smoking ok.

Location: In town; 3 mi. to beach; 3 mi. to airport.

Located at the foot of Bunker Hill in downtown Charlotte Amalie, this convenient guest house is just steps away from shops and restaurants and around the corner from a laundromat. Bunkers' Hill View also boasts some of the most reasonable lodging rates on the island, especially in off-season, and a full breakfast is included. Rates are higher in the suites and duplexes (two-bedroom suites) that provide good family accommodations.

Caribbean Bed & Breakfast

The white with pinkish-red trim guest house, which consists of three buildings that climb the hillside, was originally built as an apartment complex. The present owners renovated it about four years ago. An interesting maze of staircases unites the three buildings, all offering some hillside views.

The choice of accommodations at this b&b include, as mentioned, guestrooms, suites and duplexes. All of the guest accommodations are carpeted and have television, air conditioning and inter-room phones. The only shared baths are in the two-bedroom suites which are usually occupied by one family. These suites include a large kitchen and patio as well. All of the suites feature kitchenettes.

The accommodating rates at Bunkers' Hill View are matched by the very generous complimentary breakfasts served on an outside dining terrace. Bacon, eggs, toast, juice and coffee are offered to guests as they rise between 7:30 a.m. and 10 a.m.

For other bargains offered at Bunkers' Hill guests might like to talk with manager Angela Rawlins. Ms. Rawlins is happy to arrange reductions on major car rentals, a VIP shopping and dining card with savings at certain establishments as well as reductions for stays of seven days at Bunkers' Hill View Guest House.

Galleon House
P.O. Box 6577
St. Thomas
U.S. Virgin Islands 00801
(809) 774-6952
(800) 524-2052

U.S. Virgin Islands

Inn; 9 units; Inexpensive-Mod./ Inexpensive-Mod. CP; No credit cards; Children ok; Smoking ok.

Location: In town; 3 mi. to beach; 3 mi. to airport.

This small, friendly b&b inn is just a short walk from the heart of Charlotte Amalie, at the same time affording impressive views of the harbor and the red-tiled abodes below. The inn itself is somewhat hidden behind the Au Bon Vivant Restaurant (a separate business) and next door to the better known Hotel 1829. Several unassuming flights of stairs lead to the informal, central veranda that overlooks the inn's attractive pool. Here is where guests congregate for the complimentary morning meal as well as for friendly conversation day or night.

The nine guestrooms are located in two buildings, an older structure and a recently completed building, both watched over carefully by a penned-in guard dog that resides half-hidden between the two structures.

The original guestroom structure is apparent in the interesting antique molding with gold leaf designs that graces the long hallway leading to the guestrooms. In contrast, a large refrigerator is conveniently located in the same corridor to store food and cold drinks for the guests. All of the guestrooms in this building share baths except for one, the "Prince Royal," which is also a favorite of honeymooners. This spacious room with unusual "shingled" walls, king size bed and blue and white accents offers a nice, informal charm. The remainder of the guestrooms off the corridor, all named in brass plaques on the doors, are individually appointed and feature pretty printed sheets, fabric wallhangings, cheerful bedspreads and either ceiling fan or air conditioner. Note that although these units share baths, most share with the room on the other side of the bath, and each boasts a door from the guestroom directly into the bath—thus, no "down-the-hall." Also, the shared baths are pleasantly spacious and modern with double sinks.

The newer building at the Galleon has been blended with the older structure nicely, sporting turn-of-the-century detailing and the nicest views of the harbor. These more private units have attractive ceramic tile floors, some televisions, private baths and feature verandas with gingerbread coverings that take full advantage of the spectacular view.

The complimentary breakfast fare at the Galleon House

Caribbean Bed & Breakfast

changes each day, but includes juice or fresh fruit and French toast, pancakes or eggs, making the already reasonable accommodations hard to beat.

The inn is proud of its return clientele who enjoy the safety, seclusion and hospitality of its gracious innkeepers; Cordell and Elise Tittle and staff. As in many of St. Thomas' special offerings, it is wise to reserve early.

Harbor View
4-5 Gamle Nordsidevej
P.O. Box 1975
St. Thomas
U.S. Virgin Islands 00801
(809) 774-2651
Rep: American/Wolfe International

Historic inn; 8 units; Moderate/ Moderate CP;
AE,VI,MC; Children ok; Smoking ok.

Location: In town; 3 mi. to beach; 3 mi. to airport

This late-1800's former French consulate still has the ambience of a prestigious, private West Indian manor house. The Harbor View is located high on a hilltop in a residential area of Charlotte Amalie. Its guests ring the doorbell upon checking in, one of the many elite touches the guest will experience in this personal and sophisticated b&b.

Guests at the Harbor View actually enter through the back door, from an area with spacious parking, into a small entry area that also accesses the inn's renowned restaurant dining areas. Here the guest is greeted by the finest features of the establishment—the original old stonework walls, black wrought-iron accents, assorted antiques and the old Danish ovens. The formal dining area is plushly carpeted and decorated in a rich blend of rattan and antiques. A crystal chandelier and candlelight provide soft evening lighting to the room that has muted gray walls covered in antique mirrors and fancy wood molding that curves with the archway entries.

U.S. Virgin Islands

Walking around the old manor house, you'll discover a gracious, red marbled-tile terrace with a profusion of plants and brown shutters that open onto the sea. Then, proceeding on to the actual front of the house you come to the enclosed terrace called the "Gallerie." This lounge area which looks over the garden-set pool and the picturesque harbor earns the inn its name, Harbor View. A piano bar here provides nighttime entertainment and has attractive green and white tile floors and orange-cushioned black wicker furnishings with an occasional wrought-iron settee. The complimentary continental breakfast (which can be expanded at an additional cost) is served on the surrounding terrace with the same inspiring views.

The eight guestrooms at the inn are all different, but share a similar, good-looking brown and white color scheme with coordinating everything. The tastefully decorated rooms are furnished in carefully selected antiques such as brass or canopy beds (twin), armoires, marble-top dressers and antique mirrors. Special touches include rich tobacco-brown carpeting, pretty brown shutters with views of the harbor or town, old paintings, velvety blanket coverlets and live plants. All of the guestrooms feature air conditioning and private baths with modern fixtures and shower stalls.

Guests at Harbor View might well decide to make the inn their meal headquarters as well, for it has a gourmet menu of delicious French, Italian and other specialties that include various crepes, pasta dishes and homemade pies.

This charming b&b has been in operation since 1961; owners and managers Arlene Lockwood and Lenore Wolfe and staff (most there for over 15 years) try hard to keep Harbor View reminiscent of St. Thomas before tourism surged. Harbor View accomplishes this task nicely in a manner that can only be attributed to 22 years of careful attention and care.

Note:
The inn is in operation November 1 through Labor Day.

Hotel 1829
30 Kongens Gade
P.O. Box 1567
St. Thomas
U.S. Virgin Islands 00801
(809) 774-1829

Caribbean Bed & Breakfast

Hotel 1829

Historic inn; 14 units; Moderate-Del./ Moderate-Exp. EP AE, MC,VI; No children under 12; Smoking ok.

Location: In town; 3 mi. to beach; 3 mi. to airport.

Located next to the historic "99 Steps" on Government Hill and a block from the main shopping streets of town, the Hotel 1829 offers superior accommodations coupled with old-world charm. The European flavor of the establishment might well be attributed to the fact that the hotel, originally a private residence, was built by a French sea captain, designed by an Italian architect in a Spanish-style motif and constructed by Danish labor.

Careful restoration of the 1829-built inn, in operation since 1939, shows in every detail. The salmon-pink structure with green awnings is located on a steep grade and is a part of the city's historic walking tour. The brick-step entry leads to wrought-iron gates that open to massive wooden doors at the top. The front entry is actually the terrace dining area with comfortable rattan tables and chairs, thick wooden shutters, planters over-brimming with red poinsettias and a tranquil fountain.

The 14 guest accommodations on different levels are positioned around an interior courtyard that is every bit as charming as the exterior. Victorian benches, occasional antique cupboards and sideboards and "tulip-shaped," turn-of-the-century

U.S. Virgin Islands

lighting fixtures grace the exposed corridors as boungainvillaea drapes colorfully over the old brick walls.

The guestrooms themselves are all different, ranging from moderate poolside rooms to deluxe rooms and suites overlooking St. Thomas' boat-filled harbor. The suites and deluxe accommodations feature queen size beds, H.B.O. color television, completely outfitted wet bars and private balconies. The more moderately priced rooms are nestled around the pool and terrace, but all the guestrooms feature such special touches as rich terra-cotta tile (that blends nicely with the 200-year-old Moroccan tile in the dining area), air conditioning, warm brick-exposed walls, wooden-shuttered windows, coordinated fabrics and designer sheets and stained-glass accents. All accommodations have private baths with ultra-modern fixtures and ceramic tile.

The 1829 Restaurant offers gourmet specialties by Chef Gerhard Hofmann with appetizers such as escargot eva, which features a roquefort glazing and the finest Beluga caviar. Broiled specialties include a filet mignon topped with gooseliver pate and various foods from the sea. The indoor dining room, lined with the old brick walls of the hotel, has a large stained-glass artwork as a focal point and a hanging planter in the center of the room. The tables are set with attractive china and fresh flowers.

The bar of Hotel 1829 was the original Dutch kitchen with the old Dutch oven intact, the 200-year-old floors and special touches such as stained glass and games for guests. The hotel registration is handled here by an efficient and pleasant staff.

The Inn at Mandahl
P.O. Box 2483
St. Thomas
U.S. Virgin Islands 00801
(809) 775-2100

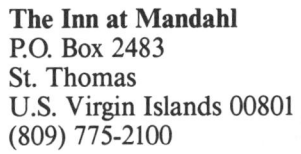

Inn; 8 units; Moderate/Moderate CP;
AE,MC,VI,DC; Children ok; Smoking ok.

Location: Mandahl Beach; 5 mi. to town; 8 mi. to airport.

Caribbean Bed & Breakfast

This cliff-hung, intimate inn offers spectacular views of the magnificent bay below and the British Virgin Islands as eyed through Drake's Passage. Situated at the top of a winding mountain road and near the prestigious Mahogany Run golf resort, the Inn at Mandahl provides comfortable, secluded accommodations about ten minutes from town.

The eight spacious and airy guestrooms are in one modest-looking building a short walk from the restaurant/lobby/bar. The guest accommodations, all in a row, share the same panoramic view that can best be appreciated from their large, private terraces overhanging the mountain side. The immaculate, but simple interiors feature polished, white tile floors, freshly painted wood paneling, open beamed ceilings with overhead fans (that are quite adequate with the ever-present trade winds), large closets and private baths with shower stalls and modern fixtures. The comfortable furnishings include king size, rattan four-poster beds with tropical print bedspreads, matching chairs and a small refrigerator.

A creative b&b routine at the Inn at Mandahl that promotes the sense of privacy is achieved cleverly with a simple, wicker bicycle basket hung outside each door. Every morning between 8 and 9 a.m. a continental breakfast consisting of thermos bottles of hot coffee and cold orange juice and foil-wrapped, hot muffins with butter and jams is placed in the door-side receptacles. A nice set-up of coffee mugs, juice (or wine) goblets and utensils are already in the room, ready for guests to breakfast on the outside terrace or even in bed! On Sunday mornings the routine is altered when the restaurant beckons guests, as well as local people, to their famous banana pancake brunch between 9 a.m. and 2 p.m. The same unbeatable view is combined with delicious banana pancakes, a variety of omelettes, eggs benedict and assorted libations, making it a meal worth "coming out of hiding" for!

The Inn at Mandahl Bar and Restaurant serves delicious, often gourmet, menus Tuesday through Saturday at fairly reasonable prices. The menus change daily, but feature fresh seafood, steak and pasta specialties, all served in the casual elegance of the cliff-perched dining room. Mr. Nibbs, the bartender, is famous for his Planters Punch, and the restaurant offers a nice selection of wines that you may choose to finish on your private terrace.

The reception area is friendly and comfortable with peacock wicker chairs facing backgammon boards, tropical print sofa and

U.S. Virgin Islands

chairs, piano and assorted reading material and brochures. The friendly staff will help in your travel planning and loans out snorkeling equipment and beach towels. A small, inviting pool dangles over Mandahl Beach, just 250 feet below and gives the sensation of swimming in air.

The Inn at Mandahl, owned and managed by a few Louisiana couples and their friends, is a pleasant discovery and has recently become a time-sharing hotel. So, if you are really sold on this friendly, secluded spot, you may choose to make it a permanent "home away from home."

Island View Guest House
P.O. Box 1903
St. Thomas
U.S. Virgin Islands 00801
(809) 774-4270
(800) 524-2023

Guest house; 9 units; Inexpensive-Mod./ Inexpensive CP; No credit cards; No children under 15; Smoking ok.

Location: Near town; 2 mi. to beach; 2 mi. to airport.

Situated midway between the airport and Charlotte Amalie on a secluded and lush tropical hillside, 545 feet above St. Thomas' harbor, is the Island View Guest House. The casual and private spot on Crown Mountain offers a reasonable vacation and friendly environs.

The neat, blue and white, 25-year-old concrete building was originally a private home; it was nicely converted to a guest house in 1969. Hospitable managers Barbara Cooper and Norman Leader have kept guests at Island View contented and the establishment well maintained for six years now.

The main floor of the b&b features the "Gallery," the hub of guest activity which overlooks the attractive pool and the town and harbor in a breathtaking way. Guests enjoy comfortable lounging in the spacious room with several small conversation areas as well as an extensive honor bar. A telescope here provides more detailed viewing of the interesting sights below.

Caribbean Bed & Breakfast

The complimentary morning fare consisting of toast, juice and coffee is served in the "Gallery" between 8 and 10 a.m. For bigger appetites a full breakfast is available at a modest charge. Sandwiches are prepared for lunch, and if a guest can't break away from the view and seclusion of the inn, the kind innkeepers have been known to make sandwiches available in the evening as well.

The pleasant and cheerful guestrooms at Island View include one suite, four poolside rooms with private baths and four mainfloor rooms that share 2 1/2 baths. All accommodations boast views of the harbor and are furnished modestly, but pleasantly with pretty bedspreads and shower curtains and absolute cleanliness. The suite features a large terrace and sleeps four.

The large pool with pretty tile and a spacious sundeck surrounding clings to the the steep hillside affording the same spectacular views. Please note that although an unobtrusive railing on the cliff side of the guest house provides adequate safety for the inn's adult guests, it is not an ideal situation for small children. For this reason Island View does not accept children under 15 years of age.

Maison Greaux Guest House
23 Solberg
P.O. Box 1856
St. Thomas
U.S. Virgin Islands 00801
(809) 774-0063

Guest house; 9 units; Inexpensive/ Inexpensive CP;
No credit cards; Children ok; Smoking ok.

Location: Near town; 3 mi. to beach; 3 mi. to airport.

Tucked away on a quiet, residential cul-de-sac 600 feet above town is this three-story, 25-year-old white guest house with orange trim. A small sidewalk lined with coconut palms and tropical plants and flowers surrounds the building; a staircase climb leads to the outdoor terrace/lounge—a friendly gathering place for the b&b guests.

The outside terrace, cooled by pleasant breezes and furnished with simple tables and chairs, offers a television, a popular honor bar and 180-degree views of Charlotte Amalie and

U.S. Virgin Islands

the harbor. The generous, complimentary morning meal is served here as well. Orange juice, eggs (any style), bacon or sausage, toast, cereal or "island" French toast and coffee are served cheerfully by the congenial innkeepers Mae and Don Bussiere each morning between 8 and 10 a.m. Mae is quick to add that the coffee is on by 6:15 a.m. for early risers, and she has been known to start breakfast at much earlier hours when the guest so desires.

The Bussieres took over management of Maison Greaux in July, 1984, and have since been upgrading little by little with new curtains and fresh paint. The nine guestrooms are all different, and five have private baths. The cheerful rooms are cooled by the refreshing trade winds and feature modest furnishings that are dressed up with pretty printed bedspreads and curtains. A convenient, full size refrigerator is located at the rear of the building for guests' use.

The management at Maison Greaux has additional plans for remodeling and refurbishing at this friendly b&b, but Mae and Don stress that any plans take second priority to making their guests feel welcome.

Miller Manor Guest House
27 & 28 Princesse Gade
P.O. Box 1570
St. Thomas
U.S. Virgin Islands 00801
(809) 774-1535

Guest house; 22 units; Inexpensive CP/ Inexpensive EP;
No credit cards; No children under 4-5; Smoking ok.

Location: In town; 3 mi. to beach; 3 mi. to airport.

Once a private home, the immaculate and homey 100-year-old structure has expanded to a second building to house guests in both comfortable guestrooms and full apartments. The prim, steel-gray hillside home is accented with attractive white gingerbread trim, thick spiral pillars and shutters. A white

Caribbean Bed & Breakfast

iron gate and a patio entry with a profusion of tropical plants keep the guest house private even though it is just a short walk from town.

The parlor of the old house reflects the warmth of its owners for over 30 years, the Millers. Decorated in comfortable antiques and memorabilia, the room is separated from the adjacent dining room by a wide, open arch. The formal dining room, not used by guests for actual dining, adds to the atmosphere of the establishment with its interesting lincrusta ceiling, ornate crystal chandelier and pretty antique furnishings. The polished ceramic floors of the two common rooms along with paintings, fresh flowers and lots of reading material make the area as inviting as "grandmother's" home.

Directly off the formal dining room of the house is a large veranda offering beautiful views of the harbor. The complimentary breakfast is served to guests (in on-season only) here on the attractive wrought-iron tables. The abundant winter fare includes a menu with a wide selection of juices or fresh fruit followed by a choice of cereal with fruit, eggs and bacon or pancakes and bacon plus coffee or tea. The breakfast meal is served daily from 7:30 to 9:30 a.m. Although no other meals are offered at Miller Manor, guests are enrolled in the "Bottle Club" and may stock their own liquor to go with the plentiful mixes provided there.

Proceeding down a short, steep staircase from the main floor, you will discover 100-year-old brick pillars and arches of the house and a rooftop terrace lounging area with guestrooms and apartments nearby.

The guestrooms and apartments at Miller Manor include a few antique-decorated rooms in the old house and more contemporary furnishings in the five-story newer structure. Overall, the furnishings are cheerful and comfortable with pretty curtains and bedspreads and are extremely clean. All of the homey accommodations boast private baths and many of the rooms are quite spacious. Some of the apartments, which are ideal for families, have full kitchens, two complete bedrooms and living room. Rates on apartments are also very reasonable.

This well-manicured bargain with homestyle atmosphere fills up sometimes a year in advance, so try to reserve early. Aida Miller, the manager/owner, takes delight in seeing her many friends who return each year, some for nearly 30 years now.

U.S. Virgin Islands

Villa Santana
Denmark Hill
St. Thomas
U.S. Virgin Islands 00801
(809) 774-1311
(800) 524-9142

Historic inn; 11 units; Moderate/ Inexpensive EP;
No credit cards; Children ok; Smoking ok.

Location: Near town; 2½ mi. to beach; 2 mi. to airport.

This historic, island-colonial villa was built by General Santa Ana of Mexico during his third exile in 1857. The mansion, with an interesting combination of Danish and Mexican architecture, sits on two acres of land on a spectacular hilltop location, 200 feet above town. A winding road leads to the estate, and a cobblestone driveway continues on to a picturesque courtyard with gardens, paths and old fountain and to cottages in the rear.

The mansion with white wooden siding and shutters and black wrought-iron trim features a wide veranda with matching wrought-iron furnishings overlooking the breathtaking views of the town and harbor. The parlor of the villa has comfortable furnishings, mainly rattan, but is enhanced by the interesting antique wall and door moldings (that curve with the wide arch entry), polished wooden floors and coved wooden ceiling with an old ceiling medallion and wrought-iron chandelier. A billiard table area and small office connect to the parlor and feature the original black and white marble floor of the house.

The guestrooms at Villa Santana are all different in size and decor; many have interesting antiques. An ornately carved four-poster with canopy may have been in the house originally and occupies one of the rooms. All of the spotlessly clean guest accommodations have private baths, the original wooden floors, pleasant, cheerful furnishings and an intercom to the manager.

Caribbean Bed & Breakfast

One accommodation offers a kitchenette with full-size refrigerator.

Villa Santana's owner and manager, Luisa Euwema, takes a special interest in the estate, which has been handed down through her family, and treats guests as company in her prestigious home.

Note:
The inn will be closed for refurbishing until an anticipated reopening December 15, 1985, but check to be sure.

St. Croix

The largest island in the U.S. Virgins, St. Croix totals 84 square miles of mostly hilly terrain with pastures and tropical foliage and has two main towns, Christiansted and Frederiksted. Christiansted, the one-time Danish West Indies capital, founded in 1734, is a National Historic Site and charms the visitor with its old-world architecture and reminders of history. The town lies in a reef-sheltered bay surrounded by hills and boasts an abundant amount of restored Danish structures. Well-preserved Fort Christiansvaern was built in 1749 of Danish ballast. Other preserved examples to view include the Old Danish Customs House, the Scale House and the Governor's House. The small streets of town are lined with quaint boutiques and cafes, and alley-tucked arcades provide more of the same. World famous Buck Island Reef, a glass-bottom boat ride from town, is the only U.S. National Monument that is underwater. The park includes 850 acres with sandy beaches and a reef with two major underwater trails.

Frederiksted is a picturesque harbor town that is characterized by largely Victorian architecture due to a fire in the late 1800's that destroyed most of the structures in town. The town, which greets cruise ship passengers who visit the island, is renovating many of its quaint, gingerbreaded buildings. Since the entire town has been named a National Historic Site, Kodak has led the way with a renovation investment of over one-half million dollars in a new facility there, and others are following suit.

The visitor to St. Croix will not only enjoy boundless recreation, but also the green countryside filled with historic sugar mill ruins. Visitors may view the Whim Greathouse, a 1700's

U.S. Virgin Islands

restored plantation and the St. George Botanical Garden consisting of 160 acres of lush woods and rich land along with the ruins of an 18th-century sugar cane village and rum factory. For those more into the libation itself than its history, the Cruzan Rum Pavilion gives regular tours that culminate with a complimentary rum cocktail.

Cane Bay Plantation
Estate Cane Bay
P.O. Box G
King's Hill Station
St. Croix
U.S. Virgin Islands 00850
(809) 778-0410

Plantation; 34 units; Moderate-Exp./Inexpensive-Mod. EP; MC,VI,AE; Children ok; Smoking ok.

Location: 40 yds. to beach; 10 mi. to town; 8 mi. to airport.

A scenic country drive meandering through gently rolling hills with views of the sea takes you to this 22-acre plantation at the foot of Mount Eagle and opposite Cane Bay. The grounds of the over 200-year-old plantation climb a hill to the overseer's original residence, now lobby and restaurant, and continue on to the various cottage accommodations that house guests in addition to a more contemporary structure at the base of the old residence. A profusion of tropical vegetation and grand 200-year-old trees fill the tranquil areas between the various structures.

The sugar plantation overseer's house is painted white, as are the other buildings, and has black trim and black wooden shutters. The long, arched "gallery" on the front contains an antique grip test machine that sits beside the lobby entrance framed by tall white and black double doors and white peacock-

Caribbean Bed & Breakfast

fanned rattan chairs. The lobby or guest lounge offers an informal and comfortable atmosphere for enjoying the television, piano or good conversation with the added bonus of relaxing cross-breezes.

Just off the guest lounge is the terrace dining area with spectacular views of the ocean. The semi-open area is decorated in pleasant blue and white Caribbean print tablecloths, with white director's chairs and lots of hanging plants. A sunken tile bar adjoins, and a cannon in the far corner of this area is a reminder of its age. All three meals are served in this idyllic spot. If you decide to picnic on the beach across the road or on a special spot on the grounds, the inn will pack a picnic lunch with sandwiches and fruit. Dinner is by romantic candlelight, and entertainment featuring a steel band, folk singer or perhaps dance music is offered three nights per week.

Guestrooms at the Cane Bay Plantation are located in a two-story building near the entrance to the plantation or in one of 11 cottages that were once slave quarters or storage areas of the old plantation. Each of the guest facilities boasts a private bath, a decorating theme that features wicker headboards on twin or double beds, desks, dressers, Haitian paintings, cheerful bedspreads and blue drapes. The newer rooms offer sliding doors and balconies with views of the ocean, and the cottages are outfitted with screened-in porch areas in their more isolated locations.

Two freshwater pools are located on the plantation grounds. The main pool is directly below the terrace dining area and bar and is surrounded by spacious wood decking and pretty potted plants. The same dramatic views of Cane Bay can also be enjoyed while swimming or sunning there. For more private tanning a second pool is located farther away from the inn activity in a country setting. The gracious management headed by Deborah Ellis is glad to arrange boating and fishing activities in Christiansted; the inn is the closest lodging establishment in St. Croix to the Fountain Valley Golf Course.

Note:
The inn is closed in the summer.

The Lodge Hotel
43-A Queen Cross Street
Christiansted

U.S. Virgin Islands

St. Croix
U.S. Virgin Islands 00820
(809) 773-1535
(800) 524-2026

Inn; 16 units; Moderate/Inexpensive EP;
AE,MC,VI; Children ok; Smoking ok.

Location: In town; 1 block to beach/harbor; 8 mi. to airport.

The Lodge Hotel is located right in the heart of Christiansted, blending harmoniously with the quaint Danish facades of the various boutiques and restaurants that make up the shopping quarter of the town. The street-fronting structure of the inn is an 1800's townhouse with an intimate courtyard tucked just behind. To the rear of the old Danish abode and connecting is a 1960's-built structure that contains the 16 guestroom units of the hotel.

The upstairs of the old Danish townhouse contains the Moonraker Bar, known to many tourists and local people as a popular entertainment spot. Live entertainment is provided here nightly on-season and three nights per week during off-season. The bottom portion of the townhouse holds the office of the inn. You are likely to find the new co-owners of the inn, Simon Marks and John Pickles, here or tending to guests at the bar. Marks and Pickles, brothers who grew up in the hotel business, acquired the Lodge Hotel in January, 1985, and are very busy instituting renovation plans. Their goal, to be achieved in 1985, is to redo rooms and begin breakfast service in the pleasant courtyard area.

A shaded courtyard with a giant mango tree draped in vines is the focus of the small inn. Protected by buildings and walls, the cozy area is surprisingly immune to the noises of downtown and gives a relaxed atmosphere for lounging or breakfasting. Ornate, white Victorian chairs and tables will dot the planter enclosed area and provide a graceful, old-fashioned feel.

The guestrooms at the inn are to be decorated in simple rattan-style furnishings; all with private bathrooms, air

Caribbean Bed & Breakfast

conditioning, telephones, television and small refrigerators. The decor will be modest, but new, and it should make for very reasonable accommodations in a convenient downtown location. The owner-brothers are friendly and quick to see to guests' needs at this intimate lodging establishment, making this a good budget choice for those who want to be in the "pulse" of things.

Pink Fancy
27 Prince Street
Christiansted
St. Croix
U.S. Virgin Islands 00820
(809) 773-8460
(800) 524-2045

Historic inn; 13 units; Moderate/Moderate CP;
No credit cards; Children ok; Smoking ok.

Location: In town; 2 blocks to harbor/beach; 8 mi. to airport.

Undoubtedly one of the most charming inns in the Caribbean, the Pink Fancy Hotel offers historic charm, modern amenities and in-town convenience along with guest house friendliness and security. The small hotel, owned and meticulously renovated by Sam Dillon, incorporates four small buildings that take up most of a corner block a few streets away from the downtown boutiques and seaplane launch. The picturesque, weathered brick walls and arches are topped by a white-shingled second story that features pastel-pink wooden shutters and small-paned windows. As you enter through the ornamental and privacy-conscious black iron gates to the brick arcade entrance, you first note the well-earned plaque on the wall reading "Pink Fancy, 1780--Registered in the National Register of Historic Places...1966." This building offering several of the 13 guest accommodations was once a 1780 Danish townhouse, and the remaining three buildings, focused on an attractive central courtyard, were constructed in 1880.

When Mr. Dillon acquired the property a few years ago he chose to restore its 1950's use as a lodging establishment (then

U.S. Virgin Islands

a haven for many famous artists and writers), but not before investing over $1 million into the careful renovation program. Saving the original walls and structures themselves, Dillon created guestroom accommodations of varying proportions within the four historic buildings. Although individually decorated, each of the guestrooms has the same airy, fresh feel created by the use of white on the walls, on the quaintly shuttered windows and on the chenille bedspreads. The effect is dramatized by the use of tropical prints, pretty brick or walnut flooring and luscious pink towels in the baths. Each guestroom features a comfortable sitting area, a compact efficiency kitchen (often cleverly hidden by French doors) with all the necessities and air conditioning and fans. The townhouse building features an impressive central air conditioning system. In addition each room has a clock radio, color television and modern, spacious baths with tub/shower combinations. Because of its odd shape, one unit features a corner tub that has a spa look.

The names of guestrooms were derived from old estates on the island and, at the same time, seem to apply nicely to a stay at this intimate inn. You might like to try the "Morning Star," the "Bonne Esperance," the "Work and Rest," "Recovery Hill" or "Hard Labor." If you can't identify which room you want by name alone, then note that "Work and Rest" might be combined with "Recovery Hill" for a spacious suite with antique corner nook and reading tables and batik prints. "Hard Labor" is the largest guestroom with attractive slanted ceilings that follow the roofline, and the "Parasol" is a more intimate unit near the gazebo with views of the pool.

The small grounds of the inn are well utilized with pretty gardens and a protected courtyard with inviting pool and large palm. In this area the guest will enjoy the "Limetree Bar," the self-service complimentary bar that is well stocked and used freely by guests. The bar is also the site of the complimentary morning fare consisting of Danish, orange juice, coffee, milk or tea. Guests are free to enjoy the breakfast outside on the patio or in the privacy of their rooms. Next door to the bar is the office that contains a small library for guests' use. Just above the courtyard are smaller sitting areas terraced on various levels. A gazebo area offers attractive outside relaxing, and a side patio is a favorite site for impromptu barbecues organized by the guests.

Assistant manager Eustace Simon knows the inn from the inside out having worked on the hotel from the beginning of its renovation. He, like the rest of the staff at the hotel, reflects a well-deserved pride in the establishment and is eager to share his enthusiasm with guests. Eustace is quick to point out the personal nature of the inn where "guests all know each other within 24 hours–unless they want their privacy." Both attitudes are readily respected at the Pink Fancy.

Royal Dane Hotel
13 Strand Street
Frederiksted
St. Croix
U.S. Virgin Islands 00840
(809) 772-2780

Historic inn; 15 units; Inexpensive-Mod./Inexpensive-Mod. CP; AE,VI,MC; No children under 14; Smoking ok.

Location: In town; ½ mi. to beach; 7 mi. to airport.

This small yet elegant inn is located on a prominent harbor-facing corner in the town of Frederiksted. A part of the National Historic District of the town, the 1790-built townhouse is surrounded by buildings of the same 17th-century Dutch persuasion. The Royal Dane Hotel, renovated in 1984 by new owners Michael Zullo and Warren Singer, was one of the first gingerbread-adorned structures to make the move towards renewal and has led the way with class and style. Warren and Zullo, an energetic team, have enthusiastically renovated the abandoned property into a well-appointed lodging establishment with popular restaurant in less than a year.
The 200-year-old ballast walls of the inn with white Victorian trellis and green shutters lead to a charming central courtyard with garden where guests congregate, dine and enjoy the hot tub. The restaurant at the inn is becoming well known for its fine West Indian and continental cuisine and is open nightly for dinner except Sunday when a special brunch is served. Flamboyant trees, cedar trees, Spanish moss and a profusion of orchids and poinsettias surround the courtyard area that also contains small goldfish ponds and local artwork. A hot tub is situated in a private corner.

U.S. Virgin Islands

The guestrooms at the Royal Dane are all newly renovated and boast air conditioning as well as ceiling fans in most, private baths and rattan furnishings. The walls are brightly painted, and the building's design makes for interesting room shapes and sizes. The upstairs units feature quaint peaked ceilings, and one room (#7) is referred to as the honeymoon suite due to its romantic antique furnishings with four-poster bed and its spectacular view of the harbor out its shuttered windows. The modernized rooms, along with the rest of the hotel, are decorated in attractive art prints or original, local artwork.

An upstairs gallery serves as a harbor-view breakfast spot for this b&b's complimentary meal of juice, coffee and freshly baked goods. The gallery featuring Victorian trim is also a guest lounge and activity center that might host an art exhibit on its tall, white walls that reach up to the peaked 20-foot-high ceiling. Warren claims you can view the green flash (a bright flash of green light on the horizon that some people claim to see at sunset) from the gallery windows that stare out to the ocean horizon. Even if you're not one of the "charmed" who catch a glimpse of green, the view is inspiring.

Innkeepers Zullo and Singer put a lot of effort into keeping guests contented at their moderately priced inn. In addition to a complimentary breakfast, they greet guests with a "welcoming cocktail" and provide free transportation to the beach one-half mile away. They also show popular or classic movies on Monday nights and have arranged use of the Grange Beach Club facility for guests of the Royal Dane. The inn, which could also be called a guest house, offers a quiet and friendly atmosphere for its special guests.

Sprat Hall Plantation
P.O. Box 695
Frederiksted
St. Croix
U.S. Virgin Islands 00840
(809) 772-0305
(800) 524-2026

Caribbean Bed & Breakfast

Plantation; 20 units; Moderate/Moderate EP;
No credit cards; Children ok (except great house); Smoking ok (except great house).

Location: 200 yds. to beach; 1 mi. to town; 7 mi. to airport.

Not only is the Sprat Hall Plantation the oldest great house in the Virgin Islands and the only French plantation house left intact, it also holds the impressive title of the oldest building in private hands in the Caribbean. The majestic, white great house surrounded by pastoral scenery was built in 1670 by French colonists who constructed it exactly like the original in Brittany. In fact, a guest of the historic inn experienced a real case of deja vu when he arrived at the plantation on vacation, sight unseen, to discover it the duplicate of his own home in Brittany—the original great house upon which Sprat Hall was modeled. Owners Jim and Joyce Hurd, whose families have been in St. Croix since the 1700's, will happily tell you this and more about the history of Sprat Hall and the island they call their home.

The plantation, consisting of over 20 acres of pasture, 5 acres of lawn, ancient trees and flowering shrubs, is a serene country inn that offers the only riding stables in the Virgin Islands. Like everything at the inn, the stables are a family endeavor, run by daughter Jill whose lifetime ambition was to do just that, and she prides herself on being the first breeder of thoroughbred horses on the island. Part of the acreage at Sprat Hall Plantation is devoted to raising the fresh fruit and vegetables used to make the wonderful homemade food served at the inn.

Guests arrive at the plantation by way of a lazy country road flanked by bright flamboyant trees. The only sounds are of the long-tailed green parrots or cockatoos that populate the country terrain or the knoll-top breeze that carries the soothing rhythm of the waves 200 yards away. The gracious great house greets you on its hilltop with views of the sea and hills for miles. Lazy trees, potted plants and palms surround the structure with curved-arch gallery, green wooden shutters and old stone steps. An Oriental carpet in greens and blues ushers the guest into the parlor, the original dining room of the house. The parlor, enjoyed by guests, has light blue walls with white trim and is furnished in an interesting combination of antiques.

U.S. Virgin Islands

Jim Hurd, an antique expert, will relate the history (if known) of each piece and has a workshop constantly full of new pieces to renovate and replace in his own rotation-like system. A built-in hutch holds books, a television is cleverly blended with the old, and the result is both comfort and a fascinating touch of the past.

The dining room, adjacent to the parlor, is one of the two restaurants of the inn. The other is the more informal, beachfront eatery a few hundred yards away. This formal dining room, the original ballroom of the great house, features a blue and white Royal Copenhagen decor from the elegant table china to the draperies tied back at the windows. The room is all antique with old wooden floors, another built-in china hutch with antique glass pieces and antique mahogany tables and chairs. Nighttime diners are treated to candlelight supplied by individual hurricane holders and candelabra that surround the room. All three meals are served at the plantation with an emphasis on homemade and homegrown.

A bar is located at the rear, bottom-level of the house and is a casual gathering spot. Upstairs are the four guestrooms of the great house, each a study in antique history and very individual. These prized rooms are not offered to smokers or children with good reason. Behind each door is a bevy of one-of-a-kind antique beds and family mementos that have been lovingly restored by the Hurds. One room features French antiques and has the only original great house antique, an ornately carved pineapple canopy bed. A cane settee and twin rockers, a marble writing table and an armoire are set off by the pink walls, green shutters and large pink and green woven rug. The other three guestrooms, all with private bath, include a "Danish" room, an "English" room and a small single room decorated in a family member's antique furnishings, keepsakes and photographs.

The remainder of the guest accommodations at the plantation are located in a 1948-built, two-story structure, in 1969-constructed bungalows and also in two-, three- and four-bedroom houses. These other guest lodgings are decorated in more modern furnishings of rattan or teak and color-coordinated fabrics.

Over 36 years of owner-management of the Sprat Hall Plantation have perfected the informal and congenial atmosphere of the inn. Whether lounging on the beach a short stroll away, horseback riding through the plantation's rain forest or soaking up local history, the guest will find this historic inn a relaxing, country retreat.

Caribbean Bed & Breakfast

Also on the Island

Anchor Inn
58-A King Street
Christiansted
St. Croix
U.S. Virgin Islands 00820
(809) 773-4000
(800) 524-2030

Directly on the waterfront in the heart of downtown Christiansted is this 30-guestroom inn with small swimming pool and popular terraced restaurant. The inn is also accessible off the main shopping street, down one of the town's hidden alleyways. The U-shaped, two-story complex is in intimate quarters, giving it a rather European feel. Guest accommodations include twin beds, color television, refrigerator, bath, air conditioning, telephone and small balconies. Suites offer double beds, but no balconies. The decor is fairly similar in all the rooms, offering contemporary, pleasant furnishings in an orange motif. The restaurant serves all meals and features continental and West Indian cuisine.

Club Comanche
1 Strand Street
Christiansted
St. Croix
U.S. Virgin Islands 00820
(809) 773-0210

Located in the very heart of downtown, surrounded by the quaint boutiques of a popular alley shopping arcade is the Club Comanche with its notable hydraulic caged elevator, awning-covered bridge that spans tiny Strand Street and unique guestroom offerings. Guest accommodations at the 46-unit inn include impressive split-level suites, four-posters and antiques and more contemporary units. The "landmark" accommodation of the Club is the Mill Room, which is actually a restored sugar mill that has been converted to a tri-plex guest suite right on the water's edge. Two restaurants, one inside the hotel and the other on the terrace, offer excellent dining and a lengthy wine list.

U.S. Virgin Islands

St. John

The smallest of the inhabited U.S. Virgins with only 28 square miles of territory, St. John is perhaps the loveliest with its verdant, mountainous landscape surrounded by sugar-white beaches and tourmaline sea. Due to Laurence Rockefeller's foresight and generosity, more than two-thirds of the island is overseen by the National Park Service for perpetual safekeeping and preservation. This 7,028-acre preserve offers beaches with panoramic views, woodland trails and wildlife sanctuaries as well as spectacular underwater trails at Trunk Bay that delight snorkelers.

Although St. John may certainly be a travel destination by itself, many visitors from St. Thomas arrive for the day. A pleasant, double-decker ferry from St. Thomas' Red Hook dock arrives in St. John's Cruz Bay on a frequent daily schedule. The ride, with gorgeous island and ocean views included, takes only 20 minutes and is one of the best bargains in the U.S. Virgin Islands! Cruz Bay is a cute little town with a few shops and restaurants around a small square. Here taxis, which are really trucks equipped with benches and red- and white-striped awnings, take visitors to any of the fine beaches or to the Caneel Bay Plantation. The cost is reasonable, but jeeps and mopeds may also be rented here.

Trunk Bay is probably the most popular tourist destination on the island with its crystal-clear water and underwater trails. A good hamburger stand is there, as are changing rooms, bathrooms and outdoor showers.

Caneel Bay
P.O. Box 720, Cruz Bay
St. John
U.S. Virgin Islands 00830
(809) 776-6111
Rep.: Rockresorts Reservations

Historic inn; 156 units; Deluxe/ Deluxe AP;
AE,VI,DC,MC; No children under 8; Smoking ok.

Caribbean Bed & Breakfast

Location: On beach; 2 mi. to town.

This full resort facility that caters to the wealthy, honeymooners or those seeking a relaxing off-season bargain in luxury has developed on 170 acres of scenic land filled with beautifully maintained tropical gardens, seven white-sand beaches, the remains of the 18th-century sugar mill (now restaurant) and the little villas and estate houses that lodge the guests.

Guests at Caneel Bay have the lovely option of being active every moment or not doing anything at all in this serene, former plantation environment. Activities, all included in your stay, can include tennis at one of the seven courts, sailing, cruising or fishing aboard one of the Caneel Bay boats, swimming, snorkeling or scuba in the clear waters, bicycling, sightseeing excursions and more. Or for pure relaxation, the guest at Caneel Bay may choose to stroll around the beautiful grounds and take in the surrounding hills of the Virgin Islands National Park or just laze on one of the comfortable lounges on the beach of his or her choice.

All three meals are included in the rate. At Caneel Bay guests may dine atop an 18th-century sugar mill, on a terrace overlooking the ocean or on the patio of a restored manor house. The inn's Sugar Mill Kitchen restaurant is one of three dining spots and is popular with the day visitors who stop for lunch. A delightful patio bar offers nighttime entertainment with local color.

The guestrooms at the plantation range from garden terrace rooms that are situated away from the bay to the most expensive premium rooms that are really small villas situated along the beach. The rooms are all fairly spacious and attractively decorated in contemporary furnishings with natural color tones. The serenity of the getaway resort is insured with a lack of television or telephone (soundproofed public phones are located near the reception area). Ceiling fans provide adequate ventilation as do the louvers and patio doors. As a nice touch, a welcoming bottle of Virgin Island rum awaits the guest upon checking-in.

While Caneel Bay is far from an intimate resort in terms of size, it has the space and peacefulness that can allow for an intimate stay. Personal service is not easy to achieve with the brisk business that goes on here even in off-season, but

U.S. Virgin Islands

professional service is a requirement at this popular resort on one of the loveliest islands in the Caribbean.

Huldah Sewer's Guest House
P.O. Box 25, Cruz Bay
St. John
U.S. Virgin Islands 00830
(809) 776-6378

Guest house; 28 units; Inexpensive-Mod./ Inexpensive-Mod. EP; AE,MC,VI; Children ok; Smoking ok.

Location: In town; 1 1/2 mi. to beach.

This modest guest house complex is an easy walk from the ferry boat landing towards the residential area of town, near the school. It offers 24 motel-type rooms and 4 apartments; all feature private baths. The guestrooms have small refrigerators and the apartments, with one bedroom, are completely furnished and can rent by the week for additional savings. Huldah Sewer's, managed by Oswin A. Sewer, is geared for the budget traveler to St. John.

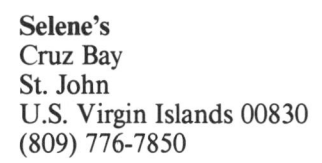

Selene's
Cruz Bay
St. John
U.S. Virgin Islands 00830
(809) 776-7850

Inn; 6 units; Moderate/ Moderate EP; MC,VI; Children ok; Smoking ok.

Location: In town; 1 1/2 mi. to beach.

This relatively new inn on a hilltop overlooking town is a pleasant addition to St. John's vacation offerings. The

Caribbean Bed & Breakfast

contemporary structure, a short walk from the shops and ferry, houses six full apartments that are rented at reasonable rates by the night or by the week. The suites can easily sleep four and are attractively and comfortably furnished.

The light and airy units are quite spacious and feature lots of fresh plants, attractive contemporary furniture and area rugs, pretty wall prints, a sleeping area with double bed and a convertible couch in the living room area. A modern bath with pretty tile and full kitchen with dining area are also a part of each apartment. Four of the six units have view balconies.

No meals are offered at Selene's, but with a fully equipped modern kitchen it is probably not necessary. But if requested, Selene's will prepare a gourmet meal and serve it in the privacy of your own apartment. A good deli-type restaurant with homemade goodies is located a few steps away as well.

Resident owner and manager Ellen Shapiro is the one who insures that guests feel welcome at her small establishment. Fresh flowers and a bottle of Virgin Islands rum await you upon arrival, and Ellen will even meet you at the ferry with advance warning. For the traveler to St. John who desires a comfortable and affordable stay with many personal touches, Selene's is certainly an attractive option.

12

British Virgin Islands

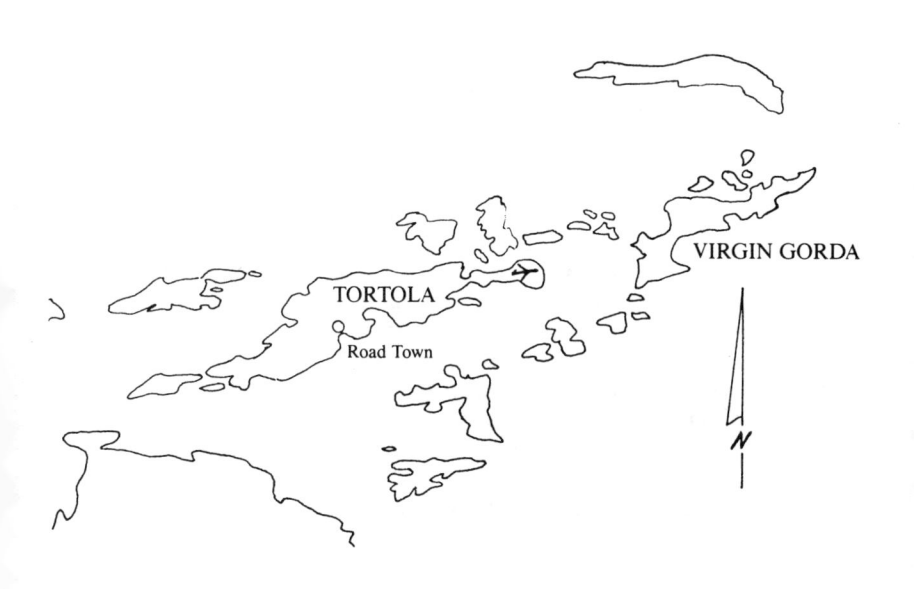

Caribbean Bed & Breakfast

More than 50 islands, rocks and cays situated in these incredibly clear, turquoise waters form the British Virgin Islands, although many of these volcano-produced formations are uninhabited. Best known in the British Virgin Islands are Tortola and Virgin Gorda; less talked about islands include Jost Van Dyke, Norman Island, Peter Island, Salt Island and Beef Island, which connects to Tortola by bridge and is the site of the British Virgin Island's airport. Anegada is the only coral (non-volcanic) island in the chain.

Getting to these islands, located just 60 miles east of Puerto Rico, is easy by air, although non-stop flights are not available. Daily connections from St. Thomas, St. Croix and Puerto Rico, as well as connections from other Caribbean islands are plentiful. Air BVI offers many inter-island and other Caribbean destination flights as well. High-speed ferry services connecting Tortola, Virgin Gorda, St. Thomas and St. John are numerous. A small departure tax is collected when leaving these islands. The U.S. dollar is the official currency, and the language is English. A passport, birth certificate or voter's registration card is sufficient for entry here. The British Virgin Islands are on Atlantic Standard Time (one hour earlier than Eastern Standard Time) except during Daylight Saving's season when clocks in these islands are the same as those in the Eastern U.S.

Recreation equals water-related sports and leisure in the British Virgin Islands. The clear, calm waters and protected cays and coves make sailing, windsurfing, scuba and snorkeling extraordinary. Fishing is considered excellent, but the colorful tropical fish are not to be caught and, like the coral, are for "looking" only. Hundreds of uncrowded, white sandy beaches make relaxing and shell collecting favorite activities in these islands. Divers enjoy their sport here year-round with visibility of 50 to 100 feet or more.

The hilly terrain, ancient ruins of sugar mills, pirate caves and rain forests make hiking, bird-watching and exploring popular pastimes as are golf, tennis and horseback riding. The nightlife on the islands is restricted mainly to informal gatherings.

For more information on the British Virgin Islands contact:
British Virgin Islands Tourist Board
370 Lexington Ave.
New York, New York 10017
(212) 696-0400

British Virgin Islands

Tortola

This 12-mile-long by 3-mile-wide island has a population of 9,000 and contains the capital of the islands, Road Town, where the main shops, banks, hospital and government buildings are located. The southern shore of the island has jagged mountain peaks rising to 1,800 feet, and the northern shore boasts white, powdery beaches and tropical groves. The Mount Sage National Park offers glimpses of a primeval rain forest on its slopes.

Although tourism has increased in the last 15 years with the advent of additional hostelries, Tortola is still a rural, slow-paced island with marauding goats, lambs and chickens and friendly people. Shopping is still minimal; local shops are located in or near Road Town. Car rental agencies are plentiful, but none are located at the airport. A taxi will take you to the car agency of your choice in town, but note that neither car rental companies nor shops are open on Sunday.

Connected by the 300-foot Queen Elizabeth Bridge is the small Beef Island, a hunting ground during the pirate days, now providing airport service to the islands. Near Beef Island is Marina Cay, a six-acre island brought to fame by the book and movie entitled *Our Virgin Island.*

Buccaneer Inn
Sopers Hole
P.O. Box 441
Road Town, Tortola
British Virgin Islands
(809) 495-4212/495-4559

Inn; 6 units; Inexpensive/Inexpensive EP;
No credit cards; Children ok; Smoking ok.

Location: 100 yds. to beach; 10 mi. to town; 18 mi. to airport.

Nestled between the West End ferry and seaplane shuttle launches, this small inn is certainly convenient for those intending to island-hop between the various British and U.S. Virgin islands destinations. The inn looks over the harbor and offers a few wooden benches and chairs on a cement patio stretching out to the water's edge. There is no real swimming beach here, but the boat activity is lively, and you can swim from the boat ramp.

Caribbean Bed & Breakfast

The 1982-built, two-story building is of white stucco construction highlighted by brown trim and tiny murals of fish and birds. A dining terrace with rough, wood-beamed ceilings, lots of hanging plants and nautical decor dominates the front of the inn and is supported by stone columns. The restaurant at the Buccaneer serves all three meals with dinner by advance reservation only. A stereo and television are located in the dining area, and a party-night is held here once a week. For a little more excitement, a restaurant with live entertainment is located about 50 yards away.

The six guestrooms of the inn are airy with a light brown decor featuring beige, flowered curtains and simple, comfortable furnishings. The modest accommodations include two rooms with private baths and four that share bathroom use. All rooms have twin beds.

This unpretentious inn with pretty views of the natural harbor and the emerald-green hills in the near distance offers simple, budget accommodations for those who enjoy the yachting activity of these islands.

Fort Recovery
P.O. Box 239
Road Town, Tortola
British Virgin Islands
(809) 495-4354
Rep: Anita MacShane

Inn; 9 units; Moderate-Exp. wkly/Moderate-Exp. wkly;
No credit cards; Children ok; Smoking ok.

Location: On beach; 7 mi. to town; 16 mi. to airport.

This is not really an inn, but a small assemblage of villas that surround an original 17th-century Dutch fort of the same name. Fort Recovery offers nine completely equipped villas that are rented mainly by the week, but are sometimes available for shorter periods. Their location is idyllically private and

British Virgin Islands

quiet, off the main road from town and fronting an intimate, private beach and small boat dock. The grounds themselves add to the overall tranquility with ample bougainvillaea, oleander and hibiscus around the grassy areas dotted with palms.

Each unit is very private, with its own semi-enclosed patio draped in purple bougainvillaea, fully equipped kitchen, spacious living room and separate bedroom; each bedroom boasts a separate entrance as well. All the villas are air conditioned and decorated tastefully, and maid service is provided daily. A two-bedroom, two-bath villa is also available.

Original owner Anita MacShane is in charge of reservations and the overseeing of Fort Recovery. Although her office is in New York, she visits often, and a full-time manager is on the premises at all times. If you care to rent a car or need a babysitter, she is happy to make those arrangements and take care of any other details that will make your stay happier.

For the traveler in need of a little rest and relaxation, coupled with modern comforts and quiet, Fort Recovery certainly lives up to its name. What could be more restful than listening to the waves lap gently a few feet away and watching the sailboats, silhouetted against the nearby islands, glide by all day long.

Long Bay Beach Resort
P.O. Box 433
Road Town, Tortola
British Virgin Islands
(809) 495-4252
Rep: American/Wolfe Int.

Inn; 37 units; Moderate-Exp./Inexpensive-Mod. EP; No credit cards; Children ok; Smoking ok.

Location: On beach; 10 mi. to town; 19 mi. to airport.

This secluded resort is located on its own mile-long sweep of incredibly white sand with aquamarine water. The 50-acre complex offers only 37 units blended cleverly around the grounds

Caribbean Bed & Breakfast

that consist of beachfront cabanas on stilts and hillside units and villas that are terraced among the grape trees, hibiscus and frangipani.

The landscaped estate has a private club feel from the moment you enter the grounds. The ruins of an old sugar mill containing an informal restaurant greet you. Guests may have breakfast, luncheon or dinner here within the sugar mill walls or on the patios that extend to the white sand beyond. The menus are more casual here than in the main dining room, but very tasty with banana pancake breakfasts or curry dinners. The inviting swimming pool is a step away from the restaurant, and the beach, complete with comfortable lounges, is only a few yards away.

A lazy, country road leads the guest to the tennis courts of the resort as well as the nine-hole pitch and putt golf course. Just a short stroll across the road is the other dining room of the hotel and bar just below. Guests are treated to a daily selected menu here in a more formal atmosphere. The bar is a gathering and socializing spot for guests in the evening. Children are discouraged in the main dining room, but the hosts are happy to arrange babysitting.

The guest accommodations at Long Bay can suit about any taste, ranging from complete, two-bedroom villas with kitchens and living rooms to standard twin-bedded rooms with balcony overlooking the ocean. The beachfront cabanas feature an elevated bedroom with twin beds, kitchenette and sundeck as well as covered patio on the sand. Furnishings include nicely tiled, modern bathrooms and attractive decor featuring rattan, wicker, tropical prints and windows that take advantage of the inspiring views.

This quiet escape has a friendly, safe feel that enables the guest to wander the countrified grounds day and night without hesitation. In fact, there are no locks on the doors. The manager of Long Bay is also the former owner; a sense of personal attention is apparent from the start at the resort. At Long Bay the guest never signs for a meal or anything else for that matter—your face is your only signature!

Sebastian's on the Beach
Little Apple Bay
P.O. Box 441
Road Town, Tortola
British Virgin Islands
(809) 495-4212

British Virgin Islands

Inn; 24 units; Moderate/Inexpensive EP;
AE; Children ok; Smoking ok.

Location: On beach; 10 mi. to town; 19 mi. to airport.

Located on a scenic stretch of beach at Little Apple Bay is this popular, informal inn consisting of beachfront, modern rooms and an older complex across the road that houses guestrooms as well as a store with an interesting medley of groceries, souvenirs and supplies. The active spot attracts its share of surfers in the winter when surf at the hotel draws aficionados from Hawaii and New Zealand to Sebastian's.

The guestrooms in the newer complex that nearly touches the surf are nicely decorated in coordinated rattan furnishings with flowered bedspreads and attractive wood-beamed ceilings. The rooms boast modern, private baths with showers, mini-refrigerators and airy, spacious square footage. Some of these accommodations in the contemporary, two-story buildings have views of the ocean, while others face the central courtyard where the activity seems to gravitate. More moderately priced accommodations are offered in the 25-year-old, maroon-colored structure just across the road.

The restaurant at Sebastian's is noted for its American, European, French and West Indian specialties. Reservations are a must for dinner, and the day's selection is posted on a chalkboard at the store desk. The combined restaurant and guest

Caribbean Bed & Breakfast

lounge has comfortable seating, nautical decor and an adjoining beachside patio. Breakfast and lunch are also offered in the open-air bistro at moderate prices.

Sebastian's on the Beach, owned and operated by the owners of the Buccaneer Inn, offers an informal, beach-oriented stay for those who seek the company of fellow guests and the sound of the waves a few feet away. It is the kind of cozy spot you can visit with just a bathing suit for daytime and a not much fancier outfit for night and be right in style.

Sugar Mill Estate Hotel
Apple Bay
P.O. Box 425
Road Town, Tortola
British Virgin Islands
(809) 495-4355

Rep: International Travel & Resorts
Historic inn; 21 units; Expensive/Moderate EP;
AE,VI,MC; Children ok; Smoking ok.

Location: 75 yds. to beach; 9 mi. to town; 18 mi. to airport.

Take two travel and food writers from California who long to experience the romanticism of innkeeping from the other side of the typewriter and add one quaint, historic inn and restaurant on a beautiful Caribbean island, and the result is the Sugar Mill Estate--a pleasant blend of island informality and romantic charm. That is how owners Jinx and Jeff Morgan recall their advent into innkeeping, and the resultant inn and gourmet restaurant reflect their sophisticated touches and good humor in many delightful ways.

The Sugar Mill Estate was originally a 1600's sugar mill plantation built from the stone and brick ballast from British ships. At the entrance to the hillside grounds are the walls of the sugar mill and rum distillery; the ancient walls have been used to house the main dining area of the hotel. The restaurant, which has won wide acclaim, features a spacious, open-air pavilion with tropical planter. There is also a more intimate

British Virgin Islands

dining terrace with undisturbed views of the ocean just across the road. Both have views enhanced by the tropical flora that covers the estate. The terrace with comfortable straw seating, tropical birds that patrol for crumbs from the rafters and the old stone walls is a delightful breakfast spot. A large silver urn holds help-yourself coffee, a doily-lined basket serves up homebaked muffins and coconut bread, and individually formed butter patties are placed lovingly next to the homemade jelly. It is a congenial spot where guests compare travel notes, and the resident dog and cat wander by to say good morning. Reservations are taken for the four-course dinners with varying menus that are served each night.

Drinks are enjoyed in the adjacent bar stocked with reading material as well as at the pool honor bar behind the restaurant. Luncheon is served at the dining patio on the Sugar Mill beach a few steps away. The sign here sets the mood: it requests visitors to "kick off your shoes" and relax. Lounge chairs and tables set with crisp, blue tablecloths are provided for hamburger, sandwich or lobster salad mid-day dining. A small, sandy beach is inviting for a swim or lounging or as a backdrop to dining.

The guestroom accommodations at the inn, consisting of a mixture of wood-sided bungalow buildings and contemporary stucco structures with arches and patios, are nestled around the grounds between the hibiscus and various tropical trees. The modern suites, cottages and studio apartments, set against the lush hills, all offer panoramic views of the ocean. The interior decor is neat, clean and attractive.

A circular swimming pool lined in pretty blue tile is inviting and boasts an "over the rooftops" view of the ocean. A plentiful supply of lounges and Ping-Pong are provided here for guests' enjoyment.

Note:
The inn is closed in August and September.

Also on the Island

Fort Burt Hotel
P.O. Box 187
Road Town, Tortola
British Virgin Islands
(809) 494-2587

Caribbean Bed & Breakfast

This small inn with only seven guest accommodations is situated on a knoll with views of the sea and yachting traffic. Built partially out of the ruins of a 300-year-old Dutch/English fort, the hotel offers a restaurant, small pool, bar and sports club. A boat takes guests to a private beach.

Moorings-Mariner Inn
P.O. Box 139
Road Town, Tortola
British Virgin Islands
(809) 494-2332

This 40-guestroom inn features tennis, swimming pool, restaurant and bar. The accommodations with some kitchenettes and covered terraces overlook the marina.

Treasure Isle Hotel
P.O. Box 68
Road Town, Tortola
British Virgin Islands
(809) 494-2501

This hotel near Road Town has an inviting swimming pool with porthole views of the ocean and a pleasant, outdoor dining terrace, as well as tennis and marina facilities. All 40 guestrooms are air conditioned.

Virgin Gorda

This rural, quiet island is characterized by mountains in the north and flat, dry land with giant boulders, scrub and cactus in the south. Exploration highlights include an abandoned copper mine, about 20 beautiful, turquoise and white sand beaches and a unique rock formation called The Baths which consists of huge boulders with sea caves that are dimly lit by sunlight filtering through.

Virgin Gorda, with a modest population of about 1,000 is a popular stop-over for sightseers and the yachting set. Daytrippers can take a 20-minute ferry from Tortola and dock right at Yacht Harbour. A few small boutiques and pubs are located right at the harbor, and Little Dix Bay is a pleasant walk away.

Everything is still very low-key on the island, and although Little Dix Bay was established as an exclusive resort in 1964, tourism

British Virgin Islands

did not really hit the island until ten years ago. Other than by foot, getting around the island can be accomplished by car rental or by taxi, but beware of the expense of hiring a taxi and discuss the rate first.

Olde Yard Inn
P.O. Box 26
Virgin Gorda
British Virgin Islands
(809) 495-5544

Inn; 12 units; Deluxe MAP/Moderate CP;
VI,AE; Children ok; Smoking ok.

Location: 1/4 mi. to beach; 1/2 mi. to town; 1/2 mi. to airport.

Owner-innkeeper Ellen Devine of the Olde Yard Inn theorizes that the many faithful, repeat guests of the inn keep coming back for the incredible library, for the personal attention they receive and for each other. In this casual, yet stimulating spot, the guest finds that these three attractions are just part of a list that also includes a tranquil setting, top cuisine and on-foot convenience.

Probably at the top of most lists would be the interesting and gracious innkeepers themselves, Ellen and Joseph Devine, who have placed making the guest feel welcome and comfortable in front of the mechanics of running an inn for the past 13 years. The inn still manages to survive with this priority in mind, and it is what makes the casual hostelry so enchanting. Ellen was the daughter of a diplomat, and her many travels are apparent in the unusual antiques and furnishings that grace the various rooms at the inn, each one an echo from the past. Joseph was a lawyer who decided law was much too serious and relates freely his childhood dream of owning a bar.

The inn is anything but fancy, but full of special touches. The grounds, about a 15-minute walk from town, are spacious and rambling with tropical flora and untamed paths. The main

Caribbean Bed & Breakfast

building contains a few guestrooms as well as the guest lounge, bar and dining room. The guests congregate here at all times under the high, banana-thatched ceiling on comfortable orange- and yellow-cushioned couches fronted by backgammon games. The bar here with Ellen's own tole-painted, Swedish hutch serves all the usual tropical concoctions. The dining room adjoins, offering all three meals (breakfast and dinner included in the stay in on-season; breakfast only included in off-season). The intimate dining spot with batik and bougainvillaea decorations serves renowned French and Caribbean cuisine. Daily choices include homemade soups or pate, escargots or coquilles, local fish or lobster and their own seafood specialties.

Without a doubt the most fascinating aspect of the Olde Yard Inn is the library, crammed floor to ceiling with carefully cataloged books on almost any subject. Especially interesting is the inn's collection of rare titles. The double, octagonal buildings with wooden decks are informally decorated with comfortable seating, writing desks, a piano and game tables. The inviting area is quite conducive to reading, playing or just relaxing.

The guestrooms at the inn number a dozen and are located in the main building as well as in a two-story structure to the rear. The guestrooms are all simply decorated and boast interesting pictures, colorful bedspreads and private baths. A few of the rooms come with balcony, and one unit offers a four-poster bed for the romantics.

Fellow guests form the entertainment at this quiet inn, making it a good hide-away for those wanting to retreat in good company.

Also on the Island

Biras Creek Hotel
P.O. Box 54
Virgin Gorda
British Virgin Islands
(809) 494-3555

This exclusive and quiet resort features more than 150 private acres with the 32 guest accommodations sprinkled carefully about. The resort offers luxury guestrooms as well as

British Virgin Islands

full facilities including restaurant, beach, bar, swimming pool, tennis and all water activities.

Bitter End Yacht Club
P.O. Box 46
Virgin Gorda
British Virgin Islands
(809) 494-2746

The elegantly furnished villas, 35 in all, are perched on the hillside of this yachting resort; all boast views of the water. This yachting club spot offers unlimited use of the 65 sailboat fleet owned by the hotel as well as snorkeling, scuba and windsurfing.

Little Dix Bay
P.O. Box 70
Virgin Gorda
British Virgin Islands
(809) 495-5555
Rep: Rockresorts Reservations

This Rockefeller resort lives up to its reputation for natural beauty and modern comforts. Located walking distance from town, the 500-acre landscaped grounds are dotted with private guest bungalows, cacti and boulders and pretty gardens. The beach at the hotel is secluded and protected, providing delightful air mattress lounging in crystal-clear water. The hotel offers full facilities including restaurant, bar, tennis, all water sports, horseback riding and bicycles.

Dieppe Bay

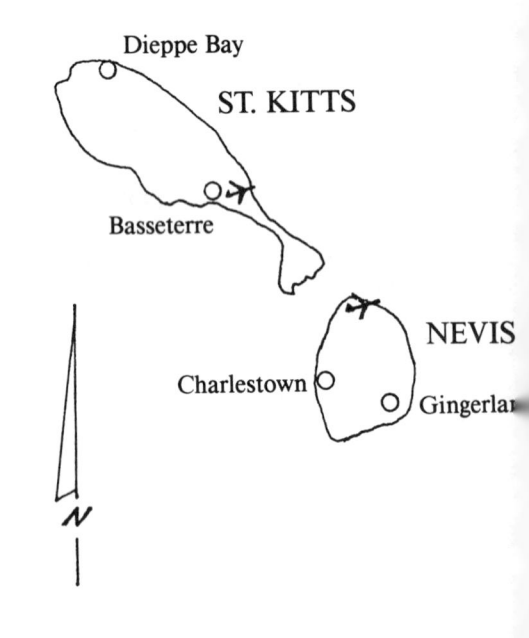

ST. KITTS

Basseterre

NEVIS

Charlestown   Gingerland

N

13

The British Leeward Islands

Caribbean Bed & Breakfast

Located between Guadeloupe and the U.S. Virgin Islands are the British Leeward Islands, boasting sugar-white beaches and "island-hopping" proximity to each other. Antigua and perhaps St. Kitts were the major tourism islands here until relatively recently when visitors began to discover the charms of "Irish" Montserrat, mountainous Nevis and the eel-shaped little island of Anguilla. The money system on all of the British Leeward Islands is the Eastern Caribbean dollar (EC$), although U.S. dollars are often accepted as well. The British Leeward Islands are in the Atlantic Standard Time zone except during Daylight Savings season when the time on these islands is the same as Eastern Daylight Time.

Antigua

Antigua and its 62-square-mile neighbor island 30 miles away, Barbuda, share a common history of British Colonial rule and today make up an independent nation administered by a Prime Minister and Upper and Lower Houses. Their combined population is around 75,000 with 30,000 in the capital city of St. John, Antigua.

Cooling trade winds and a lower humidity level keep both islands pleasant year-round, with temperatures fluctuating between 71 and 86 degrees. Antigua, 108 miles square, is characterized by gently rolling hills and pastoral fields not dissimilar to the California countryside, with highlands rising to 1,330 feet and a rain forest region that is perpetually green. Barbuda, a coral island, is low with tall shrubs and trees and little rainfall.

Antigua has one international airport, modern and well kept, that is served by several major airliners and many local carriers. Antigua is a favorite port-of-call for cruise liners. Both islands are just minutes away by air from the rest of the British Leeward Islands.

Both Antigua and Barbuda are surrounded by protective reefs and miles of sandy, conch-filled beaches, the color pink in Barbuda. Off the coast of Barbuda are many famous shipwrecks; exploring them is a favorite with divers. Visitors to Barbuda also enjoy the Frigate Bird Sanctuary and The Caves, a chance to explore fascinating underwater caves. Antigua's dry climate and topography make sports plentiful. The visitor will see many cricket fields (the national sport), two excellent golf courses

British Leeward Islands

and water activities including scuba, diving, waterskiing, windsurfing, para-sailing and deep-sea fishing. Tennis enthusiasts are treated to two professional tournaments in January each year. Carnival takes place the end of July with lots of local color and flowing rum. The last week of April is "Sailing Week" featuring yacht races and more parties and rum. Several rental cars and taxis are available for touring whether it be for sport, enjoying the clear, blue-green water or maybe just counting sugar mills. When renting a car, take into consideration that the roads are bumpy and slower than you might anticipate. Also, the roads are not well signed, but the friendly local people who happily offer directions more than make up for that deficiency.

Many local artists produce crafts in Antigua. A popular handicraft is the Warri Board, a seed game played on a board originally from Africa. A visit to the Seaview Farm and its potters is interesting.

The capital city of St. John was severely damaged by an earthquake in 1974; restoration work is under way. An unusual walk-in, outdoor cinema and small shops can be found there.

Nightlife on the islands is limited to hotel offerings that are often colorful shows with limbo dancers, calypso and fire-eaters. The development of luxury hotels and condominium complexes to meet the increasing tourism needs of the island has brought a casino and many fine restaurants to Antigua. A common local food served there is black pudding, a well-seasoned dish made of intestines and rice. Antigua is also famous for its very sweet pineapples grown in black sand.

For more information on Antigua and Barbuda contact:
- Antigua and Barbuda Department of Tourism
  610 Fifth Avenue, Suite 311
  New York, New York 10020
  (212) 541-4117

The Admiral's Inn
Nelson's Dockyard, English Harbour
P.O. Box 713
St. John's, Antigua
West Indies
(809) 463-1027
Rep.: American/Wolfe Int.

Caribbean Bed & Breakfast

The Admiral's Inn

Historic inn; 14 units; Moderate/ Inexpensive EP;
No credit cards; Children ok; Smoking ok.

Location: 1/2 mi. to beach; 12 mi. to town; 14 mi. to airport.

Situated right at the entrance to the historic Nelson's Dockyard complex, Admiral's Inn is composed of two 1799 former offices and storage buildings of the old naval service center. The weathered brick buildings with blue shutters and white French doors boast their own waterfront terrace and lawn areas on this quiet corner of the dockyard.

The high-ceilinged structures have original beam ceilings and the old stonework walls. The lounge is decorated in comfortable seating with tropical-printed rattan sofas and chairs, a cozy bar and captain's chairs on the adjacent terrace overlooking the lawn and harbor.

The 14 guestrooms at the "nautical" inn are all different and decorated simply but comfortably in period style with twin beds, fans or air conditioners and private baths with showers. One of the guestrooms features a pretty four-poster with canopy.

If the guest wishes, dinner and breakfast may be included for an additional rate; the menu is varied with several choices at each meal. Luncheon is served on the terrace or a box lunch may be ordered for a day of beach-going or sailing. Steel bands play at the inn each Saturday night and sometimes local bands provide dancing in this informal atmosphere.

Ethelyn Philip has been the congenial manager of the Admiral's Inn for many of its 23 years in operation and will personally see to it that your stay is relaxing and comfortable.

British Leeward Islands

Note:
The inn is closed the month of September.

The Blue Heron Beach Hotel
Johnson's Point Beach
P.O. Box 185
St. John's, Antigua
West Indies
(809) 462-0407

Inn; 40 units; Moderate/ Inexpensive-Mod. EP;
MC,VI; Children ok; Smoking ok.

Location: On beach; 7 mi. to town; 12 mi. to airport.

This brand new hotel of moderate size for resort- and condominium-splashed Antigua is at first rather average looking with its white contemporary exterior accented with wooden railings. But, as a guest here, the traveler will delight in the personal service of the Belizaire family who operate the small hotel and will enjoy the attractive, modern decor of the interior of the units. Of course, the superb location of the Blue Heron should be convincing all by itself. This almost-deserted stretch of beach known as Johnson's Point is an unspoiled delight with its reef-protected clear water, sugar-white sand overflowing with pink conch shells and no tourists except your fellow inn-goers. The guestrooms, located in two-story buildings, are situated right on the sand with balconies stretching out to the sea.

A lagoon signals you have reached the Blue Heron with its circular drive and front parking area. The reception area and attached bar/lounge areas are open and lead to the main dining room. Guests at the Blue Heron may pay an additional sum per person for breakfast and dinner to be included, and whether or not you choose the MAP program, you'll want to dine here some of the time. The elegantly set tables are matched only by the excellent service and gourmet food. If you would like to stay in your room and enjoy dinner from the terrace, the friendly staff is happy to provide room service, all at moderate costs. Each evening's menu is typed in the morning and available at the reception desk. Dinner entrees include such delectables as lobster thermidor, roast spring chicken grand mere, broiled lamb chops with mint jelly and local West Indian specialties.

The guestrooms at the Blue Heron include 30 superior

Caribbean Bed & Breakfast

offerings and 10 standard, all just a few steps from the beach. The pretty interior decor features rich wall-to-wall carpeting, coordinated fabrics on bedspreads and drapes, a modern and spacious bathroom with tub/shower combination, color television (although viewing is limited in Antigua), big closets and queen size beds.

To be sure the guest enjoys this beachside location in every way, the staff at the inn offers all the non-motorized beach sports free by contacting their Watersports Hut and will arrange waterskiing, boat tours and scuba diving. A little beach bar and comfortable lounge chairs are provided on the beach.

The Copper and Lumber Store
Nelson's Dockyard, English Harbour
P.O. Box 184
St. John's, Antigua
West Indies
(809) 463-1058
(401) 683-0858 (U.S. answering service)

Historic inn; 14 units; Moderate-Deluxe/ Moderate EP;
AE,VI,MC; Children on approval; Smoking ok.

Location: 1/2 mi. to beach; 12 mi. to town; 14 mi. to airport.

The Copper and Lumber Store is more than a beautifully restored inn—it is a slice of maritime history that has become a glorious addition to the Nelson's Dockyard complex of various dockyard buildings from the 18th century. The grounds around

British Leeward Islands

the inn are dotted with various antique dockyard structures at different stages of renovation and usage. The Dockyard Supply and Service Company occupies one of the old stone and shuttered buildings and another houses a tea shop and local art gallery that bring in revenues for the further renovation of the dockyard. Right next door to the inn is a white wooden structure with grey-blue shutters that is filled with maritime museum pieces. However, many of the original buildings stand waiting for attention, and, according to Copper and Lumber Store owner and manager Jill Gutteridge, that is just what is in store. This busy and gracious innkeeper has high hopes that Nelson's Dockyard will someday be the "Williamsburg" of the Caribbean; under her careful direction it is safe to assume that this will come to pass.

When Jill and her husband Gordon retired they set out for England to buy a castle and fulfill their dream of opening an old, restored inn. But on the way they stopped in Antigua and discovered this 1782-built store, a charming 18th-century, English-crafted building in need of much renovation and investment. After completing extensive historical research on the building and the period, the meticulous owners began the design and renovation of the 14 suites that surround a picturesque stone courtyard. Although Jill claims the renovation is still happening, it is hard to tell. Even the guestrooms that have not yet been "authentically" restored are charmingly decorated and elegantly comfortable.

The beautiful old brick building with steel-blue shutters and distinctive symmetrical, curved protrusions has an ornately carved ship's lady over the doorway, a reminder of its origins. A stately palm in front of the inn has a plaque that reads "planted by her majesty Queen Elizabeth II 20 February 1966." The guest enters through a small reception area into the guest lounge filled with Oriental rugs, antique leather couches and formal chairs—all contrasted warmly against the old exposed-brick walls. Antique dining tables and chairs, a freelance bar built into a brick archway, restored wood columns and wonderful old wooden beams further enhance this both comfortable and elegant living room area. Every detail is authentic here, and throughout the inn old map prints, silver and copper decorative pieces and beautiful brass lamps are apparent.

Upstairs are the guestrooms, all situated around the lovely courtyard. All of the guestrooms are suites and boast fully equipped kitchens and full maid service. The one-bedroom suites have a spacious living room area with day beds or a queen size sleeper-couch. But, beyond these similarities, you will find very little the same in each of the authentically and individually decorated units. Furnishings, which are a combination of antiques and reproductions, are of 18th-century vintage and include many four-posters and unusual pieces. Marvelous wooden floors, some with stenciled borders, antique-patterned wallcoverings, baths with brass fixtures and mahogany-lined showers, fancy scrolled wooden bannisters in split-level units and decorating details such as brass lamps, old china, coordinated fabric prints and Williamsburg design bedspreads, fresh plants, Oriental carpets and authentic wall prints fill each unit with the past.

Some of the units have dormer windows overlooking the harbor, and all open to the balcony overlooking the courtyard. It is this interior courtyard that will be the site of a restaurant in the near future. The tranquil Georgian feel of this area with its exposed brick archways will undoubtedly set a perfect tone for the Gutteridge's current renovation project. Jill has high hopes that the restaurant will be in operation by early 1986. In the meantime, there are five other restaurants nearby.

The individual units at the Copper and Lumber Store may also be purchased by guests and leased out to other guests who visit the inn in a time-share sort of arrangement. If you buy one of these gems, you may end up with Sophia Loren or Princess Margaret in your home—both have stayed here.

Spanish Main Inn
East Street
P.O. Box 655
St. John's, Antigua
West Indies
(809) 462-0660

Historic inn; 15 units; Inexpensive year-round EP;
Credit cards accepted; Children ok; Smoking ok.

Location: In town; 2 1/2 mi. to beach; 3 mi. to airport.

This restored 1780 townhouse facing St. John's Park was the first governor's residence built in St. John's from public funds. The historic inn with white, wooden siding and rust and black

British Leeward Islands

shutters shows its age and is somewhat weathered from the outside.

The guestrooms are on the second floor of the inn and are furnished simply, yet comfortably, in rattan and bamboo. All units have a private bath and twin beds. All three meals are offered in the inn's restaurant on the garden level. It features good American and West Indian specialties and has an impressive following that has grown through the years.

The atmosphere is comfortable and relaxed at the Spanish Main due to the low-key hospitality of its hosts and owners for over 19 years, Julian and Janice Branker.

Also on the Island

The Inn at English Harbour
P.O. Box 187
St. John's, Antigua
West Indies
(809) 463-1014

This medium-sized inn at the entrance to historic English Harbour offers 28 guestrooms and suites in two-story buildings near the sand. The mainly beachfront accommodations on pretty Freeman's Bay contain twin beds, patios or terraces and contemporary decor. The English-style pub overlooks the picturesque bay; all watersports are available.

Long Bay Hotel
P.O. Box 442
St. John's, Antigua
West Indies
(809) 463-2005

This family-run hotel gives its guests, who return faithfully, special attention in its very private peninsula location. The 20 guestrooms are located in two-story buildings that are near the sheltered, coral beach and boast private baths and comfortable, modern decor. Five cottages are also available. Long Bay Hotel has a country inn feel with chintz fabrics and wicker and offers guests a library and game room. The 1/4-mile-long beach at Long Bay provides good snorkeling and scuba.

Caribbean Bed & Breakfast

St. Kitts and Nevis

The sister islands of St. Kitts and Nevis are situated in the northern part of the Leeward Islands and are separated by a strait just two miles wide. The two islands gained full political independence from Britain in September, 1983, and the 44,000 population is governed by a democratic form of government. The islands have an average temperature of 79 degrees, with northeast trade winds keeping the otherwise hot days quite pleasant.

Getting to St. Kitts and Nevis by air is achieved via connections with local Caribbean airliners that fly directly from other islands in the Caribbean. Because these islands are so small it is not difficult to get anywhere; taxis are available for tours as are comfortable sightseeing buses. The taxi drivers on St. Kitts attend classes on tourist information and are quite knowledgeable about the sights. They are also quite willing to take you to a destination and return at a requested time. Rental cars and cycles are available from several rental agencies, but a temporary license must be obtained. Driving is on the left side of the road. A 45-minute ferry operates on a regular schedule between St. Kitts and Nevis for fairly easy island hopping. Wednesday is the favorite ferry-day for tourists when the schedule allows for an all-day visit to the sister island. Upon leaving the two islands a nominal departure tax is collected.

English is the principal language of the islands, but electrical current is not North American, requiring adapters in most of the lodgings. Shopping specialties on St. Kitts and Nevis include locally produced batik and tie-dye clothing and fabrics, homemade jellies and jams and hand-embroidered items. The Romney Manor, located down a peaceful country road, is famous for its Caribelle Batik factory, but is most notable for its lovely gardens and picturesque, 350-year-old "rain tree."

For additional information on St. Kitts and Nevis contact:
St. Kitts-Nevis Tourist Board
Eastern Caribbean Tourist Association
220 East 42nd. St., Room 411
New York, New York 10017
(212) 986-9370

British Leeward Islands

St. Kitts

St. Kitts is the larger of the two islands and is made up of rich rolling sugar cane fields, rain forests with exotic birds and vegetation, pastoral scenes and golden and black sand beaches in its 65-mile-square area. The capital is Basseterre, an 18th-century British town with white colonial houses on palm-lined streets. People congregate at the town's active harbor; at the town square, Circus, with its tall green Victorian clock; and at Independence Mall (formerly called Pall Mall), the former slave market that is now a lovely square surrounded by large, Georgian-style homes. Fresh vegetables, fruit and tropical flowers from the fields are brought to market there now.

Visitors to St. Kitts will also be interested in the Brimstone Hill Fortress, a leftover from British and French battles over the island, with 360-degree views of the hills and ocean. Mt. Misery is the island's looming volcanic crater. There is talk of changing the name to Mount Limauiga, the original name given St. Kitts by the Carib Indians. A guided hike through the rain forest can be strenuous, but natural waterfalls and glimpses of the island's famous "Velvet Monkeys" make it well worthwhile.

The nightlife in St. Kitts consists of a few bars and discos as well as a gambling casino at the Royal St. Kitts Hotel. The hotels in St. Kitts sometimes organize brass and steel band and calypso shows. Restaurants specialize in West Indian and creole foods.

Fairview Inn
P.O. Box 212
St. Kitts
West Indies
(809) 465-2472/465-2473
Rep: International Travel and Resorts

Historic inn; 30 units; Moderate/Moderate EP;
VI,MC; Children ok; Smoking ok.

Caribbean Bed & Breakfast

Location: 1/2 mi. to beach; 3 mi. to town; 5 mi. to airport.

This country inn and cottage complex climbs a knoll a few miles out of town and offers breathtaking views of the ocean and St. Kitt's sister island, Nevis. A French, 18th-century great house, which may have been the residence of the commander of the French troops based in the area, is the traditional part of the lodging establishment, and the dozen cottages that have been added around the garden-filled grounds offer a more contemporary choice in lodging. The Fairview opened as the pioneer resort hotel of the island in 1969 under the skillful direction of owners and managers Fred and Betty Lam. The Lams converted the private residence into a quaint West Indian inn and restaurant and have earned the respect of many return guests, including some royalty.

The quiet inn with sugar fields in front and hills to the rear is filled with sweet smells of the ever-flowering gardens. The 1700 home with white, wooden siding, shingled roof and fancy trim sits up proudly from the manicured garden and features a long, front brick-lined veranda. You first view the reception area, parlor and dining room when entering it. Oriental rugs fill the polished wooden floors, and the vaulted ceiling bears pretty, carved beams and a brass chandelier. Only a pair of etched-glass doors separate the period rooms that are decorated in antiques, stained glass and plants. Three guestrooms are located in the home itself and are usually rented only when the cottages are full or on special request.

Although the cottage accommodations represent a more contemporary offering in age and furnishings, the Lams took great care to include a pleasant blending of the old in the design. The cottages, dotted around the hillside grounds in back of the main house, were built from old stone found on the property; many feature stained-glass windows over the doorways. All of the units have wood-beamed ceilings and a unique character. The cottages uniformly contain built-in closets, tile or carpeted floors, modern baths with shower stalls and contemporary furnishings. Either air conditioning or fans are available as well as twin or queen beds. Some of the units are suites containing a hide-a-bed in the living room area to sleep four comfortably as well as a private patio. The cottage units are well spaced with lots of grassy area in between and flower-lined paths leading to each.

Caribbean Bed & Breakfast

A sparkling blue pool surrounded by lounges and offering inspiring views of the ocean sits next to another grassy lawn with picturesque fountain to the side of the house. A greenhouse-looking terrace with white latticework, wrought-iron chairs and tables and plants, along with the inn's bar, connects. Spacious guest baths by the pool area add a nice touch.

The West Indian cuisine at the Fairview has received many praises and features fruit and vegetables fresh out of the gardens of the inn. The sea-view patio is the locale of most meals at the Fairview; these are served cheerfully by the friendly, Kittitian staff.

The Golden Lemon
Dieppe Bay
St. Kitts
West Indies
(809) 465-7260
Rep: Scott Calder International

Inn; 15 units; Deluxe/Deluxe MAP;
No credit cards; No children; No smoking in rooms.

Location: On ocean; Countryside; 14 mi. to airport.

Over 20 years ago Arthur Leaman, a former decorating editor for *House and Garden Magazine*, decided to put his skills to practical work in a beautiful spot with a more than challenging subject. The abandoned building with a 17th-century French West Indian downstairs and an 18th-century Georgian West Indian upstairs, used originally as a private home and then warehouse, gave Mr. Leaman ideas that only decorating expertise, fortitude and a large bankroll could realize.

Leaman completely remodeled the building adding bathrooms, electricity, a kitchen wing and additional rooms. He walled in the property and landscaped it with tropical gardens, a freshwater pool and an English rose garden. The result is as might have been predicted--a special inn with an elegant charm amid tropical informality. Of course, this elegance does not come inexpensively. The Golden Lemon is one of the higher priced establishments in this guidebook, but it offers an antique-lover's splurge that is a little more affordable during off-season, especially with two delicious meals and afternoon tea included.

The Golden Lemon sits on a small, gray-sand beach lined with palms. Located on the north end of the island, it is about 14 miles from Basseterre. Guests at the Golden Lemon are able to enjoy its elegance and freedom to do nothing at all or can explore the island in either direction.

A few white structures with bright lemon-yellow trim signal you've reached the inn. Inside the front walls is the gallery of the house, a delightful spot for breakfasting overlooking the sea and garden. Or guests may enjoy the morning meal in the privacy of their rooms. Directly inside the house is the formal dining room, a truly elegant room filled with Oriental-patterned accents and china, vases with fresh flowers, chair coverings and large, china chandeliers—all in blue and white. Hurricane globe candles sit on the antique tables, and old paintings and prints decorate the walls. The dinner, included in the stay, is served here in romantic candlelight.

Just off the formal dining room is a back garden eating patio or lower gallery. This tranquil spot with ferns, palms and tropical flowers is a perfect luncheon retreat when timed before or after a possible tour bus full of visitors who also want to soak up the elegant ambience and partake of the excellent West Indian cuisine. The waitresses wear crisp yellow uniforms with white trim and the white, wrought-iron patio tables are set in cheery lemon placemats with coordinating lemon-design glasses. One of the freshwater pools is located to the side of the back patio and features a petite waterfall that drips down the old stone walls that enclose it on two sides. A sunken, private sunning area with thick, yellow chaise pads connects; a latticed drink area alongside has a garden feel.

The guestrooms at the Golden Lemon are each unique and filled with four-poster canopies, armoires, fans, tastefully selected antiques, modern baths and fresh flowers daily. Last year four condominium units for guests, each with private pool, were added to the grounds and range from studio facilities to two-bedroom units on the beach.

The service at the Golden Lemon, supervised by manager Kathleen Fallon, matches the special decor at this intimate inn, making your stay at the Golden Lemon an elegant, gracious retreat.

British Leeward Islands

Rawlins Plantation
P.O. Box 340
St. Kitts
West Indies
(809) 465-6221
Rep: Rawlins Plantation, Mass.

Plantation; 9 units; Deluxe/Deluxe MAP;
No credit cards; Children ok; No smoking.

Location: Countryside; 1 mi. to beach; 14 mi. to airport.

You have to look carefully for the sign on the telephone pole that leads you up a long, winding dirt road through sugar cane fields to the plantation estate that sits atop a hill with masterful views of the fields below as well as the ocean in the distance. The drive sets the tone of the resort, a tranquil country inn that blends plantation history with homey accommodations.

Owned by the Walwyn family since 1790, the plantation's original home burned down several years ago, and in 1970 Phillip and Frances Walwyn built new structures to mix carefully with the ruins on the estate grounds. An English country house contains the dining room and guest lounges of the inn; several cottages are widely spaced on the rolling, grassy acreage that surrounds. The main house, like the cottages, is constructed of white cement and has attractive yellow shutters and Victorian gingerbread trim and latticework. The old stone used on the buildings blends lovingly with the ruins that are found about in various stages of restoration.

The upstairs terrace of the main house has comfortable seating with inspiring views, and the connecting parlor boasts pretty wooden floors, a mixture of rattan and antique furnishings, a large library to fill the lazy hours here and wide French doors. The adjacent dining room has an antique table and chair set, a large built-in bookcase, candles for elegant dinner

Caribbean Bed & Breakfast

settings and a silver tea service. An outside terrace provides a less formal eating area with an arched stone wall entrance, white lattice and white wrought-iron tables and chairs.

The cottages at the Rawlins Plantation resemble little houses and are beautifully private with lots of rolling lawn and tropical flowers in between. Most notable is the Windmill Suite, a tri-level unit built into the ruins of the plantation windmill. A white iron bed with canopy and a dressing table with old-fashioned skirting occupy the top level of the suite; the middle level is a large landing with baskets and china figurines, and the bottom of the suite consists of the living room with attractive French doors and bright flower prints. The bath has a clever, deep shower built into the curve of the windmill's old, stone walls.

Recreation at the plantation includes a large, tiled pool with gazebo overlooking the grassy fields and tennis courts below as well as horseback riding and croquet. For those staying at Rawlins for a week or more, the Walwyns extend a special treat of sailing on their 75-foot catamaran. There is a reasonable additional fee for day sails as well as for a two-day trip to St. Barts.

The stay at Rawlins Plantation includes breakfast, dinner, free drinks and an afternoon tea, making the rate more reasonable than it might first appear. A buffet lunch or box lunch is also available so that you need never leave these peaceful grounds steeped in family hospitality.

Also on the Island

Ocean Terrace Inn
P.O. Box 65
St. Kitts
West Indies
(809) 465-2754/465-2380
Rep: American/Wolfe Int.

Overlooking the bay of Basseterre is this hillside-terraced hotel that has grown from its original "small inn" status to hotel in recent years. The charm is still evident throughout the beautifully landscaped grounds with fountain, old-fashioned swing, flowing lawns and antique cannons. The 44 spacious

British Leeward Islands

guestrooms are nicely furnished with telephones and radios, air conditioning and patios or balconies; some boast television and mini-refrigerators. Self-contained condominiums are also available. The inn offers a swimming pool, bar, entertainment in the evenings, good Caribbean cuisine and shops.

On the Square
P.O. Box 81
Basseterre
St. Kitts
West Indies
(809) 465-2485

This small guest house with five guestrooms is situated in the heart of town facing Independence Square, the former slave mart. The structure was originally a plantation owner's residence in the 1800's and boasts attractive Georgian architecture in common with the other buildings that surround the historic square. The accommodations are modest, but clean, and feature wall-to-wall carpeting, double beds (except one twin) and air conditioning. Two rooms have private baths and small kitchenettes; the remainder share a bathroom. No meals are offered at the guest house, but several fine restaurants are within walking distance. Those looking for in-town convenience and modest rates will find the small guest house nicely adequate.

Nevis

The island of Nevis was settled by the British in 1628 and in the 18th century became the "Queen of the Caribees" as the leading spa of the West Indies, due to its hot mineral springs. Sea island cotton is the principal crop today, but Nevis boasted prosperous sugar cane estates at one time. These estates of yesterday have been transformed into beautiful inns, many discussed in the bed & breakfast listings that follow. Touring these fine, historic inns is also the main tourist activity on the small island.

Nevis is an island of unspoiled beauty with miles of white sandy beaches lined with palms. Some consider Pinney's Beach to be one of the best beaches in the Caribbean. A strenuous, but

Caribbean Bed & Breakfast

popular, hike 3,500 feet up Mt. Nevis to its extinct volcanic crater is an all-day event.

The capital of Nevis, Charlestown, is known for its distinctive houses built out of locally quarried volcanic stone. The ferry from St. Kitts docks right in the heart of the little town, and rental cars and taxis await just steps away. A rental car can be obtained, allowing for a leisurely all-day tour around the small island. The roads on Nevis are bumpy and curvy, but lined with lush, tropical vegetation, pretty ocean vistas and numerous sugar mill ruins.

Golden Rock Estate
Gingerland
Nevis
West Indies
(809) 465-5346
Rep: Scott Calder International

Plantation; 13 units; Deluxe/Expensive MAP;
No credit cards; Children ok; Smoking ok.

Location: 1 mi. to beach; 3 mi. to town; 10 mi. to airport.

This former plantation is hidden from the road up a winding drive lined with tropical groves. The estate house, dating back to the early 1800's, is constructed of ancient stone and accented by pale yellow wooden shutters, arched doorways and cascading bougainvillaea. Inside, the guest lounge offers comfortable seating and an abundance of books amid the old stone floors and walls with low, yellow-beamed ceilings. A short flight up is a bar built into the stone with an adjacent billiard and games room. The unusual gameroom ceiling has a fishing net that holds untamed ivy instead of the usual nautical touches. Another step up places you in the dining room with the same stone walls, antique buffet and silver tea service. Plants and ivy decorate the walls here and small baskets of fresh posies are centered on the blue tablecloths.

The hillside grounds of the inn contain the dozen cottages that provide guest accommodations, the Sugar Mill suite, an inviting pool, tennis courts and rambling, tropical gardens full of the sounds and sweet smells of the rural countryside. For a slight additional fee and on arrangement only, the Sugar Mill suite, the 1811 renovated mill of the plantation, can be reserved for up to four or five people, although it is a favorite honeymooner's retreat. This duplex features double four-poster beds with canopies downstairs and a massive king-size canopy bed upstairs with intricate, antique carvings. The staircase of the mill curves with the turn of the old stone walls. The remainder of the guest accommodations, located in cottages about the grounds, offer attractive furnishings such as custom bamboo four-poster beds and dressing rooms and private baths. Each unit is very private and provides a private patio where you may choose to breakfast in the morning.

Owners Frank and Pam Barry (Pam a descendant of the original plantation family) are known for their hospitable nature at this small inn. The plantation owns two beaches and offers use of its sailing vessels to guests. They also take guests to town twice a day and are happy to make car rental arrangements. The relaxing stay at Golden Rock includes breakfast and dinner with wine.

Montpelier Plantation Inn
Charlestown
P.O. Box 474
Nevis
West Indies
(809) 465-5462
Rep: Ray Morrow Associates

Plantation; 16 units; Expensive-Del./Moderate MAP;
No credit cards; Children ok; Smoking ok.

Location: 3 mi. to beach; 2 mi. to town; 10 mi. to airport.

The Montpelier Plantation is nicely tucked away down what might be called a residential lane by local people, but a rural country road with ruts and chickens to anyone else. Once you get there, you are glad it is hidden, in hopes not many others will discover its charming attributes and turn it into a less personal retreat. The gracious owners, James and Celia Milnes Gaskell, will probably not let such a thing happen anyway because it is obviously their home as well; you feel that special, homestyle touch in every detail at Montpelier.

Eight guest cottages are scattered on the vast grounds of the plantation along with the attractive West Indian great house, a pool, bar, dining area and the plantation's exceptional, organic gardens—the pride of its owners. The plantation's organic farm and orchards along with its fishing boat supply the basis of the delicious homemade, natural cuisine of the inn.

A large swimming pool at the plantation retains an impressive mural with Nevis scenery on the privacy wall and blends well with the surrounding tropical vegetation. Overlooking the pool is a semi-enclosed bar with attractive rattan seating covered in a blue and rust tropical print. A few steps up lead to the dining room, facing a handsome mill ruin, with a stone planter in the middle, walls with colorful murals and white tablecloths set in pretty blue and white china. The patio surrounding the dining room is a tranquil luncheon spot where a generous buffet is offered among the stone arches dripping with plants.

The great house, framed in front by an ancient weeping fig tree, has an English country house look featuring large rooms with polished wood-inlaid floors, domed ceilings, French doors and arched-stone entries. The furnishings are warm and elegant, boasting antique tables, old portraits, a hoosier with china and coordinated orange chintz sofas and draperies. Plants bring the peaceful outside in, and a large veranda on one side provides intimate nighttime dining. The parlor also contains the nighttime bar and is the gathering spot after the sun goes down.

The pastel stucco cottages housing guests are scattered along a winding path with manicured lawns in between. The cottages contain two units each and are decorated attractively in comfortable rattan furnishings with pretty print draperies. The cottages, with private patios, boast ocean views and quiet surroundings.

In addition to the pool, a tennis court surrounded by coconut trees is located on the spacious grounds, and the Gaskells provide free transportation to the nearby beaches.

Both breakfast and dinner are included in the stay at Montpelier and lunch is available. The full breakfast fare includes tropical fruits, a main course and homemade bread and marmalade; dinner is table d'hote with three courses brimming with fresh, local ingredients. The food at the inn, which can be described as sublime, is made from whole wheat flours; all

British Leeward Islands

that can be is homemade. The coconut cream pie is a real specialty.

For a true "home away from home" experience on this quiet, little island the Montpelier never fails to provide a personalized getaway for its special guests.

Nisbet Plantation Inn
Nevis
West Indies
(809) 465-5325
Rep: Nisbet Plantation Inn, Minn.

Plantation; 30 units; Deluxe MAP/Moderate EP;
No credit cards; No children under 10 (on-season),
Children ok (off-season); Smoking ok.

Location: On beach; 8 mi. to town; 1 mi. to airport.

Although no one could quibble that the Nisbet Plantation presents a beautiful picture from the front, there are few plantation scenes that can surpass the Nisbet's view from its upper-back terrace. Guests may dine on this pretty outdoor patio on quaint burgundy-printed china and gaze at the sweeping vista of the ocean 500 yards ahead through a perfectly placed path lined with giant coconut palms. If you dare turn your eyes from the tree-lined focus, you'll also take in the well-manicured, grassy grounds, tropical gardens, tennis courts and the various cottages that house the small group of guests at the plantation.

The Nisbet Plantation is nicely situated on a pretty half-mile beach on grounds spacious enough that you might want to request a cottage either near the beach or near the main house. A walk in either direction is a pleasant, tranquil stroll. The inn was built on the site of an 18th-century sugar plantation; some of the historic ruins, with tropical vegetation pushing out of the cracks and crevices, are visible in the curve of the front circular drive. The estate house itself was rebuilt around the turn of the century and has fancy gingerbread trim, coral

Caribbean Bed & Breakfast

stonework, white shutters and a second-story, screened-in sunporch reminscient of those graceful days.

The guest parlor and dining room of the house feature antique furnishings, country chintz fabrics and comfort. The dining room has walls of gathered pink material and subtle wallcoverings in the same old-fashioned theme. The tables of the formal dining area are punctuated with small china vases filled with petite flower arrangements; a built-in shelf displays antique china and glassware. The attractive wooden floors are bare except for an occasional straw mat. The sunporch and connecting bar at the inn add a more casual touch and are decorated in a mixture of antiques and island furnishings of bamboo and rattan.

The 15 cottages of the inn are sprinkled about the 30-acre grounds, granting maximum privacy and solitude. Most of the cottages house two guest facilities, and each guestroom is named after an old plantation on Nevis. Most of the cottages are more contemporary than the main house, while the more interesting appear about the same vintage. The later-built cottages are attractively designed with vaulted ceilings, walk-in closets, modern baths with large shower stalls and views of the ocean and are furnished in rattan, pretty fabrics and some antiques. The older cottages have the same fancy gingerbread, white frame and lattice construction as the estate house and details such as French doors with matching shutters. The "Gingerland" is a favorite at the Nisbet and features two ornately carved, twin canopy beds with patchwork quilt spreads. But not to forego comfort, the bath is quite modern.

The on-season stay at the plantation includes both breakfast and dinner with wine; during off-season, guests may make meals optional. The continental breakfast may be enjoyed in the room, while lunch, afternoon tea and dinner are served at the main house. Dinner is handled family-style, allowing guests to get acquainted in their elegant yet intimate surroundings. A beachfront restaurant at Nisbet also offers lunch as well as dreamy moonlight barbecues. A boutique on the plantation sells island handicrafts and necessities.

Old Manor Estate
P.O. Box 70
Charlestown, Nevis

British Leeward Islands

West Indies
(809) 465-5445

Plantation; 10 units; Expensive/Moderate EP;
No credit cards; No children under 12; Smoking ok.

Location: 1 mi. to beach; 3 mi. to town; 10 mi. to airport.

This small plantation-inn is appropriately named, since a first impression of the secluded establishment is of an exclusive estate. The plantation is also referred to as "Croney's Old Manor Estate" (Croney was a former estate owner). The restored plantation dates back to a 1690 land grant; several of the stone-constructed buildings were built in the late 1700's through 1832.

The Cooperage dining room is a separate building where barrels for the sugar mill were once made. The eating spot now holds rattan tables and chairs and a pleasant veranda connects with views of the sea. Breakfast and dinner are available on the MAP plan throughout the year. The garden with ruins of the kitchen stone hearth is a favorite locale for lunch and the Friday night steak and lobster buffet.

The guestrooms at the plantation are located in restored buildings around the Sugar Mill and the great house. The attractive furnishings in guestrooms and suites include king size or twin canopy beds and modern conveniences.

The staff at the Old Manor Estate provides free beach and town transportation and welcomes the guest with a drink. A picturesque, freshwater pool is nestled within the lush, tropical grounds in this most relaxing and intimate spot.

Also on the Island

Zetland Plantation
Nevis
West Indies
Rep: Resort Villas International

Caribbean Bed & Breakfast

This 750-acre plantation resort is situated on a high bluff that grants panoramic views of the ocean. The pastel-colored cottages that dot the property and manicured lawns contain suites that are all basically the same: attractive, modern interiors with living rooms, bedrooms, baths and kitchenettes. A converted sugar mill also houses guests. Delicious meals are served from the estate's own gardens; the resort offers tennis courts, a large, inviting pool, a restaurant, lounge, bar and boutique. Complimentary transportation is provided to town and to the beach where the Zetland Plantation has its own sunning pavilion.

Muriel's Guest House
P.O. Box 472
Charlestown, Nevis
West Indies
(809) 465-5491

This small guest house lodging establishment is built on the ruins of an 1810 plantation. It consists of two buildings, one the former horse stable that now houses visitors. The grounds are still partly ruins, containing overgrown tennis courts and an old round swimming pool and sundial. The very hospitable owners, Mr. and Mrs. Leverock, are originally from Saba and retired 21 years ago to Nevis. The pair has worked hard to convert the former horse carriage room and kitchen to guest quarters offering three bedrooms and two baths, a sitting room, dining room and kitchen. The modest guest house is ideally suited to a one-family rental.

Montserrat

Montserrat, 12 miles long and 7 miles wide, is located some 27 miles from Antigua. The lush, green mountainous scenery traversed by numerous rivers and streams is often compared to Ireland, and the little island has adopted the shamrock as a symbol of these similarities. Actually, the first European settlers in 1632 were Catholic-Irish fleeing from religious persecution, and these settlers left evidence of their existence in the island's various place names.

English is the spoken language on the island. The current population is 12,000 in this British Dependent Territory with a

British Leeward Islands

resident Governor appointed by the Queen. Montserrat is reached through connection in Antigua, the closest international airport, which offers several 15-minute flights daily. The electrical current does require a transformer for U.S. appliances.

Plymouth, the island's capital, has a population of 4,000 and boasts many fine Georgian houses. The Post Office and Treasury, located in a lovely colonial structure, produces the beautiful postage stamps sought after by collectors.

Fine tennis and golf are available as well as nature trails that lead hikers by waterfalls to the steaming center of the island's volcano. History can be relived by exploring the ruins of an old rum distillery in the highlands or by visiting the island's museum housed in an old, restored sugar mill. Beach-goers will enjoy Montserrat's unusual black sands.

The local specialties on Montserrat range from roasted fresh coconut chips, called hospitality chips, to beautiful handcrafted tapestries made of yarn, cotton or linen.

>For more information on Montserrat contact:
>Montserrat Tourist Board
>c/o Eastern Caribbean Tourist Association
>220 East 42nd St., Room 411
>New York, NY 10017
>(212) 986-9370

Coconut Hill Hotel
P.O. Box 337
Plymouth
Montserrat
West Indies
(809) 491-2144/ 491-2423

Plantation; 9 units; Moderate/ Moderate MAP;
No credit cards; Children ok; Smoking ok.

Location: Near beach; 1/4 mi. to town; 6 mi. to airport.

This former plantation mansion with graceful upper and lower verandas was converted to an inn around the turn of the century by the son of the original owner. The Osbornes, who run the Vue Point Hotel on the island, are the present owners and

Caribbean Bed & Breakfast

keep the family feel alive for all who stay at this charming, antique-filled inn.

Coconut Hill is located in a quiet residential area within an easy walk to the beach and with views of the same. A casual atmosphere prevails on the park-like grounds that surround the one-time mansion.

The guestrooms at the country inn contain a mixture of antiques and more contemporary furnishings and are very pleasant. The accommodations boast private baths, balconies, double beds and a few romantic four-posters.

Both breakfast and dinner are included in the stay here, and guests are treated to delicious West Indian specialties in the dining room of the inn that traverses the rear of the house and grants tranquil views.

The congenial manager of Coconut Hill is Joseph Fergus who makes sure the service matches the homestyle hospitality of the intimate inn.

Anguilla

Surrounded by white beaches and turquoise waters, the eel-shaped island of Anguilla is often referred to as "the best-kept secret island paradise in the world." Located on the northern tip of the Leeward chain, the 16-mile-long by 4-mile-wide island is almost flat and treeless. The highest point is Crocus Hill with a 213-foot elevation. Its surrounding waters reveal several offshore cays and coral reefs.

Anguilla is a British Colony with a population of 7,000 of mainly African descent, but with European, especially Irish, influences. The monetary system is the Eastern Caribbean dollar, but U.S. money is widely accepted. Electrical voltage is compatible with U.S. appliances.

The nearest jet airports to Anguilla are in St. Maarten, Antigua, St. Kitts, St. Thomas and Puerto Rico; all offer direct, regularly scheduled flights to Anguilla. An efficient ferry system operates between St. Maarten and Anguilla daily docking at Anguilla's Blowing Point Harbor. The trip takes just 35 minutes. Visitors to the island are required to have a valid passport and must pay a departure tax upon leaving. Taxis are available on the island and several firms rent cars. The roads in Anguilla are good, and driving is probably the best way to really explore the island. Vehicles travel on the left.

British Leeward Islands

The beaches of Anguilla, some 30 in all, are immaculately clean with white coral sand and hidden coves and grottos. Crescent-shaped Rendezvous Bay is a beautiful sunbathing and shell-collecting beach. Charter boats with fishing, scuba or snorkeling equipment are available at several spots. Lobster diving is an integral part of the local economy, and abundant tropical fish may be viewed or spearfished.

Sights to see around the island include the Salt Ponds, two currently harvested salt lakes; the Irish fishing village of Island Harbour; the Fountain, a huge underwater cave of fresh water; and the Ruins of Dutch Fort, the scene of the 1796 French invasion of Anguilla. A few true desert islands are in close proximity to Anguilla and are reached by charter fishing boats or power boats. The main town on the island, The Village, is a settlement near Crocus Bay where the French landed in the 18th century.

The main industry of Anguilla is building boats, which are richly colored and designed for speed. Not surprisingly, the national sport is boat racing with races held almost every holiday.

The entertainment on the island is limited to small bands at the hotels or restaurants. Island cuisine features freshly caught seafood and fish (red snapper a favorite) often cooked creole-style. Beach barbecue pits are set up to feed beach-goers a fish snack or even to cook the latest catch fresh off the boat while you wait.

For more information on Anguilla contact:
    Anguilla Department of Tourism
    Caribbean Tourism Association
    20 East 46th Street
    New York, New York 10017
    (212) 682-0435

Florencia Guest House
The Valley
Anguilla
West Indies
(809) 497-2319

Guest house; 5 units; Inexpensive MAP year-round;
No credit cards; Children ok; Smoking ok.

Caribbean Bed & Breakfast

Location: Near beach; 1 mi. to town; 1 1/4 mi. to airport.

This small guest house run by Mrs. Wilfred Daniel offers very modest accommodations that are convenient to the beach, town and airport. The guest house is situated on the second floor of a street-fronting, green and white building; a grocery store occupies the ground level. The five guestrooms offer both private and shared baths, radio and some kitchenettes and balconies. The decor is quite sparse but tidy. Mrs. Daniel includes a breakfast and dinner of her own tasty homecooking at this spot for the budget minded.

Inter-Island Hotel
P.O. Box 194
Anguilla
West Indies
(809) 497-2259

Guest house; 12 units; Moderate MAP year-round;
No credit cards; Children ok; Smoking ok.

Location: Near beach; 2 mi. to town; 2 mi. to airport.

Mr. Arrendel Lewis, proprietor of the Inter-Island, makes sure that guests feel like part of the family at this guest house. The two-story building with upper and lower verandas has views of the sea and St. Martin. Guestrooms with simple furnishings include single and double rooms with bath as well as a one-bedroom apartment and a two-bedroom apartment. Breakfast and dinner are included in the reasonable rate and are served in the first-floor restaurant. The guest house has a homey parlor for its guests to enjoy.

14

Dutch Windward Islands

ST. MAARTEN
Philipsburg

SABA Windwardside
The Bottom

ST. EUSTATIUS

N

Caribbean Bed & Breakfast

On his second voyage to the West Indies, Columbus was said to have sighted this lovely group of islands on the name day of San Martino (St. Martin of Tours). The largest island, surrounded by sparkling white beaches, then became known as Sint Maarten or Saint Martin, depending upon the Dutch or French point of view. After changing hands 16 times, the island of Sint Maarten has held two peacefully coexisiting nations for over 330 years.

The three Windward islands of St. Maarten, Saba and St. Eustatius (Statia) combined with Aruba, Bonaire and Curacao form the Netherlands Antilles islands of the Caribbean. The six islands are governed by a representative of the Queen of the Netherlands, and a parliamentary democracy allows each island territory a representative in the Island Council.

Regularly scheduled flights from North America into the Dutch Windward Islands, as well as from other Caribbean islands, are available, and cruise ships make frequent stops in St. Maarten. Day sails and charters out of Philipsburg to Saba, Statia and other nearby islands make island-hopping possible. A valid passport, birth certificate or voter's registration card will admit U.S. citizens to the islands, and a nominal departure tax for persons over two years of age is collected upon leaving.

The official language of the Dutch Windwards is Dutch, but English is spoken widely and used on local television and radio programming. The currency is the NA florin or guilder. Both traveler's checks and credit cards are accepted in most establishments, but it is wise to check ahead. The electrical power is compatible with North American appliances. Getting around the islands is easy with both rental cars and taxis available, and traffic moves to the right. The island is on Atlantic Standard Time (one hour ahead of Eastern Standard Time) all year. During Daylight Savings season, the time on St. Maarten and in the Eastern U.S. is the same.

For further information on the Dutch Windward Islands contact:
St. Maarten, Saba and St. Eustatius Tourist Office
25 West 39th Street, Suite 1003
New York, New York 10018
(212) 840-6655

Saba

Just 15 minutes by air from St. Maarten is this 5-mile-square "unspoilt Queen of the Caribbean." Lushly green Saba is

Dutch Windward Islands

made up of four villages—The Bottom, Windwardside, St. John's and Hell's Gate—that are connected by a single cross-island road full of hairpin turns through the mountains and ravines. Before the road, the villages on this volcanic cone-shaped island were united only by hundreds of steps chiseled by the 1640 Dutch settlers. Unlike most of the Caribbean islands, Saba has no real beaches; its surrounding rugged cliffs meet the sea below.

A trip through Saba, perhaps to the highest point at Mt. Scenery (2900 feet), can be made by taxi or on foot and is filled with breathtaking views and jagged rocks and boulders covered with orchids, lilies and begonias. Along with nature's beauty are the charming villages of Saba with their gingerbread-trimmed cottages clinging to the mountain sides, gabled roofs and flower- and fern-filled gardens. Saba, really a mountain top, is cooler than the other Dutch Windward islands, averaging 78 degrees, with brief showers keeping the gardens and wild tropical flowers plentiful.

Saban women began their craft of intricate needlework when the men on the island took to the sea, although present-day Saban men are employed by the oil refineries of Aruba and Curacao. The Artisans Foundation promotes and sells silk-screened fabrics and clothing handmade by the Sabans; this has become an integral part of the local economy.

Captain's Quarters
Windwardside
Saba
Netherlands Antilles
(011-599) 4-2201

Historic inn; 10 units; Moderate/Moderate EP;
No credit cards; Children ok; Smoking ok.

Location: Residential; Near town; 5 mi. to airport.

This early 1900's sea captain's home that forms the main house of the inn was built by Captain Henry Hassell for his daughter. It was used at one time in its history as a hospital, but opened as a charming turn-of-the-century lodging in 1965.

Caribbean Bed & Breakfast

Cuddled in the leeward slope of the village, this intimate group of three gingerbreaded houses with red tile roofs and Dutch blue shutters overlooks the sea 1,400 feet below.

The old sea captain's house with its old-fashioned verandas is now the office, library and kitchen of the inn and holds a few of the guestrooms. The sitting room is furnished in a pleasant assortment of antiques and paintings. Adjoining the home is a shaded breakfast porch where guests may enjoy a full American fare in the tranquil surroundings. A few steps away is the arbored dining pavilion, a charming open-air patio decorated in rattan and Mexican trestle tables and surrounded and shaded by breadfruit and mango trees. This garden dining spot serves lunches and dinners of freshly caught lobster, grouper and snapper along with steak, veal, lamb and other specialties.

A separate bar sits next to the inn's freshwater pool, which is surrounded by a spacious sunbathing deck on two sides and aromatic trees and flowers; the ocean view from here is exceptional. Light lunches are also served in this scenic spot.

The guestrooms at the Captain's Quarters all boast modern, private baths and relaxing verandas or balconies with views of the tropical blooms that surround, the green hillsides and the sparkling sea. These spacious rooms vary in size and decor, but all are furnished in a delightful mixture of mahogany antiques and island rattan and wicker. Romantic four-poster beds grace most of the accommodations.

Manager Steve Hassell is on hand to provide guests with a truly relaxing stay among friends in this intimate and quaint inn.

Cranston's Antique Inn
The Bottom
Saba
Netherlands Antilles
(011-599) 4-3203

Historic inn; 6 units; Inexpensive CP year-round;
Credit cards accepted; Children ok; Smoking ok.

Location: In town; Near ocean; 5 mi. to airport.

This 1850-built inn in Saba's capital city has a congenial history of housing visitors. The 130-year-old frame structure

Dutch Windward Islands

that fronts the small roadway was a government guest house that regularly hosted Dutch officials, including Queen Juliana. For over 35 years Mr. J.C. Cranston has been continuing the hospitality of the antique inn by offering six charming guest accommodations to island visitors.

The country inn is clean and cozy, decorated in a mixture of original house antiques and those collected by Mr. Cranston. The pretty hardwood floors add warmth as do the printed curtains and bedspreads. Most notably, every guestroom hosts an impressive four-poster, the most formidable asset of each room. Queen Juliana's room is available to guests who want to relive history; it is on the second floor and boasts a tranquil garden view. Only one room at the inn has a private bath, and the remaining quarters adequately share two bathrooms.

This b&b offers the complimentary morning meal on the covered garden terrace, as well as lunches and dinners of tasty local food and vegetarian specialties.

Nestled between the green, volcanic hillsides of the island, Cranston's Antique Inn is within walking distance of picturesque Ladder Bay, a network of over 500 steps leading to the coast.

Scout's Place
Windwardside
Saba
Netherlands Antilles
(011-599) 4-2205

Guest house; 8 units; Inexpensive MAP year-round;
No credit cards; Children ok; Smoking ok.

Location: In town; 3 mi. to harbor; 2 mi. to airport.

This 1920's-built guest house once housed government officials and passed through many hands until Scout Thirkield purchased the property and turned it into a modest, well-run lodging establishment. Very recently Scout sold the small inn to local Diana Medero who, along with manager Harold Levenstonel, is carrying on the guest house's reputation for congeniality most ably.

The old building, of Dutch architecture, holds a guest parlor with some Victorian furnishings and a color television. Five guestrooms are located here and feature some four-posters

Caribbean Bed & Breakfast

and antiques as well as views of the flower-filled courtyard and the sea beyond. The homey accommodations include three rooms with private baths and two that share a bathroom. The other three guest lodgings are contained in separate cottages on the garden grounds and have full utensils and furnishings.

This tranquil inn is right in the heart of things, in the center of town, and set gracefully on the ledge of a hill. The staff is friendly and the pace is quiet. Future plans for Scout's Place include a freshwater swimming pool.

St. Maarten

Thirty-seven-mile-square St. Maarten, half Dutch and half French, is considered the smallest existing territory shared by two sovereign states. (See Chapter 15 for information about the French half.) The northernmost Antilles island, St. Maarten boasts a year-round average temperature of 80 degrees with cooling trade winds, over 30 coral beaches, popular duty-free shopping and active gambling casinos.

The capital of St. Maarten, Philipsburg, was founded in 1763 by Commander Hohn Philips, a Scotsman in Dutch employ, and it is distinguished by unique shingled architecture. Philipsburg's shops line the two main thoroughfares, and little lanes called *steegjes* connect the streets with still more quaint stores. St. Maarten is a duty-free port with no local taxes imposed and some very reasonable rates on all kinds of merchandise, from designer jewelry and cameras to Holland cheeses. To the southwest of town are the ruins of 17th-century Fort Amsterdam, the first Dutch fort on the island.

St. Maarten's crystal-clear bays and coves offer superior snorkeling and scuba with visibility of 75 to 125 feet. Deep-sea fishing charters for half or full day, coastal and lagoon cruises as well as glass-bottom boat trips are available for exploring the countless coves and bays around the island.

Mary's Boon
P.O. Box 278
St. Maarten
Netherlands Antilles
(011-599) 5-4235
(800) 223-5608

Dutch Windward Islands

Inn; 12 units; Moderate/Moderate EP;
No credit cards; No children; Smoking ok.

Location: On beach; 5 mi. to town; 2 mi. to Dutch airport.

The original owner of Mary's Boon, Caribbean innkeeper Mary Pomeroy, is the "Mary" in question, but the second half of the inn's name, meaning "welcoming benefit," might be relevant to anyone who visits the intimate inn in search of a private stretch of beach and friendly surroundings. The small inn, located down a long private road on the snow-white sand of Juliana Beach, is now owned and managed by Rushton Little, who carries on the 1970-built inn's tradition of hospitality.

Mary's Boon is made up of gingerbread-adorned buildings and cottages with wooden balconies and verandas that boast elaborate hibiscus trim. The structures are situated directly on the sand with gardens of shrubbery, sea grapes and coconut palms growing in profusion. The desertion of this stretch of beach is interrupted only by an occasional plane landing or taking-off from the airport runway that nearly touches the edge of the inn property. Even with that one inconvenience, the inn is still a favorite of a generous return clientele.

Guestrooms at Mary's Boon are really apartments; each is quite unique. The dozen spacious studios all boast private baths with tiled shower stalls and lots of fresh-air ventilation, tile floors, ceiling fans, kitchenettes and private, seaside patios. The decor is light and airy with louvered windows, beamed cathedral ceilings, Haitian paintings and a nice combination of wicker, bamboo and antique furnishings.

All three meals are served at the inn and offered on a pleasant open-air gallery with wood panelling and beamed ceiling. The bistro with small tables and romantic nighttime lighting fronts the picturesque bay. Guests at Mary's Boon enjoy a varied Dutch, French and West Indian menu while gazing at the sparkling Caribbean a few feet ahead. An honor bar at the inn allows guests to help themselves day or night. A lounge area in the main building has a grand piano for informal entertainment and comfortable, tropical seating.

Note:
The inn is closed the months of September and October.

Caribbean Bed & Breakfast

Mary's Fancy Hotel
P.O. Box 420
St. Maarten
Netherlands Antilles
(011-599) 5-2665

Historic inn/Plantation; 11 units; Expensive/Inexpensive-Mod. EP; Credit cards accepted; No children under 13; Smoking ok.

Location: Near beach; Near town; 5 mi. to Dutch airport.

This historic plantation is filled to the brim with tropical beauty, eclectic decor and special service for its intimate family of guests. It is an oasis of exotic delight where guests may return and return and never get bored, for each room at the inn is an adventure in color, theme and feel.

Mary's Fancy was named after an early island settler—Mary Van Ramondt—who, given a choice of any piece of land on the island, "fancied" this fertile acreage in the valley near Philipsburg. The soil turned it into one of the richest sugar plantations in St. Maarten; a great house built on the lushly landscaped grounds was later to become the Governor's Mansion. The mansion is now the inn's restaurant, Gianni's, and carries a fine reputation for Italian and continental cuisine.

The great house sits at the end of a tree-lined drive and is entered by way of a handsome pink and white striped awning-covered walkway. The restaurant offers romantic terrace dining or dinner within the private dining rooms of the house, each possessing its own charming atmosphere and decor. One such dining room was the former governor's bedroom and hosts antique cabinets and a red Oriental screen. Only fine china and linens are used along with gold plates to set the glass-top tables of the restaurant, and guests sit in gracious, high-backed Mandarin wicker chairs. Dinner is by reservation only. Breakfast is served on the terrace on the same elegant gold plates; lunch is not available.

The guestrooms at Mary's Fancy are all located around the tropical grounds in seven very individual cottages hidden by the huge trees and tropical foliage of the plantation. These pastel-colored cottages contain 11 guest suites, some with full kitchens and large sitting areas and all with imaginative and eclectic decor that follows an excitingly unique theme. The cathedral-

Dutch Windward Islands

beamed ceilings, turn-of-the-century fans and collector's items within each room are augmented by perhaps a Tudor four-poster, a Chinese bamboo bed, matching Edwardian brass beds, a red and white Chinese scroll or a hand-quilted bedspread. The themes are harmonious and eclectic at once, and the result is more than pleasant.

The five-acre grounds of the inn are lush with gardens of oleander and frangipani, huge oaks and even a 200-year-old silk tree all reached by meandering walkways lined with bright blooms. A wooden bridge spans an ancient slave wall to a meadow that leads on to the inviting free-form pool and surrounding sun patio.

The guest at Mary's Fancy gets all this and tip-top service too provided graciously by manager Nicky Guyt. According to Guyt, "Mary's Fancy is just paradise in a tropical garden—we just love it!" And for a unique stay, you will too—especially when paradise is a very hospitable 50 percent lower in off-season.

Pasanggrahan Royal Guest House
P.O. Box 151
Philipsburg
St. Maarten
Netherlands Antilles
(011-599) 5-3588
Rep: American/Wolfe International

Historic inn; 27 units; Moderate/Inexpensive-Mod. EP;
No credit cards; No children under 12 on-season,
Children ok off-season; Smoking ok.

Location: On beach; In town; 7 mi. to Dutch airport.

Pasanggrahan, an Indonesian word, means "the guest house" and is an appropriate name for this typical guest house: a relaxed, casual, friendly, informal and small hostelry. This guest house, however, happens to convey a little more—a piece of local history. It was the late-1800's Governor's Mansion where Queen Wilhelmina and Princess Juliana stayed during WWII and was later used to house various other government VIP's. Today, the Pasanggrahan has the notable title of the oldest guest house or hotel on the island.

Caribbean Bed & Breakfast

Located between the narrow, bustling main street of the town and the white sand beach, the Dutch colonial guest house holds court under tall trees and hosts a long, white veranda. The guest lounge is decorated in a few period antiques and a portrait of Queen Wilhelmina dominates the room.

The Garden Cafe, pleasantly taken over by the overgrown tropical gardens and coconut palms, is where all three meals are served family-style. They feature good American and West Indian cuisine in a homey atmosphere. The private beach is a short walk from here through the untamed tropical shrubbery.

The guestrooms at the guest house are located alongside the Cafe in the two-story building with veranda or in a newer annex building on the other side of the garden area. The informal tropical foliage surrounds and adds privacy to the guest quarters that all boast private, tiled shower baths and ceiling fans. A few of the rooms have air conditioning, kitchenettes, four-poster or king size beds, and all have attractive bedspreads. The simple, pleasant decor includes a few antiques.

Guests at this charming inn are treated to the manager's weekly cocktail party hosted by owner-manager Peter de Zela. The friendly staff and management also provide complimentary coffee, tea and snacks each day.

Also on the Island

The Horny Toad
P.O. Box 397
Philipsburg
St. Maarten
Netherlands Antilles
(011-599) 5-4323
Rep: Sontheimer-Hazlett Ltd.

Owners and innkeepers Betty and Earle Vaughan stayed at the Horny Toad as guests in 1979 and "fell in love with the guest house," purchasing it in June 1981. This simple and casual guest house, known affectionately as "the Toad," is really a small assemblage of housekeeping apartments (eight) that offer a separate bedroom, fully equipped kitchen, living area and private gallery overlooking the pretty, white sand beach. The guest house was originally the island governor's residence and boasts a large covered balcony as do each of the guest units. The guest accommodations are decorated individually in rattan, wood paneling and cheerful tropical prints. This quiet and private spot gets some occasional noise from the nearby airport runway, but still offers plenty of seclusion. No children under 7 are allowed, and credit cards are not accepted. The moderate rates include daily maid service and the hospitable, personal service of the Vaughans.

Oyster Pond Yacht Club
P.O. Box 239
Philipsburg
St. Maarten
Netherlands Antilles
(011-599) 5-2206
Rep: David B. Mitchell & Co.

This castle-looking inn with towers and curved stone walls sits high on a promontory on the remote eastern edge of the island. The 16-year-old inn has recently undergone a costly renovation that has made the 20-room inn even more appealing. An open-air lobby is decorated in white wicker from France and colorful flower arrangements; the central courtyard with copper sculpture fountains offers large white umbrella seating. The guestrooms are all decorated individually with the same imported white wicker, including rockers and peacock headboards. Four tower suites have cozy window seats. Guests enjoy all three meals from a gourmet menu, tennis, watersports, a marina, mile-long Dawn Beach and a staff that believes in pampering. No children under 10 are allowed, and prices in on-season are in the deluxe range.

St. Eustatius

Referred to as the "Golden Rock," St. Eustatius or "Statia" was once the trading hub of the Caribbean. The 8-mile-square dot 30 minutes by air from St. Maarten has two extinct volcanos, the Quill and Little Mountain, with sweet potato and yam fields nestled in between. The climate is drier than Saba's, but the island enjoys fresh prevailing sea winds. Statia's prosperity waned when it was no longer needed as a transit port for American colonies; today, the Golden Rock is trying to shine again with a growing tourism trade.

Caribbean Bed & Breakfast

Sightseeing, hiking and beach-going are the most popular pastimes on the tiny, informal island. Car rentals or taxis will take the visitor around the island; vehicles travel American-style, to the right. A visit to the cliff-perched capital city of Oranjestad will reveal 18th-century buildings and Fort Oranje, the present seat of island government and the former defender of security. Some of the original 17th- and 18th-century buildings that were situated on the waterfront have sunk into the sea and have become a major attraction to scuba divers and snorkelers.

The Quill, a volcano with an exceptionally beautiful rain forest in its crater, can be reached by burro with a guide. For a totally unique activity, visitors may hunt giant crabs here by moonlight and bring them back to town for tempting stuffed crab dishes. Another point of ecological distinction for Statia is the twice-a-year beaching of sea turtles here while they lay their eggs.

The Old Gin House and
Mooshay Bay Publick House
P.O. Box 172
St. Eustatius
Netherlands Antilles
(011-599) 3-2319
Rep: Scott Calder International

Historic inns; 20 units; Expensive/Moderate EP;
AE,VI,DC,MC; No children under 12 or
on approval; Smoking ok.

Location: On beach; Near town; 1 mi. to airport.

This charming pair of inns has been reconstructed with historical authenticity and personal comfort guiding the way on the site of a 1700's warehouse and cotton gin, now filled with bougainvillaea and palm trees. Ex-New York advertising executives Marty Scofield and John May are responsible for the stunning results in their quest to provide a truly pressure-free getaway for other executives amid history, charm, gourmet food and modern conveniences—a blending almost too ideal, but one they aptly succeeded in achieving. The two men own and personally manage both the establishments, which are located across the road from each other, and, likewise, guests mingle

Dutch Windward Islands

back and forth between the properties, partaking of their individual offerings.

The Old Gin House was the original transformation and the pair's inspiration. The 19th-century cotton gin factory was actually a conversion from a 1710-built warehouse. Located right on the beach at Oranjestad, the site was an ideal spot for their lodging endeavor. Brick ballast brought from Holland was used in the construction of the inn. Guestrooms boast balconies facing the sea.

The Old Gin House proved so popular that the owners purchased what was to become the Mooshay Bay Publick House just across the road. This old stone-constructed building is reminiscent of an 18th-century structure and is located on the ruins of an original molasses warehouse. The age-worn cistern on the property was transformed into an inviting little swimming pool, and the overseer's gallery is a charming library and backgammon room abrim with warm antiques and island memorabilia.

The 20 guest accommodations can all be rated excellent in comfort, decor and modern conveniences. Antiques, mainly from the 18th century, are tastefully mixed with practical pieces and locally handcrafted items at the Old Gin House; the modern, private bathrooms at both inns boast hot water showers. Guestrooms at Mooshay are furnished mainly with handmade island furniture and offer poolside rooms that overlook the swimming pool and lush, tropical gardens. Paintings, flowering pots on terraces and gentle colors all contribute to the sophisticated feel of each room's setting.

The Mooshay Publick House's dining room is the splendid locale of the inns' gourmet dinners. Classical music and candlelight set the tone for each evening's selected menu served on delicate Delft china. (The inn's cuisine was featured as a cover story in *Gourmet Magazine's* January 1979 issue.) Dinner is served among the rafters and bare brick walls. Breakfast and lunch are served on the beachfront terrace decorated in maritime antiques and surrounded by palms and ferns.

The pace at the Old Gin House and Mooshay Bay is casual and relaxing, the service sublime and the setting beautifully nostalgic—owners Scofield and May practically guarantee it!

Note:
The inns are closed September 1 through October 15.

Grand Case **ST. MARTIN**

ST. BARTHELEMY
Gustavia

N

15

French West Indies

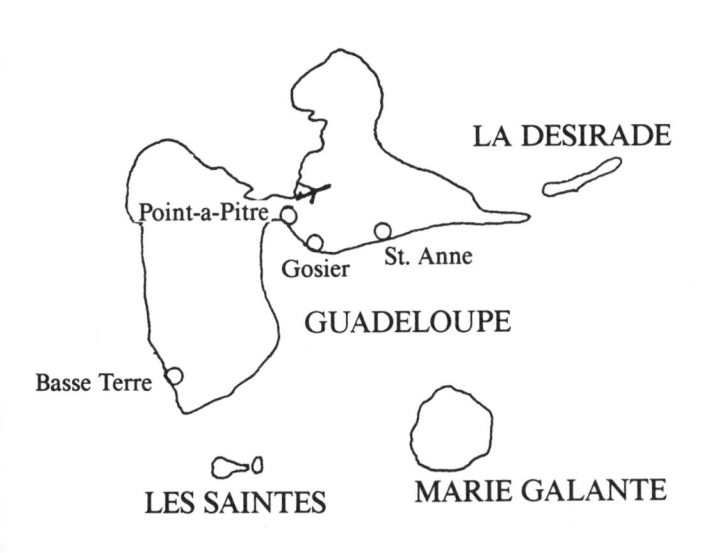

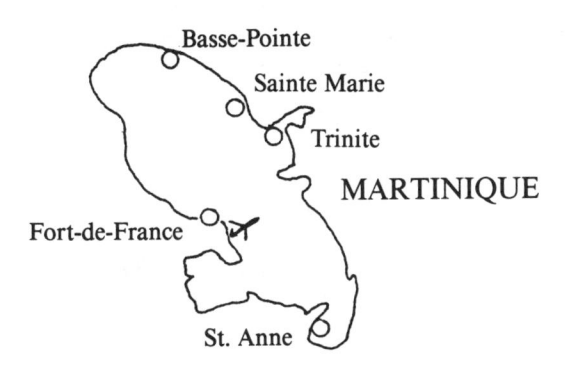

Caribbean Bed & Breakfast

Martinique, Guadeloupe, St. Martin (French-side), St. Barthelemy and a small scattering of tiny offshore islands make up the French West Indies, a part of France itself and not merely colonies of the European nation. The ambience of France lends itself beautifully to these tropical isles located in the curve of the Lesser Antilles.

Regularly scheduled flights from North America arrive here daily; U.S. citizens are required to show a valid passport and a return ticket for entry. On the islands, taxis operate on set rates per car for up to four persons with rates slightly higher at night. It is wise to settle upon the exact fare before leaving for your destination. The roads in the French West Indies are fairly good and car rental agencies are plentiful. Driving is American-style with traffic on the right, and the primary rule of the road is that priority always goes to the vehicle on the right. Gasoline prices are higher here, but the cars are economy models. Also note that no speed limits are set, and the French drivers tend to be impatient. Organized tours by cars or buses go to all parts of the islands, and various sailing vessels and boats offer trips to the French Indies' offshore islands.

The beautiful, tropical climate of the French West Indies is cooled year-round by *les alizes* or trade winds. Slightly wetter weather can occur September through November, but it lasts only briefly with lots of sunshine.

French, the national language of the islands, is tempered with an interesting Creole dialect. The French tourist bureau suggests that the visitor take along a phrase book, and they furnish one as well which is a good idea since a majority of the population does not speak English. The currency is the French franc, but American dollars, traveler's checks and credit cards are accepted widely. The electricity is 220 volts and requires a converter, available at some inns, to operate North American appliances.

Beach nudity or the European fashion of "topless" is often associated with the French West Indies islands. The visitor should be aware that there are no beaches reserved for nudists on Martinique and the practice is not permitted on public beaches. The topless fashion is prevalent at many hotels and on some of the beaches. There are a few designated nudist beaches on the island of Guadeloupe.

French West Indies

For additional information on the French West Indies contact:
French West Indies Tourist Board
610 Fifth Avenue
New York, New York 10020
(212) 757-1125
or
French Government Tourist Office
9401 Wilshire Blvd.
Beverly Hills, CA 90212
(213) 271-6665

Martinique

The Carib Indians originally named Martinique *Madinina*, meaning "island of flowers," and it lives up to its name with a rich, plentiful offering of tropical flowers and plants. Colorful hibiscus, rose laurels, oleander, bougainvillaea and more are accompanied by hummingbirds, turtledoves, tiny frogs, "forest kids" and crickets that provide magical background music to the tropical evening lit up by fire flies. The island is also submerged in a profusion of palm, bamboo, mahogany, mango, orange, pineapple and papaya trees as well as endless fields of sugar cane.

Martinique, population 350,000, has been a French Department since 1946, and its rich history is displayed in the numerous monuments and remains scattered about the island. Its 417 square miles of land are surrounded by white beaches with five bays and dozens of coves and rise gradually to mountains connected by hills called *mornes*.

Fort de France, the island's capital, is a bustling city bathed in pastel shades. Historic Fort Saint Louis stands guard over the boat-filled harbor where nearby open-markets are held. In the center of town is La Savane, a flower- and fountain-filled park with a white marble statue of the Empress Josephine. Overlooking the city are two more forts from the 18th and 19th centuries as well as Sacre-Coeur de Balata, a miniature version of the basilica in Montmartre. The beautiful high-cheekboned, statuesque women of Martinique clothed in sophisticated fashions or in the island's colorful red, green and orange plaid can be seen on the city's busy shopping streets.

Martinique offers many interesting and picturesque towns to explore and well-signed roads to make the sightseeing

Caribbean Bed & Breakfast

enjoyable. The towns of Sainte Anne and Sainte-Luce boast magnificent white sand beaches and nearby forests. Rivere Pilote, on the way to Sainte Anne, is a charming village with European flavor and turn-of-the-century lightposts. The "Little Paris of the West Indies," Saint-Pierre, was the capital of Martinique until 1902 when Mt. Pelee erupted, killing all but one of its inhabitants. Ruins and relics of the town can be viewed on the spot and at the Franck A. Perret museum. Also, the birthplace of Empress Josephine and a sugar mill and church from 1765 may be found in the town of Trois-Ilets.

The island is known for its fine cuisine, both creole and French or a combination of the two. Dining often begins with a *petit punch blanc/vieux*, meaning punch made of light or dark rum with sugar cane syrup, lime (only for the tourists) and ice. Besides fine restaurants, Martinique offers an array of nightlife with two casinos and several cabarets and discotheques.

Outdoor activities are plentiful on Martinque. Ample coral beds and reefs make underwater exploration popular. Fort de France is known as one of the safest and most beautiful bays in the Caribbean for sailing and yachting. Martinique offers a championship 140-acre golf course at La Pointe du Bout. The golfer can take a break here with a Planter's Punch while rocking leisurely in one of the clubhouse rocking chairs.

Relatively recent is the island's Regional Natural Park, covering 232 square miles or half the island's total area. This park area has been developed to provide hiking, camping, horseback riding and nature excursions for both the residents and the island's visitors.

Martinique time is one hour later than Eastern Standard Time. However, when the East Coast is on Eastern Daylight Time, Martinique and East Coast time are the same.

Manoir de Beauregard
97227 Sainte-Anne
Martinique
French West Indies
(011-596) 76-73-40
Rep: Robert Reid Associates

French West Indies

Historic inn; 32 units; Moderate/Inexpensive CP; AE,MC,DC; Children ok; Smoking ok.

Location: Near town; 2 mi. to beach; 26 mi. to airport.

On a sunny hill just above the quaint seaside town of St. Anne is this impressive 18th-century manor house-turned-inn-and-restaurant. A picturesque drive through small towns and pretty countryside brings you to this tranquil resort near one of the finest beaches in Martinique. The manor was built in the early 1700's and may have been named after one of the first owner's daughters who married a knight named de la Touche de Beauregard. Although the history of the estate is still being researched, the idea of preserving the house and its contents was a high priority when the inn conversion took place a few years ago.

The manor house sits on a quiet piece of the countryside with panoramic views of the hills and trees. The tropical growth is informal and dotted with small sitting areas that take advantage of the quiet. The manor house, containing all but five of the guest accommodations, is white with old stone and wooden shutter detailing. You enter the house through a side door that is fronted by a colorful parrot in a cage. The first impression of the almost cavernous reception room and lounge is that of an old castle or perhaps church. The marble-tiled floor is the original and the stone walls are untouched, only accented with old portraits and rich tapestries. Deep, arched recesses are filled with antique settees, cane rocking chairs and a grandfather's clock, and a scrolled, green iron grating with gold leaf that once graced a 19th-century church now forms doors and staircase railings. The polished wood-beamed ceilings of the two common areas hold spectacular gilded chandeliers.

The restaurant of the inn connects to the far side of the lounge, mingling the old and the new. This spacious room with pleasant cross breezes is decorated in a few antique hoosiers displaying china and in several tables with straw chair seating. The tables are gaily covered in a Martinique-plaid. All three meals are served in the restaurant; the complimentary breakfast for guests includes a continental fare of juice, fresh fruit, rolls and coffee. To the left of the lounge is a small boutique selling handsome hand-painted items of silk.

All of the guestrooms at Manoir de Beauregard boast private baths, air conditioning and telephones, and all of the

Caribbean Bed & Breakfast

guest accommodations in the manor house happily boast antique decor. In fact, most of the furniture in the house is authentic and entirely handmade of native wood; these pieces are at least 100 years old. One room downstairs holds identical, double four-poster beds, an antique rocker and dressers. French doors lead to the room's own, private patio overlooking the pool and hills. Upstairs rooms are reached through halls spiced with antique pieces, prints and attractive flower arrangements from the gardens.

Though lacking the charm of the manor house, a few additional guestrooms are available in a row building to the rear of the house. This building covered in pink and yellow tropical blooms has five guestrooms with more standard, contemporary decor.

Horseback riding is available at the estate, and an inviting L-shaped pool to the front of the old house offers the same pastoral views. Just a few minutes drive away is a beautiful, white sand beach that might cause you to divide your time between this serene resort and its warm, blue water.

Plantation de Leyritz
97218 Basse-Pointe
Martinique
French West Indies
(011-596) 75-53-92/75-53-08

Plantation; 50 units; Moderate/Inexpensive-Mod. CP; VI,MC,AE,DC; Children ok; Smoking ok.

Location: Countryside; 15 mi. to beach; 35 mi. to airport.

A scenic drive through winding roads lined with lush tropical vegetation and small towns leads to a smaller road that bumps past banana fields to this charming, 16-acre plantation resort. On a secluded hill overlooking the Atlantic in the distance, Plantation de Leyritz feels remote and displaced from the rest of the world, wrapped in 18th-century history and

French West Indies

working agricultural fields. Of course, this ideal picture is not at all times serene since the plantation is a favorite of bus tour passengers who travel miles to sample the delicious French cuisine and soak up the centuries of history and sheer beauty of the location. Fortunately there is enough tranquility and beauty to share with the occasional day-visitor here.

Plantation de Leyritz is owned and operated by a gracious couple, Charles and Yveline De Lucy De Fossarieu, whose well-respected family lines date back to the early 1600's. The plantation was built around 1700 and has been restored lovingly by the present owners. At the core of the plantation is the original planter's house with 20-inch-thick stone walls, beamed ceilings, tile and flagstone floors and an expensive and rare Vienna wood staircase. The coral-colored building with old wooden shutters and shingled roof holds a gracious parlor with beautifully restored antiques and Oriental rugs. In fact, the antique parlor dining table flanked by antique china cabinets with silver pieces and rich, old paintings was the site of the 1974 Meeting of the Presidents with presidents Ford and Giscard d'Estaing in attendance. Located upstairs are antique-filled guestrooms of the inn that were under renovation at the time of this writing. Also, a main house restaurant was in the planning stages; given the intimacy and antique beauty of the home, it is sure to be a special dining spot.

The rest of the guest accommodations at the plantation are located in various cottages that surround the grounds, most of those former slave quarters. One especially attractive unit was the former kitchen of the plantation and grants spectacular views. The various wood shingle- and stone-constructed buildings are decorated in a mixture of antiques and contemporary decor, but mostly convey an antique feel. All of the guest accommodations are different, but commonly offer private bathrooms, air conditioning and telephone. At this writing renovation of the bamboo former married slave quarters was well underway, and a few new stone bungalows were under construction. It was reassuring to view the care taken with the new construction to make it appear old and blend with the other guest bungalows on the property. All of these units are being constructed of stone taken from the plantation, and the tiles have been perfectly matched to the originals with an estimated two years of weathering to make the difference in age indistinguishable.

Caribbean Bed & Breakfast

A formal French garden offers some of the best views over the banana fields and the pretty plantation swimming pool with antique marble dolphins. Two fountains, one a waterfall and the other a basin, highlight the botanical gardens that boast trees with name plaques, bright red poinsettias and traveler's palms.

Fronted by a flowing, manicured lawn and fish ponds is the plantation's restaurant, a former rum and sugar factory. The elegant stone dining rooms contain rough wooden beams overhead, remnants of an old chapel and red anthuriums clinging to the ancient walls. An ever-flowing sheet of water gurgles down one of the old walls, a natural waterfall when it rains and a motor-driven flow on sunny days. The effect is soothing, and the food is a sublime offering of French and creole delectables. Guests at Leyritz are treated to a complimentary breakfast here, and lunch and dinner are also available. The gourmet dishes include such entrees as coconut milk chicken, pork flambee and various "colombos" or stews.

The Plantation de Leyritz has recently opened a health spa on the premises in partnership with a couple from New York. Special spa programs that include diet and beauty treatments are available, and a doctor is in residence at this most unique health farm.

Saint Aubin Hotel
P.O. Box 52
97220 Trinite
Martinique
French West Indies
(011-596) 69-34-77

Historic inn; 15 units; Inexpensive/Inexpensive CP; AE,DC,VI,MC; Children ok; Smoking ok.

Location: 1 mi. to beach; 3 mi. to town; 20 mi. to airport.

This gingerbread-laden, pink Victorian is perched majestically on a hill overlooking the Atlantic. A drive curves gently up to the house and is lined with colorful flowers and turn-of-the-century lamp globes mounted on palm tree bases. The front of the house bears a gracious circular driveway with pink flowers in the center planter and green wrought-iron gates that

French West Indies

protect the privacy of the estate. An outside veranda with gleaming tile, scalloped pillars and green wrought-iron trim decorate the house itself.

The 1900-built home was rebuilt on the old plantation site that dates back to the 17th century. The comfortable inn with quality food is the result of two years of Mr. Foret Guy's hard work. He is the b&b's hospitable owner and manager, and he gives each letter and special request his personal attention.

The bottom floor of the house has a small reception area and guest parlor as well as the inn's dining room off a quaint pair of French doors. Old-fashioned globe chandeliers, a small bar, television and some wicker furnishings fill the parlor and reception areas while the dining area offers more traditional furnishing with seating for 50 on antique tables and chairs. The comfortable room boasts built-in hutches, pillared woodwork and unusual two-tone, inlaid wooden floors. The dining room, with views of the ocean, is just for guests of the inn and features a complimentary continental breakfast and a complete and tasty creole and French dinner menu. Lunches are not available.

The 15 guestrooms of the St. Aubin are located on the second and third levels of the house. A fancy, white-spooled bannister with oak trim leads upstairs. The second-level landing is the site of an unusual mini-flight of stairs that leads out to the veranda with panoramic views of the lush hills.

The guestrooms at the inn have all been modernized with air conditioning, wall-to-wall carpeting, up-to-date and private bathrooms, telephones and attractive wallcoverings. The guest quarters do not possess the antique charm of the house in terms of furnishings, but are very clean and comfortable. Guestrooms on the third floor, the former attic of the home, contain units that can accommodate up to four people and boast homey slanted ceilings with wallpaper coverings.

The rear grounds of the St. Aubin are as quiet and delightful as the front. An informal flower garden, wide grassy lawn and swimming pool with cabana occupy the back acreage in this intimate and hospitable spot.

Also on the Island

Hotel Bristol
0,200 km. rue Martin-Luther-King
Fort-de-France

Caribbean Bed & Breakfast

Martinique
French West Indies
(011-596) 71-31-80

This converted colonial home in the middle of town offers nine guestrooms overlooking the bay. The hilltop house has an attractive veranda that extends on all sides for pleasant, breeze-cooled lounging. Guestrooms, with twin or double beds, have air conditioning and comfortable, though not fancy, furnishings. A swimming pool is available; the beach is about ten miles away. A good creole and French cuisine restaurant is a part of the inn, serving all three meals. Overnight rates are very reasonable and include a continental breakfast. Your hospitable host is Mr. Philippe Solis.

Hotel Victoria
Rond Point de Didier
P.O. Box 337
Fort-de-France
Martinique
French West Indies
(011-596) 60-56-78
(305) 891-0323 (Miami)

Located in a residential area of the city, this medium-size inn offers 30 guest accommodations and views of the harbor. The main house is a 150-year-old colonial structure, but all the guestrooms are contained in small bungalows on the grounds. Each bungalow is air conditioned and decorated simply yet comfortably. A gingerbread-adorned veranda on the house is a pleasant spot to watch the bay while enjoying a drink from the bar. A garden swimming pool is available for guests, as well as a comfortable parlor with television. A restaurant serving delicious French specialties is a part of this family-owned hotel that is gaining a large repeat business.

Guadeloupe

The Carib Indians who originally inhabited this island named it "island of beautiful waters" which is very true of butterfly-shaped, less sophisticated Guadeloupe. This "double"

French West Indies

island's parts are separated by a drawbridge and narrow strait called *La Riviere Salee*. Grand-Terre is characterized by rolling hills and ample sugar plantations, while Basse-Terre to the west is mountainous and banana plantation- and forest-filled with a dormant volcano, La Soufriere. Guadeloupe, 580 square miles in size, has several island dependencies: Iles des Saintes, Marie Galante and La Desirade, all offshore, and the islands of St. Barthelemy and French St. Martin, which are discussed here independently.

Basse-Terre, the city, is the capital of the island, but the larger city of Point-a-Pitre on the southwest coast of Grande-Terre is the commercial center of activity. Point-a-Pitre, often called the "Paris of the Antilles," is a modern, crowded city lacking a French old-world charm; instead it is full of modern apartments and condominiums. This port city has some shopping significance, a 19th-century cathedral and some scenic squares. The open-air markets and boutique stalls around the narrow streets contain colorful displays of the local wares and people. Three miles east of Point-a-Pitre is the Fort Fleur d'Epee, an 18th-century fortress offering spectacular views of the city and the nearby offshore islands.

Other spots to visit on Guadeloupe might include Ste. Anne, a quaint village with a town hall, church and nearby beaches; Pointe-des-Chateaux, a castlelike rock formation with coved beaches; Les Chutes du Carbet, a trio of waterfalls near the town of St. Sauveur; and La Soufriere, Guadeloupe's steam-breathing volcano. The foot of the volcano's crater can be reached by car and the rim is reached by foot trails, marked for ease in colors. The walking part of the trip can take up to three hours and a guide is recommended. A popular government-run inn called the Hotel-Relais de la Grand Soufriere in St. Claude and near the base of the volcano is now closed. However, the charming town dotted with interesting colonial architecture is worth the visit.

A few stretches of white sand make swimming and sunning a pastime in Guadeloupe, but the surf on some of the island's beaches is too wild for safe swimming. An area off Pigeon Island, frequented by Jacques Cousteau, is considered one of the top scuba and diving spots in the Caribbean. For those looking inland, the Parc Naturel provides excellent hiking trails through rain forests sprinkled with waterfalls and pools.

The nightlife of Guadeloupe is accented by its dancing; Guadeloupeans claim to have begun the beguine. A casino and

Caribbean Bed & Breakfast

several clubs come alive at night. Guadeloupe offers creole cuisine and not the classic French dishes of neighboring Martinique. The island celebrates its culinary art each year at the Cook's Festival, characterized by a parade, music and dancing as well as a huge feast enduring several hours.

A tour or independent plane-hop trip to Guadeloupe's offshore islands of Iles des Saintes and Marie Galante provides wonderful sightseeing and delicate fine white beaches. Sugar mills, rolling hills, and architecturally quaint towns and squares make for wonderful strolling and picnicking.

Guadeloupe time is one hour later than Eastern Standard Time and the same as Eastern Daylight Time.

Relais du Moulin
Chateaubrun
Sainte-Anne
Guadeloupe
French West Indies
(011-596) 88-23-96

Plantation; 20 units; Moderate/Inexpensive CP;
AE,VI,MC; Children ok; Smoking ok.

Location: Countryside; 1 mi. to beach; 18 mi. to airport.

After a pleasant drive out of the town of Sainte-Anne, traveling through picturesque countryside, you will spot a windmill ruin in the midst of green fields. Look carefully for a sign that will lead you through a palm-lined drive to the sugar mill ruin, now reception office, of the Relais du Moulin. This circular stone building was built in 1843 as a part of a working sugar plantation. The mill boasts pretty stone arches and a low wall at its base which overflows with purple bougainvillaea. A steel spiral staircase makes the climb to the top of the old mill easy and most worthwhile. The 360-degree views from this historic ruin take in the lush countryside and ocean for as far as you can see. The only sounds you hear in this tranquil setting, except for your fellow guests, are the mill's blades cutting through the ocean breezes as they spin around most of the day.

Although the encompassing views from atop the windmill are not available from the remainder of the inn's facilities, the green, tranquil countryside most certainly is. An outdoor bar surrounded by tropical vegetation sits next to the mill and serves drinks in its setting of pretty tilework and beamed ceilings; the inn's cat pays an occasional friendly visit. Across from the bar is the inn's Tap-Tap Restaurant. This enclosed and spacious eating area has the same elaborate beamed ceiling and handsome decor marked by green high-back chairs and pastel tropical-print tablecloths. The walls carry paintings and old photographs of the sugar mill, and the table centerpieces are miniature "tap-taps" or colorful buses. The complimentary morning breakfast of rolls, juice and fruit is served to guests here along with lunch and dinner.

A few steps down from the bar and restaurant area is the swimming pool, hidden by fragrant tropical foliage. Surrounded by lounges, the blue-tiled pool is most inviting and a popular gathering spot. This country inn also offers archery and horseback riding to its guests; a long beach is about a ten-minute walk away through the fields, but the surf tends to be a bit wild.

The guestrooms at the Relais du Moulin are all contained in bungalows to the rear of the mill and restaurant/bar area. Each unit is quite private and named after a different flower. The units, which are all similar, are actually mini-suites with a small living room with two daybeds and refrigerator, separate bedroom with double bed or twins, private bath with modern facilities and shower and private patio. These suites are pint-sized and decorated sparsely in a contemporary mode. The floors are of linoleum, the walls are pine paneled, the ceiling is a dropped acoustic type, and the drapery is grass cloth. The bathrooms carry a bit more charm with pretty wallcoverings and hand-painted tile. Probably the most alluring feature of the room units are the patios that sit right in the flower-filled fields. The views are tranquil, but the field-enclosed setting does invite a bit of the outdoors in. The louvered floor-to-ceiling windows are not screened at this writing and tend to allow visits from the countryside inhabitants. It is quite advisable to take along your insect repellent when visiting this country oasis.

Also on the Island

Serge's Guest House
97190 Perinette-Gosier
Guadeloupe
French West Indies
(011-596) 84-10-25

This informal guest house is nearly hidden from view by the dense tropical vegetation and colorful hibiscus that fill the front gardens. A small white gate opens to the guest house complex which includes simple guestrooms with shared baths, studio units and a few apartments in several concrete block and stucco buildings. Little red-tiled walkways connect the buildings; in one is the outdoor dining area with cheerful, West Indian tablecloths. A connecting guest lounge has television and reading material, and the two areas overlook the informal flower gardens and pool of the guest house. Overnight stays in this congenial spot include a continental breakfast of breads with marmalade, coffee, tea or chocolate. Rates are very moderate; no credit cards are accepted.

Les Saintes

Hotel Bois-Joli
97137 Terre-de-Haut
Les Saintes
Guadeloupe
French West Indies
(011-596) 99-50-38

A short boat or airplane trip from Guadeloupe will take you to this small, offshore island with a quiet pace and pretty beaches. The Hotel Bois Joli is situated on the western end of the island on a hilltop that overlooks a nice beach. The 21 guest accommodations are located in the main house, home of hosts Mr. and Mrs. Blandin, as well as in more modern cottages down the hillside. The guestrooms are simply furnished with pretty tropical prints and offer both shared and private baths. The white stucco guest house serves good creole cuisine; both breakfast and dinner are included in the reasonable rates. Note that some knowledge of the French language would be helpful here, or at least remember to bring along your phrase book.

St. Barthelemy

This tiny, 8 1/2-mile-square island commonly referred to as St. Barts is full of natural, uncrowded beauty, and it is distinguished by a Swedish influence. The beautiful green mountains and coral sand beaches combine with its toy-scaled capital, Gustavia, to make it a special spot in the Caribbean.

Discovered by Columbus in 1493, the island was named after his brother Bartholomew and settled by the French in 1648. In 1784 Louis XVI traded St. Barts to Sweden for a warehouse. The Swedes rechristened its capital Gustavia and made the island a rich trade port until 1878 when France took control of it once again.

Gustavia, home to 90 percent of the 3,200 population, includes descendants of Norman, Breton and Poitevin settlers. The harbor town is quaint and neat with Swedish Colonial and French Creole structures and French boutiques that attract the visitors. There are several small cafes for snacks and refreshments.

The town of Corossol, referred to as the "straw village," on the northwest end of the island is famous for its descendants of early French days who dress in white bonnets and sell fine straw hats and other straw souvenirs that are woven from the leaf fibers of the fan palms.

St. Barts also offers a touch of St. Tropez in its beach and cafe-life. The nights are slow and dedicated to dining and wine and just relaxing. The Festival of St. Barthelemy is a French country fair with a definite tropical influence that is held each August. Gustavia is then filled with booths, sports and lots of parties.

You can reach St. Barts by taking a small aircraft from nearby islands, on a one-hour flight from Guadeloupe, or by taking a catamaran from Philipsburg. St. Barts is on Atlantic Standard Time all year and has the same time as the East Coast during Eastern Daylight Saving season.

Eden Rock
St. Jean 97133

Caribbean Bed & Breakfast

St. Barthelemy
French West Indies
(011-596) 27-60-01

Guest house; 10 units; Moderate-Exp./Moderate CP;
No credit cards; Children ok; Smoking ok.

Location: Near beach; 1½ mi. to town; 1 mi. to airport.

This bright red-roofed gem jutting out to the sea has some notable firsts to its credit: it was the first hotel on the island, its first guests included a Rockefeller and Greta Garbo and it was built by the first pilot who landed on St. Barts. That pilot is guest house owner Remy de Haenen who was a long-time mayor of the little island and built the 1955 colonial structure as his private home.

The distinctive home and cottages that dip down the rocky hillside were built on what was a bare rock protruding into the heart of beautiful St. Jean Bay on the island's north coast. Six guestrooms are provided in the main house, and four cottages straddle the boulder towards the white sand below. All of the guest accommodations are homey and comfortable with well-worn antiques, various family pieces, four-posters and mosquito netting. The baths are private, but be warned the showers are generally cool to cold with water warmed by the sun.

An open-air terrace provides an honor bar and good West Indian cuisine with an emphasis on French cooking. Guests enjoy their complimentary morning breakfast from this pleasant retreat with ocean views on every side. Romantic dinners are served by candlelight.

The white sandy beach is just a few steps away at this peaceful and home-like guest lodging; manager Christiane Gevaudan is there to see that your stay is comfortable.

Hibiscus Hotel
Route de Lurin
P.O. Box 86
Gustavia 97133
St. Barthelemy
French West Indies
(011-596) 27-64-82

French West Indies

Inn; 11 units; Deluxe/Moderate CP;
AE,MC,VI; Children ok; Smoking ok.

Location: In town; 1/4 mi. to beach; 1 mi. to airport.

This intimate little inn attracts a mixture of St. Tropez and New York visitors who are looking for a quiet and tastefully appointed retreat on the fringe of the charming town of Gustavia. From this harbor-view spot guests may enjoy the village's offerings, take a five-minute ride to the beach (provided by the hotel) or just relax in their gracious surroundings.

Built in 1981, the Hibiscus is most contemporary and sleek with attractive color-coordinated interiors and exteriors. Guestrooms are all located in bungalows that boast lovely views of the the harbor from their private, hillside terraces. These white cottages with hibiscus flowing over and around are decorated in contemporary, local hardwood furnishings and rattan in attractive brown and white color schemes and have sheets from Descamps. All of the guest accommodations have kitchenettes with cooking facilities and refrigerators as well as air conditioning and ceiling fans and baths with showers.

The careful attention to decor and comfort is also apparent in the common areas enjoyed by guests of the Hibiscus. A terrace and entry area are furnished in rattan sofas and chairs with white cushions and with handsome terra-cotta tile floors, a green and white trellis and an abundance of potted plants and palms. The adjacent pool area has a wide wooden deck and comfortable green and white striped lounges protected by large white umbrellas.

The restaurant of the inn grants views of the pool, the harbor and the green hills beyond. This semi-enclosed terrace has a white vaulted ceiling with ceiling fans and is surrounded by pink hibiscus and macrame hanging planters. Old-fashioned cane ice cream chairs are arranged around the lace-covered dining tables, and guests enjoy their complimentary morning meal as well as French dinners on attractive pink Franciscan china. Lunches are not available.

The owner and manager of this friendly and delightful inn is Mr. Henri Thellin.

Note:
The inn is closed in September and October.

Caribbean Bed & Breakfast

Tropical Hotel
P.O. Box 147
97133 St. Barthelemy
French West Indies
(011-596) 27-64-87
Rep: Robert Reid Associates

Inn; 20 units; Expensive/Inexpensive-Mod. EP;
AE,VI; Children ok; Smoking ok.

Location: Near beach; 1½ mi. to town; 1 mi. to airport.

At nighttime this white gingerbread-decked inn has a storybook quality, its intricate scallops reflected in the small central pool and its flower garden in full fragrance. The inn is not an old Victorian home, but is actually a U-shaped, homey conglomerate of guestrooms whose porches or terraces look over the central garden courtyard or stare out to sea. The hillside inn is just a few yards above pretty St. Jean Beach.

The guestrooms at the Tropical are nicely decorated in contemporary, local furnishings. The attractive terra-cotta tile floors extend to the private balconies that are accented by the inn's fancy trimmings, and the rooms are made comfortable and cheery by the use of printed draperies, bright bedspreads and lots of fresh plants. The neat guestrooms boast radios, refrigerators, telephones, twin beds and private baths with showers.

This friendly inn provides a hospitality center for its guests with lots of reading material, music, video movies, television, a bar and comfortable wicker seating. A small freshwater pool is inviting and breakfast is served on the poolside terrace.

The owners, Alain and Mariange Jeanney, also own Caraibes Car Service, and vehicles may be rented at a reasonable price from the hotel or the airport.

St. Martin

The divided island of Saint Martin (Sint Maarten in Dutch) is in part French and partly Dutch, with complete freedom of movement from area to area. Having coexisted peacefully for over 330 years, the two parts of the 37-square-mile island offer two

French West Indies

cultures in one island stop. The most northern part of the island belongs to France and has about 21 square miles of area. French St. Martin, population 7,000, is governed from Guadeloupe; the principal town of Marigot is the seat of the municipal council.

Marigot is a tiny French village with a nearby fort offering views of the western part of the island. Most visitors here come for the shopping in the quaint boutiques, displaying all sorts of French finery and perfume. Grand Case, about 30 minutes away, is really a small fishing village with some good local restaurants specializing in creole cooking.

Although not as popular with tourists as the island's Dutch side, St. Martin is becoming a popular tourist destination with an emphasis on relaxation and friendliness. There are many fine beaches, some with nude bathing. The north end of the island has some good diving spots, and boats can be rented for deep-sea fishing.

St. Martin is on Atlantic Standard Time. During Eastern Daylight Time, the island and the East Coast are on the same time schedule.

16

The British Windward Islands

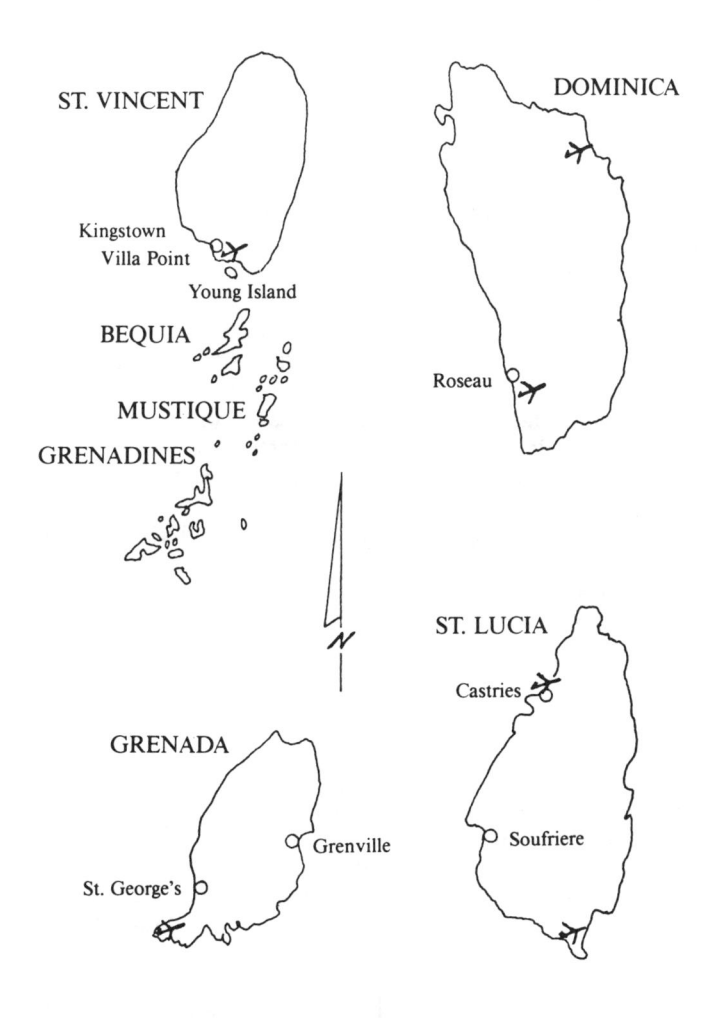

Caribbean Bed & Breakfast

These small, lushly green and mountainous islands are cooled by the ever-present northeasterly trade winds. The British Windwards, consisting of the islands of Dominica, St. Lucia, St. Vincent, Grenada and the Grenadines, are now predominantly British-affiliated, but retain influences of past Gallic or French inhabitants.

The Eastern Caribbean dollar or the "BeeWee" is the monetary currency on all of these islands, and the electrical voltage requires an adapter for North American appliances. The British Windward Islands are on Atlantic Standard Time but share the same time as the East Coast during Eastern Daylight Saving Time months.

St. Vincent and the Grenadines

St. Vincent and the Grenadines are a collection of 32 main islands and cays and numerous smaller ones scattered in the Eastern Caribbean, 100 miles west of Barbados. St. Vincent, the largest, is 18 miles long and 11 miles wide. To the southwest is the chain of smaller islands called the Grenadines, most of these islands no larger than a few square miles. Surrounded by white coral beaches and crystalline waters that range in color from sapphire blue to emerald green, the Grenadines are a diver's or snorkeler's paradise and provide superb sailing conditions.

Connecting flights to St. Vincent and the Grenadines are available from Barbados, St. Lucia, Martinique or Trinidad, and several daily flights go inter-island to and from St. Vincent.

For further information on St. Vincent and the Grenadines contact:
>Eastern Caribbean Tourist Association
>220 E. 42nd St., Room 411
>New York, New York 10017
>(212) 986-9370

St. Vincent

This volcanic island is rich in fruit, vegetables and spices. Its flatland interior with coconuts, bananas, breadfruit, nutmeg and arrowroot contrasts with its steep mountain ridges, coastal cliffs and rocky shores that dip down to the gold and black sand beaches.

Representing a real blending of cultures, descendants of

British Windward Islands

the Carib Indians still live on the northern shores of La Soufriere. British and French cultures mix in their language and customs. English is the official language and cricket and afternoon tea are traditions in St. Vincent.

Kingstown is the capital of the island and is a busy port and market town with 12 small blocks crammed with non-tourist, local shopping and commerce. Saturday morning market is colorful and well-stocked with fresh vegetables and fruit. St. Mary's Roman Cathedral, a combination of old European architecture, and Fort Charlotte, offering magnificent views of the Grenadines, are both located in Kingstown. North of town are the Botanic Gardens, the oldest in the Western Hemisphere and occupying 20 acres filled with tropical trees, blossoms and plants. Captain Bligh of the *Bounty* fame planted the breadfruit plants here in 1793. Also here is the Museum of Archeology with an extensive collection of stone artifacts.

A boat trip to the northern tip of the island takes visitors to the Falls of Baleine, a 60-foot freshwater fall with shallow pools at the base of the volcanic slopes. Hikers may climb 3½ miles up La Soufriere, St. Vincent's northern volcano, and be treated to spectacular views.

Sightseers can also visit several charming fishing villages to the west with their pastel-colored cottages and unusual black sand beaches. To tour St. Vincent a car can be rented with a small fee for a local license, but note that roads tend to be mountainous and curvy. Taxis are plentiful as well, but it is advisable to travel with a member of the island's Taxi Drivers' Association and decide upon a rate for the outing before departing.

The Cobblestone Inn
P.O. Box 867
Kingstown
St. Vincent
West Indies
(809) 456-1937/456-1938

Caribbean Bed & Breakfast

Historic inn; 20 units; Inexpensive CP;
No credit cards; Children ok; Smoking ok.

Location: In town; 3 mi. to beach; 3 mi. to airport.

    The Cobblestone Inn, a fine government-run b&b, dates back to 1814 when it was built as a sugar warehouse, later used to store arrowroot. The inn was converted to hotel use in 1972 when extensive renovation work exposed the Georgian architecture with its enchanting cobblestone walkways and arches. Local craftsmen utilized the same materials used in the original Georgian structure to complete the careful restoration.
    The inn is situated directly on the waterfront in the small capital city of Kingstown and overlooks the harbor backed by the green mountainous scenery of the island. The bar and restaurant of the hotel are located on street level, right off the tiny, but busy thoroughfare. The attractive eating and drinking areas boast the old stone walls and charming small-paned windows. The complimentary morning breakfast is served in the popular restaurant.
    An airy, stone stairway passage with green wrought-iron trim leads to the second-level reception desk and guestrooms. The guestrooms at the Cobblestone Inn are a nice blend of modern and old with limestone-carved arches framing the windows and walls of old, exposed stonework. The furnishings are all modern and attractive featuring cane headboards, dressers, modern private baths and telephones in the rooms. The 13 double and 7 single accommodations are fully air conditioned and have become a favorite of business travelers because of the Cobblestone's pleasant furnishings and in-town convenience.

Grand View Beach Hotel
Villa Point
P.O. Box 173
St. Vincent
West Indies
(809) 458-4811
(800) 223-5352
Rep: Robert Reid Associates

British Windward Islands

Historic inn; 12 units; Moderate/Moderate EP;
AE,VI; Children ok; Smoking ok.

Location: On beach; 3 1/2 mi. to town; 3 mi. to airport.

Located on Villa Point on the south coast of the island, this family-run inn offers spectacular ocean vistas, tranquility and old-fashioned hospitality. The original 1860-built cotton drying house on eight acres of beautifully landcaped gardens became the estate home of owner Tony Sardine's wife's great-grandparents. Tony's father bought the estate in 1930; Tony was born in the house. The Grand View became a charming family hotel in 1964 when Tony's father left his bakery in town to begin the lodging establishment. Tony took over the thriving business, now in its 20th year of operation--a delightful representation of a family operation spanning both sides of the Sardine family.

A scenic roadway climbs up to the point overlooking the bay and leads to the intimate resort. The inn's tennis and squash courts are to the side of the road on the way up to the house, as is a restful, thatched gazebo lookout with views of the ocean and town. The villa house with brick arches and French windows is fronted by gardens highlighted by a tranquil fountain with lily ponds and by a large veranda-type, open entry semi-attached to the house. The veranda with polished tile floors and wood coverings is a pleasant spot to sit and take in the views of the bay. In fact, Tony's mother is a regular figure here, giving the Grand View Beach Hotel another touch of homestyle quaintness.

The entrance to the old home sets the tone of warmth found within. The neutral walls are trimmed in coral shades; a painting of the home as it originally looked is displayed in the hallway. The painting shows that a balcony once fronted the house, but reveals that the home's charm has not been lost through the years. The guest parlor of the house is decorated in pretty antiques and local wood furnishings made by the family. Books, magazines and games are supplied; a corner nook displays antique china and silver pieces. Old family photos hang from the antique picture railing around the gracious room. Burgundy draperies and coordinated pillows give the room a warm, turn-of-the-century feel. The beautiful wooden floors here and throughout the house are of local cedar; the polished wooden staircase bannister to the second-story guestrooms is of rich mahogany.

The dozen upstairs guestrooms are each named after a flower

found on the lush premises. The rooms all boast private baths and a sunny, airy feel. The decor is simple, but cheery and comfortable. A pretty flower print of each room's namesake graces the walls, and rockers, vanities/desks, large closets, flowered curtains, straw-mat rugs and telephones can be found in each room. The private, tiled bathrooms feature spacious shower stalls and very hot water. The guestrooms in harmonious pastel shades of green, yellow and white or blues and lilacs offer spectacular views and either trade wind cooling or air conditioning units. The cheerful staff at the Grand View delivers a refreshing pitcher of cold water when the guest checks in, one of several hospitable touches.

Delicious meals are served at the inn, which specializes in freshly supplied local fish, lobsters, vegetables and fruit. The dining room in the house, located downstairs, has picture-window views of Great Head Bay and the lush mountains behind. Pretty coral-colored tablecloths, chair pads and draperies add warmth and cheerfulness as do the yellow walls and profusion of hanging and potted plants. A built-in hutch adds an antique touch; the room can be a bright breakfast spot or a dazzling nighttime bistro lit up by the lights of the bay. The breakfast menu is quite complete and coffee is served in a handy thermos container for easy guest refills. The honey and jams are delicious as are the large, warm-from-the-oven breakfast rolls. Lunch might be a shrimp salad or lobster sandwich on the patio or by the pool, and dinner is a choice of tasty local or continental dishes. A comfortable bar with the same great views of the bay is located off the side veranda and features a piano for informal entertainment.

To the back of the house is the pool, nearly suspended over the ocean just below. Swimmers can relax at the swim-up bar with drinks and survey nearby Young Island or lounge on the comfortable pool furniture. A grassy path lined with a mini-botanical garden of flowering tropical vegetation leads to the lower acreage of the estate as well as to the inn's small, private beach. This park-like area of grass and palms makes for leisurely strolling and serene pastoral views.

The Sardines have plans to expand on the Grand View, but without altering the day-to-day operation of the inn or its present, intimate state. They hope to add four apartment-type units above the bar area (not in the house) that will offer sitting rooms, large baths with dressing room, kitchenettes, front verandas and separate bedrooms. Although the new units will mostly attract the many European businesspeople who are frequenting St. Vincent for longer periods, they should also provide the same attraction for vacationers planning to stay on the island a little longer. For either a brief or elongated stay on the island, the Grand View Beach Hotel promises a hospitable, relaxing refuge.

The Heron Hotel
Bay Street
P.O. Box 226
Kingstown
St. Vincent
West Indies
(809) 457-1631

Inn; 15 units; Moderate year-round MAP;
VI,MC; Children ok; Smoking ok.

Location: In town; 4 mi. to beach; 2 mi. to airport.

The second-story Heron Hotel once topped an estate's plantation warehouse and was originally used as a lodging facility for the estate's owners and managers when they made trips from their northern St. Vincent plantation into town. The Georgian building, exact date of construction unknown, is remarkably the same today except for the addition of many modern-day comforts including private baths, air conditioning and telephone. It is still a favorite of businesspeople visiting town, and an air of hospitality has been added by manager Doreen McKenzie.

Caribbean Bed & Breakfast

The intimate hotel is nestled right downtown, opposite the waterfront and next to the shopping district. A small river that flows through Kingstown and past the side-rear of the hotel is responsible for the inn's name. The heron no longer resides in the river, but the hotel is in its 25th year of operation.

The upstairs entry of the hotel contains the reception desk, a bookcase brimming with readables and the dining area where all three meals are served. Breakfast and dinner are both included in the stay at this inn; breakfast is often shared with local people who enjoy the plentiful breakfast fare of fruit juice and fruit, toast with marmalade and eggs. The hearty dinner includes soup, a meat entree, vegetables, dessert and coffee. All of this is served in the cheery ambience of homey, flowered valances, lots of green plants and fresh flowers from the garden. A tiny bar here serves various hard and soft drinks which can be enjoyed in the guest lounge nearby.

Just beyond the reception area is the spacious and airy guest lounge with television, vaulted ceilings and cane and rattan furniture outfitted with brightly colored pillows. A second guest retreat can be found on the sunporch toward the rear of the building. This cozy spot looks over the South River beyond the back door of the porch and boasts comfortable chairs and a greenhouse of plants.

All of the guestrooms at the Heron are different in both size and decor; all wrap around the sides of the building with various views of town and the waterfront. All of the guest lodgings boast showers, air conditioning, pretty wooden floors, twin beds and built-in vanities. Most of the rooms convey an airy feel with walls washed in pastel shades and homey, calico window valances and lace curtains. The doors to the rooms are left open when not in use to keep them very fresh. Room #15 at the inn boasts a large sitting area, two beds and curtains in an orange and gold calico print that give the spacious room a comfortable, home-like feel.

The Heron Hotel is a simple inn that has been granting true "home away from home" hospitality and good West Indian cooking for a quarter of a century in a structure designed to do just that. Its charm is very local and represents a true bargain amid warmth and basic comforts.

Kingstown Park Guest House
P.O. Box 41

British Windward Islands

St. Vincent
West Indies
(809) 456-1532

Guest house; 22 units; Inexpensive year-round MAP;
No credit cards; Children ok; Smoking ok.

Location: Near town; 3 mi. to beach; 2 1/2 mi. to airport.

On a hilltop overlooking the town of Kingstown and granting spectacular views of the sea and emerald-green mountains is this personally run guest house owned by Miss Nesta Paynter, a retired St. Vincent government worker and all-around interesting person. At the core of the guest lodgings is the main house, a century-old plantation-style structure that was once a prestigious family home. Ten guestrooms and the dining room are located in the antique home, and the remainder of the guest accommodations are found in the newer buildings of brick and stone on the property.

The gray wooden siding of the main house is a bit frayed, but in keeping with the antique interiors. The guest enters through the parlor brimming with antiques, polished wooden floors, curios and organdy curtains. A high cathedral ceiling has been painted white, and an elegant crystal chandelier hangs from its center. The walls are covered in interesting, old photographs that were taken by none other than the innkeeper herself, who not known to many, was the first lady photographer on the island. The photos were meticulously hand-painted by Miss Paynter.

All of the guestrooms in the main house are furnished with a sprinkling of antiques. All of the guestrooms, some with shared bath, are airy and clean with an emphasis on comfort, rather than fanciness. Groups are welcome at the guest house and a common sight; the guest house receives its share of return clientele who enjoy the quaintness and budget accommodations.

The stay at the Kingstown Park Guest House includes breakfast and dinner with an emphasis on local and creole foods. The dining room is located downstairs in the main house and retains the old stone walls and beamed ceilings of the home; seating is provided at antique tables and chairs. This turn-of-the-century room leads to a pleasant backyard patio with a small, manicured garden and inspiring views as far as you can see. Although situated in a residential area, the guest house is just a five-minute walk from town.

Caribbean Bed & Breakfast

Also on the Islands

Coconut Beach Hotel
P.O. Box 355
St. Vincent
West Indies
(809) 458-4231

Hidden on a small, residential lane that leads to the ocean is this modest inn with ten air-conditioned rooms. The hotel sits directly on the water with waves lashing up to the colorful outdoor dining area; large coconut trees line the shore. Bamboo shoot doors lead to the guestrooms which are all a little different. The staff is friendly; all three meals are offered.

Mariner's Inn
Villa Beach
P.O. Box 868
St. Vincent
West Indies
(809) 458-4287

This 1936-built estate house and two buildings that were added in the last few years house the 25 guestrooms of the inn. A boat-shaped bar sits practically on top of the ocean, separated only by a low, stone wall. Lawn and gardens flow between the buildings; an open dining area is decorated in pretty, white wrought-iron tables and chairs. The guestrooms are simple, but roomy, and have private baths, telephone and some balconies.

The Grenadines

You can reach some of the Grenadine islands by air, but the least expensive means is by boat. Mail, cargo and passenger boats travel among the islands, but check schedules carefully. Boats tend to be slow and do not run every day of the week.

Young Island in the Grenadines is just 200 yards off St. Vincent and can be reached easily via a ferry that resembles a small, rustic *African Queen* that runs constantly between the two islands, taking about five minutes. The 25-acre, mountain island provides visitors with breathtaking views, tropical foliage and

British Windward Islands

an 18th-century fort sculpted from an enormous rock, 200 feet above the sea. One resort, the Young Island Resort, comprises the entire sleepy island and has a low-key bar and restaurant and cottages.

Bequia lies ten miles south of St. Vincent and, measuring seven miles square, is the largest of the Grenadines. This sea-oriented island is reached only by boat and is a favorite anchoring spot. A ferry departs daily at noon from St. Vincent and begins the return trip the following morning at six. Its gold sand beaches and quiet coves are excellent for sailing, scuba and snorkeling. The age-old traditions of boat-building, whaling and fishing are the main concerns of the tiny island. The waterfront town of Port Elizabeth offers bars, restaurants and small shops.

Mustique is a privately owned, 2½-square-mile gem. Soft green hills, white sand and turquoise waters attract the elite. Cotton House, an 18th-century converted plantation house, is the only resort there and offers magnificent and secluded accommodations that cater to the jet-set.

Other principal islands in the Grenadines include Canouan, boasting some of the best beaches in the Caribbean; Tobago Cays, with spectacular coral reefs; Mayreau; Union Island; Palm Island; Carriacou and the southernmost island of Petit St. Vincent.

Hotel Frangipani
P.O. Box 1
Bequia
St. Vincent and The Grenadines
West Indies
(809) 458-3255

Inn; 17 units; Inexpensive-Mod./Inexpensive EP;
VI,MC; Children ok; Smoking ok.

Location: On beach; Near town; 12 mi. to airport.

Caribbean Bed & Breakfast

This former family estate, still owned and operated by family members Pat and Son Mitchell, became a small inn in the 1960's. The 50-year-old seafront home with modest guestrooms has expanded in recent years with five cottages of local stone and hardwood construction. The estate with distinctive red roofs stands right on the the shore of picturesque Admiralty Bay and is a favorite of both the yachting set and locals.

The location of the Frangipani is nearly ideal. It is just a short walk away from the the St. Vincent ferry stop in Port Elizabeth and a close jaunt to beautiful Tony Gibbons Beach and Friendship Bay. The anchorage at Admiralty Bay is considered one of the best in the Caribbean, thus giving this inn world-wide recognition from the yachting set. The grounds of the family estate are casual and tranquil, boasting a nice garden and lots of mango, citrus and papaya trees.

A range of accommodations are available at the Frangipani, all at fairly reasonable rates. The most economy-minded rooms are found upstairs in the main house. These rooms share a bath, but each has its own wash-basin/vanity area for convenience. The decor is simpler here, but the guestrooms carry a homestyle charm not found in the newer cottages. The cottages with stone walls all have private, spacious bathrooms, a dressing room and a large sundeck with views of the ocean. These very private facilities are decorated attractively with ceramic tile floors, wooden louvered doors and modern furnishings.

The restaurant of the inn overlooks the yacht anchorage and is the meeting spot for guests, locals and visiting yachtsmen. All three meals are offered here, along with delicious rum punches and pina coladas made from fresh fruit juices. The reasonably priced menu concentrates on locally produced vegetables, fruit, fish, lobster and sometimes whale provided by the island's fishermen. Local musicians liven up the spot once or twice a week, and the Thursday night barbecue/buffet with live entertainment is a popular tradition.

The Frangipani does not provide any water activities itself, but the friendly staff headed by manager Marie Kingston is happy to make any arrangements for charter yachting, snorkeling, windsurfing or tennis.

Note:
The inn is closed in September and October.

British Windward Islands

Also on the Islands

Young Island Resort
P.O. Box 211
Young Island
St. Vincent
West Indies
(809) 458-4826

Just 200 yards off St. Vincent is this island with one resort, reached day and night by a rapid and complimentary ferry ride. The island, consisting of 25 acres of tropical flora, has 29 little cottages sprinkled around the dense hillsides and on the beaches. A freshwater pool, tennis courts, turtle ponds and very relaxing thatched outdoor bar and dining areas also make up this peaceful resort.

Cotton House Hotel
Mustique
St. Vincent and the Grenadines
West Indies
(809) 458-4621

This privately owned island measuring 3 miles by 1 1/2 miles has just one elite resort, the Cotton House Hotel. The 18th-century plantation house boasts public rooms decorated in exquisite antiques and serves afternoon tea on the veranda. The guest quarters include stone villas and cottages, also tastefully decorated. The once private club opened to the public several years ago and offers, along with seclusion, a hilltop swimming pool, tennis, horseback riding and all water sports on its beautiful beaches.

Grenada

Grenada, referred to as the "Isle of Spice," is one of the only spice-producing areas in the Western Hemisphere. The 133-square-mile Grenada includes the two islets, Carriacou and Petit Martinique. Grenada, 12 miles wide and 21 miles long, lies 100 miles north of Venezuela and 12 degrees north of the equator.

A new international airport has recently opened on the

Caribbean Bed & Breakfast

island at Point Salines, allowing for regularly scheduled, direct flights into the island. Major cruise ships pull into the port at St. Georges as well. Proof of citizenship is required of U.S. citizens, and a small departure tax is charged. Both taxis and self-drive cars are available for touring; local buses operate to some parts of the island.

During the dynastic wars of the 18th century, Grenada changed hands several times between the British and French, finally being ceded to the British in 1783. The country became independent in 1974, and a coup of the People's Revolutionary Government took over the government until October 1983. After a year of turmoil following the well-known "invasion of Grenada," the island is once again open to tourism and is actively promoting the industry in several ways. To boost tourism some of the room and yachting services costs have been reduced. No curfews exist and utilities have been returned to normal levels of service. Roads are currently being repaired, and tour operators have resumed full schedules of excursions.

No matter how far inland you travel you are never more than 6½ miles from one of the 45 beautiful beaches of Grenada. Its narrow roads wind through foliage-covered mountains with bamboo trees, ferns, cocoa and banana trees to farming towns and fishing villages.

Grenville, the second largest city in Grenada, is the locale of the vegetable market and the spice factory where visitors may watch nutmeg, cocoa and mace being prepared for export. Saturday is the colorful market day here when Grenadians do their own marketing. Weavers display hats, baskets, bags and placemats made from palm fronds.

Sauteurs, on the northernmost tip of Grenada, is the site of the great cliff where the Caribs leapt to their deaths rather than be captured by the French. Levera Beach nearby is a large, deserted beach ringed by sea grapes and palm trees.

The Grand Etang District with lush mountains and tropical forest is highlighted by the Annandale Falls and a profusion of orchids, armadillos and monkeys.

Dougaldston Estate in the market town of Gouyave is another spice factory where various spices are sorted by hand. Tours of the process and storage areas, as well as fresh samples, await the visitor here. Fifteen minutes from the estate is Concord Falls and nearby Betty Mascoll's Plantation, a 72-year-old plantation home built of hand-chiseled colored stones and mortared with lime and molasses. Visitors may have lunch amid the family antiques.

St. Georges, Grenada's capital city and major port, is a picturesque town of pastel buildings and red tile roofs. The Carenage is the center of activity in town; fishing boats with weekly loading on Tuesdays depart with crates and bags of fruit and vegetables bound for Trinidad. Various shops here display and sell spice- and flower-related goods: perfumes, shampoo, lotions, potpourri, teas, etc. The Grenada National Museum is set in the foundations of an old French army barracks and prison built in St. Georges in 1704. The newest addition to the town is the Marryshow Folk Theatre—Grenada's first cultural center. Plays, West Indian dance, music and poetry readings are featured in this former home of the West Indian patriot, T. Albert Marryshow. Several forts surround the city, which also boasts a zoo and botanical garden.

Carriacou, Grenada's sister island and one of its island dependencies, is 13 miles square with rolling hills and white sand beaches. It is actually the largest of the Grenadines and is a favorite stop for yachtsmen. The main streets of the island run parallel to the beach; its pier is the site of most of the activity. Visitors may tour on foot or by car. A side trip to the town of Windward is interesting because of its villagers of Scottish descent who still build wooden schooners. To reach Carriacou, 16 miles north of Grenada, you may take a daily flight from Grenada or rent a yacht. Organized tours to the island are also available.

For additional information on Grenada contact:
Grenada Tourist Office
141 East 44th St., Suite 905
New York, New York 10017
(212) 687-9554

Horse Shoe Bay
P.O. Box 174
St. George's
Grenada
West Indies
ph: 4410

Caribbean Bed & Breakfast

Inn; 12 units; Expensive MAP/Moderate CP;
Children ok; Smoking ok.

Location: On beach; 2 mi. to town; 30 mi. to airport.

This charming cottage-hotel consists of a main building crowning a hilltop and six Mediterranean-style villas that tumble down the hibiscus and bougainvillaea slopes toward the secluded beach below. The guest enters the hilltop structure with tile and arches past a giant banyan tree and rich tropical foliage. The dining room of the inn is directly ahead with its intimate nooks for dining and socializing and spectacular views out to the gardens, pool and sea.

The dining pavilion and lounge are decorated tastefully in some antiques and island paintings. The feeling is relaxed, and guests enjoy tasty West Indian cuisine by candlelight. The games room provides billiards and darts in the hospitable setting.

The guestrooms at the Horse Shoe Bay are secluded and elegantly decorated. Each of the six cottages contains two separate guest accommodations that share a kitchen and laundry center. Guests are treated to antique decor, much of it from island family estates, four-poster beds, air conditioning and private balconies with views of the sea. One example of the special service the guest receives at this intimate inn is found in the morning meal that is prepared by a maid in your kitchen and served "hot from the grill" to your private seaview balcony.

When not enjoying the luxurious quarters of Horse Shoe Bay, guests can be found at the beach-based swimming pool or partaking of the numerous watersports available such as windsurfing and snorkeling.

Ross Point Inn
P.O. Box 137
St. George's
Grenada
West Indies
ph: 4551

Inn; 12 units; Moderate/Moderate MAP;
No credit cards; Children ok; Smoking ok.

Location: On beach; 2½ mi. to town; 30 mi. to airport.

British Windward Islands

This ancestral home of the Hopkin family opened in the early 1950's as an intimate family-run inn. Its spectacular Ross Point setting with views of the harbor and Grand Anse Beach made it a natural British army gun emplacement location during WWII. No shooting ever took place, but the men who stayed there must have enjoyed the congenial environment. If not actually a case of history repeating itself, then the search for warm surroundings away from home definitely does repeat since Ross Point Inn has been home to U.S. government personnel stationed in Grenada for the last few years.

Many people think the home cooking at this inn is one of the best reasons to stay here. The authentic West Indian cuisine is made from mainly locally grown produce and prepared from family recipes. The tasty meals are served in a garden setting and are often shared with island residents who consider it the best restaurant around.

The guestrooms at the inn have been renovated in recent years and all boast air conditioning, private baths and patios. Their nicest feature is the view out to St. George's Harbour and the sparkling sea that washes up to Grand Anse Beach. Guest accommodations are located around the gardens, and a few are in the main house. The furnishings are on the simple side, but the rooms are clean and homey, and each is unique.

Guests at Ross Point enjoy the thatched-roof garden bar and a pleasant garden library. The inn has its own small beach, but spectacular Grand Anse Beach is just minutes away. The family provides transportation to the beach and offers its own cabana for sunbathing once you get there. Don't be afraid to ask for sightseeing assistance or suggestions; the innkeepers are happy to help make your stay very special.

Secret Harbour Hotel
P.O. Box 11
St. George's
Grenada
West Indies
ph: 4439
Rep: David B. Mitchell & Co.

Inn; 20 units; Expensive/Moderate EP;
AE,VI; Children ok; Smoking ok.

Caribbean Bed & Breakfast

Location: On beach; 5 mi. to town; 30 mi. to airport.

This Mediterranean-looking complex that rambles through the lush bougainvillaea-filled hillside to the sea is a dream-come-true—at least for owner and creator Barbara Stevens. The ex-accountant from Britain left "it all" to find the perfect spot for her luxurious inn, and this elegant site overlooking Hartman Bay on the south coast was to be the setting.

Red-tiled roofs, white arches and terraces dominate the exterior architecture of the inn while antiques, stained glass, colorful Italian tile and color-coordinated furnishings dominate the interiors. The overall effect is elegant and special. The lobby, lounge and restaurant are located at the very top of the hill and feature heavy beamed ceilings and wrought-iron light fixtures. Breakfast and dinner are served in the tasteful surroundings.

The luxurious suites are located in cottages close to the beach and feature double mahogany four-poster beds covered in designer-coordinated fabrics in each guest accommodation. Each spacious guest suite boasts a sprinkling of choice antiques that have been lovingly restored, a dressing room, living room area and private patio as well as an incredible bathroom with a sunken tub lined in Italian tile. Everything coordinates nicely including the towels, and potted plants add warmth and flair.

From the private cottages guests may climb a few steps up the lush hillside to the free-form swimming pool lined in the same eye-appealing tilework and to the tennis court or take a few frangipani- and palm-lined steps down to the sandy beach with convenient bar.

Also on the Island

Calabash
P.O. Box 382
St. George's
Grenada
West Indies
ph: 4234

Situated at Prickly Bay on eight acres of tropical grounds

British Windward Islands

is this hospitable inn named after a popular Caribbean gourd-like fruit. Twenty-two suites are located in the ten cottages around the grounds and close to the beach, each with its own bathroom, sitting area, kitchenette and porch. The contemporary structures of wood and stucco with louvered windows are pleasant and come with a breakfast maid who will cheerfully serve you the morning fare on your patio, in the sitting area or even in bed. One guest accommodation boasts a private swimming pool. Delicious island-food lunches and dinners are served in the natural stone pavilion covered in aromatic, tropical vines. The sheltered water and powdery sand beach make for good swimming, snorkeling and sunbathing activities. Winter MAP rates are deluxe with off-season rates dropping to expensive on the CP.

Spice Island Inn
P.O. Box 6
St. George's
Grenada
West Indies
ph: 4258

This small hotel offers accommodations directly on renowned Grand Anse Beach. Guests may enjoy the white powdery sand from 1 of 20 beachfront suites that are sheltered from beach-goers by a screen of tropical greenery or from one of the 10 suites that boast private swimming pools. All of the suites are comfortably and nicely furnished with a maximum of privacy. The main house of the inn has a dining area and dancing, and an outside patio provides meals in a tropical setting. Weekly, local entertainment is provided, and a boutique is located on the grounds. The on-season stay is deluxe MAP; off-season is expensive MAP.

St. Lucia

Like Dominica St. Lucia is green and mountainous. Its highest peak, Mount Gimie, is 3,117 feet. On this island, often identified by its twin, green volcanic mountains, are many species of exotic flowers and plants, such as orchids and anthuriums that grow wild in the dense rain forests. In contrast the southern portion of St. Lucia is characterized by flatter, somewhat hilly land. Living only on St. Lucia is the beautiful Amazon Versicolor Parrot.

The 27-mile-long by 14-mile-wide island was purchased by the French India Company in 1650 and the following 150 years saw it change hands 14 times between the English and French until being ceded to the British in 1814. St. Lucia (pronounced Loo-sha) obtained its independence from Britain in 1979 and is now a member of the Commonweath of Nations.

English is the official language of the island, but due to the French historical influence, most of the 120,000 inhabitants speak a French Creole as well.

International non-stop airlines fly into the island and inter-island airlines and on-island charters are available. Identification in the form of a passport, birth certificate or voter's card is required for U.S. citizens, and a departure tax is levied upon leaving. There is no well organized public bus system on the island, but taxis with drivers trained in a special sightseeing program as well as car rentals are readily available. A temporary driver's license is required, and remember to drive on the left side of the road. Tour operators offer a variety of tours ranging from on-island plantation, village and volcano excursions to yachting cruises to nearby islands.

Temperatures on St. Lucia are in the mid-80's year-round with a rainy season August through September. The rains are brief, leaving sunny skies most of the day.

Sightseeing around St. Lucia is sure to include several banana plantations. Bananas are the leading export and the plantations a primary island attraction. The Pitons are the towering, ½-mile-high volcanic mountains that challange mountain climbers. Soufriere, a scenic fishing village, makes a good base for exploring the Pitons and the sulphur baths once praised by King Louis XVI. The visitor will also find near here Mt. Soufriere, a "drive-in" volcano where cars actually may drive into the ancient crater allowing passengers to walk about the sulphur springs and pools.

Yachtsmen from around the world congregate at the anchorage town of Marigot Bay, locale of some of the filming of *Dr. Doolittle* and dotted with fine restaurants. Castries, St. Lucia's capital, is also a favorite port for the yachting set and is known for its colorful Saturday morning street market, shops and restaurants. St. Lucia is best known for its cane furnishings and batiks on plentiful display here. Castries is a newer town with modern concrete buildings that have replaced most of the French colonial or Victorian structures lost by fires. Still intact, however, are the Government House and a cathedral. Morne Fortune or "Hill of Good Fortune" changed hands repeatedly between the French and English and is now an exceptional location to view sunsets over the Castries Harbor.

Pigeon Point is really an island that is connected by a manmade causeway to St. Lucia. It was historically a pirate retreat and site of British forts, the ruins still present. Its white, sandy beaches make it a popular picnic and swimming spot. The beaches of St. Lucia offer not only white sand but also unique pearl-gray sand shores, along with superb sailing and every type of water sport. Glass-bottom boat trips allow glimpses of the underwater sealife through the clear water below.

Dining in St. Lucia is a blend of French, English, German and American, as well as creole cuisine. Special food offerings include pumpkin souffle and lobster creole. The nightlife here is relaxed and highlighted by steel bands that perform folk, calypso and reggae.

For additional information on St. Lucia contact:
St. Lucia Tourist Board
41 East 42nd Street, Suite 315
New York, New York 10017
(212) 867-2950

Anse Chastanet
P.O. Box 216
Soufriere
St. Lucia
West Indies
(809) 455-7355
Rep: Scott Calder International

Inn; 20 units; Expensive/Moderate EP;
AE,DC,VI,MC; Children ok; Smoking ok.

Location: On beach; 2 mi. to town; 45 mi. to airport.

Rising up from the gray-sand beach of Anse Chastanet is a hillside lushly blanketed in hibiscus, bougainvillaea and tropical greenery, with an occasional whitewashed bungalow

Caribbean Bed & Breakfast

peeking out to share the landscape. Anse Chastanet is made up of these 20, charming octagonal cottages that house guests as well as a main house at the top of the hill, a beachside restaurant and bar and a few villas that are really houses for rent.

This peaceful retreat offers guest accommodations with inspiring views of the Pitons, the island's spectacular twin peaks, and the hillsides from their wrap-around terraces. The pleasant but simple interiors include color-coordinated bedspreads and draperies and furniture of locally crafted wood, and each unit has a private, tiled bath and overhead fan.

Over 100 steps lead from the sand to the main building of the inn with impressive views and rest-stops along the way. Delicious local dishes are served in the main house dining area and at the palm-lined beach restaurant with thatched bar. Fresh fish is a specialty, often with the daily catch arriving by fishing boat directly at the beach below. All three meals are offered.

The ¼ mile-long beach provides excellent snorkeling and scuba, and the courteous, helpful staff will assist with any vacation details.

Green Parrot Inn
P.O. Box 648
Castries
St. Lucia
West Indies
(809) 452-3167

Inn; 30 units; Moderate/Moderate EP;
VI,AE; Children ok; Smoking ok.

Location: 1 mi. to beach; 2 mi. to town; 40 mi. to airport.

The Green Parrot, better known as one of the island's most prestigious restaurants, went into the small hotel business in recent years. The restaurant and inn, located on a hillside of Morne Fortune, have panoramic views of the sea, harbor and Castries. The buildings of stucco and natural stone are tucked behind pretty foliage in this residential area overlooking the capital.

The guestrooms are comfortable and rather standard with

British Windward Islands

modern amenities such as wall-to-wall carpeting, air conditioning, telephones and private baths. The nicest asset is the spectacular harbor view from the private balconies of the rooms. All of the guest quarters are convenient to the inn's swimming pool.

The Green Parrot Restaurant has an English pub feel with warm, local furnishings and personal service. The bistro is known for its local specialties made from homegrown produce, the produce often displayed in the dining room, and offers a large menu of West Indian and steak dishes that are prepared under the supervision of well-known London chef Harry. Breakfast includes omelettes and St. Lucian sweet rolls; lunch offers a large selection of sandwiches, salads and hot entrees, while dinners range from curries to homemade soups.

The restaurant offers colorful, local entertainment several nights each week. Guests might take in a fire-eater show, limbo dancing or Ladies' Night when escorted women with flowers in their hair dine free.

An informal open-air restaurant poolside serves short order food to guests, and a boutique, perfumery and car rental outlet are all located on the grounds.

Also on the Island

Boot's Guest House
36 Micoud Street
P.O. Box 392
Castries
St. Lucia
West Indies
(809) 452-2841

This residential guest house offers four double rooms to visitors about a ten-minute walk away from the stores of the capital city. The 1951-built, two-story building has no real grounds and contains modest guestrooms with shared and private baths. The pastel-painted rooms are for the economy-minded traveler who wants a budget accommodation without frills near town. The guest house's hospitable innkeeper is Miss Bouty, and b&b rates are inexpensive year-round. A few rooms have air conditioning.

Dominica

Dominica, called the "nature island of the Caribbean," is characterized by towering mountains and crisscrossing rivers, lush green valleys, fields of broadleafed bananas, cocoa and lime trees and abundant tropical foliage. In fact, the island is home to over 135 species of local birds, including the Imperial Parrot and the Red-Necked Parrot which are found only in Dominica.

Discovered by Columbus in 1493, Dominica has been British since 1805 and self-governing since 1967. English is the official language of the 80,000 population, but a French patois is common as well.

Dominica is reached by connecting flights on local airlines north from Antigua or Guadeloupe and south from Martinique or Barbados. Proof of citizenship is required for U.S. citizens, and a nominal airport departure tax is collected upon leaving the island. Getting around Dominica is best done by taxi with government-regulated rates for sightseeing, or with one of the tour companies which offer land rover safaris, boat trips, hiking guides and more. Jeeps may be rented at some of the hotels, but are not recommended due to poor roads and general driving conditions. If you do rent a vehicle, a license fee is charged.

The daytime temperature of Dominica averages between 70 to 80 degrees with cooler nights, especially in the mountain areas. Brief showers that keep the vegetation lush can come any time of the year, but mainly June through October.

Proof that nature is Dominica's main offering is even evident in the capital city of Roseau on the calm leeward coast. Rivers gurgle through the quiet town that offers little nightlife and a small amount of shopping. The Saturday market held in the square is a time to peruse the grass rugs made in Roseau as well as Carib baskets and various bamboo, coconut and "Foujere" seashell handcrafts.

The town of Portsmouth boasts the best and most attractive harbor on the island. Close to here is the Indian River, which can be explored by canoe, winding through the ancient mangrove trees that line the banks. Two miles north of the harbor town are the twin peaks of the Cabrits, upon which stand the remains of an 18th-century garrison with over 200 acres filled with major structures, lookouts and barracks. The Portsmouth Harbour and Douglas Bay are also popular areas for scuba, sailing, windsurfing and waterskiing.

Safari trips can be arranged from Portsmouth across

Dominica to explore the Tropical Rain Forest, the sulphur springs, waterfalls, the Boiling Lake, Freshwater Lakes, the Carib Indian Reservation and the Emerald Pool. The Emerald Pool in the Morne Trois Pitons National Park is reached by a one-half-mile loop trail canopied by trees and plants. The Middleham Trails here take the hiker through a true rain forest to a viewpoint overlooking one of Dominica's tallest waterfalls, Middleham Fall. Boiling Lake in the Pitons Park is five miles east of Roseau and is the world's second largest boiling lake. The temperature along the edges ranges from 180 to 197 degrees. This cauldron of bubbling, greyish-blue water is usually enveloped in a cloud of vapor and is believed to be the result of a crack through which gases escape from the molten lava below the earth.

For additional information on Dominica contact:
    Caribbean Tourism Association
    20 East 46th Street
    New York, New York 10017
    (212) 682-0435

Anchorage Hotel
P.O. Box 34
Roseau, Dominica
West Indies
(809) 445-2638
Rep: Robert Reid Associates

Inn; 36 units; Moderate CP year-round;
Children ok; Smoking ok.

Location: On ocean; ½ mi. to town; 3 mi./38 mi. to airport.

This pleasant dockside inn at Castle Comfort near Roseau offers peaceful accommodations with some local and international flavor. Owners Janice and Carl Armour, who also operate local tours on the island, are informative and hospitable hosts who can keep guests as occupied as they care to be.

The guestrooms at the Anchorage are located in a contemporary three-story building that faces the large swimming pool and the curving bay, as well as in an addition offering a

Caribbean Bed & Breakfast

few more units facing the water. Each room boasts two double beds, brightly flowered matching bedspreads and draperies, louvered windows, straw-matted floors and a private shower or tub bathroom. All of the guestrooms have either a patio or balcony that takes advantage of the sea views.

The Ocean Terrace Restaurant at the inn is a favorite of local people and yachtsmen who dock at the mooring a few feet away. The restaurant serves up good, simple Caribbean cuisine with an emphasis on locally produced vegetables and fruit as well as fish specialities. The roof-top restaurant with views of the sea is even more lively a few nights a week when local musicians play for dancing.

There is really no beach at this oceanfront inn, but water activities such as boating, fishing and waterskiing are popular as well as other island activities ably arranged by your hosts. The Carib bar at the Anchorage is another popular lounging spot for visitors, and the Armours also run the Petite Boutique, offering local handicrafts, on the inn grounds.

Note:
Try to arrange airplane reservations into the Canefield Airport near Roseau rather than Melville Hall's airport, if possible, to save yourself a long, bumpy ride to the inn. The airport accommodates smaller commuter aircraft.

Castaways
P.O. Box 5
Roseau, Dominica
West Indies
(809) 445-6244

Inn; 27 units; Moderate MAP year-round;
Children ok; Smoking ok.

Location: On beach; 11 mi. to town; 8 mi./21 mi. to airport.

British Windward Islands

Located on Castaway Beach, this hillside inn has recently reopened and been refurbished after being out of the visitor business for a while. The inn offers serenity and beauty sandwiched between lush tropical foliage and a volcanic, gray sand beach next to the sparkling Caribbean.

The palm-surrounded resort north of town has informal, simple guest accommodations, but all rooms face the sea and take full advantage of the refreshing trade winds. All of the guestrooms boast a private balcony, floral print bedspreads and matching draperies and rattan seating.

The restaurant of the inn is a popular spot overlooking the sea and serves delicious Dominican cuisine. Among the specialties are the fresh conch and stuffed and seasoned island crab. All of the meals are garnished with local fresh fruits and vegetables. A thatched beach bar is a peaceful lounging spot; each Sunday the inn hosts a beach barbecue with local entertainment.

The beach at Castaways has average swimming, but is very popular for other watersports such as skin diving, spearfishing, sailing and motor boat cruising.

Note:
As mentioned above, to save yourself a long, rocky ride from the airport, try to fly directly into the Canefield airport near Roseau rather than Melville Hall's airport.

Papillote
P.O. Box 67
Roseau, Dominica
West Indies
(809) 445-2287

Inn; 7 units; Moderate MAP year-round;
Children ok; Smoking ok.

Location: In forest; 4 mi. to town; 8 mi./41 mi. to airport.

This "little butterfly," as its name translates, is appropriately a part of the surrounding natural environment. Located in a small rain forest in the Papillote Forest, this remote and secluded inn offers a setting of begonias, hibiscus and ferns among waterfalls, rivers and hot springs. Owners and managers Cuthbert and Anne Jean-Baptiste are pleased to lead guests to the best in natural delights the tiny forest has to offer.

The Papillote offers six comfortably furnished guestrooms plus a cottage, and the architecture is basically West Indian with large, airy verandas. The fireplace in the main house is a romantic and homey spot for guests to gather on brisk evenings that are common in this shady, forested area.

The outdoor restaurant, covered by breadfruit trees and ferns, has peaceful, tropical garden views and serves superb natural and vegetarian cuisine. The gourmet health food includes freshly caught fish, salads punctuated with exotic fruit and vegetables from the garden, homemade breads and herb tea fresh from the herbal garden. Breakfast here might start with a banana or papaya plucked from a tree outside your window.

The inn is a popular starting point for nature walks, and guests may also delight in an invigorating river swim under a secluded waterfall or a soak in a natural, hot mineral bath. The innkeepers will arrange day tours and guided nature walks to rare and unusual places on request in this unique, "organic" wilderness retreat.

Note:
Guests arriving at the island's Canefield airport rather than Melville Hall's airport will save over 30 miles in travel to reach the inn.

Also on the Island

Springfield Plantation
P.O. Box 41
Roseau, Dominica
West Indies
(809) 445-1401

This Victorian plantation house with outbuildings has spectacular views of the countryside from its 1,200-foot elevation just a few miles from the National Park entrance. The turn-of-the-century house is furnished in some homey antiques and has seven pleasant guestrooms. Several cottages and apartments on the grounds can also be rented for extended stays with monthly rates available. The picturesque inn serves good island food and offers a river-fed pool to guests. Overnight rates are moderate year-round, and include breakfast and dinner. The plantation is about six miles from town and three miles from the Canefield airport.

17

Barbados

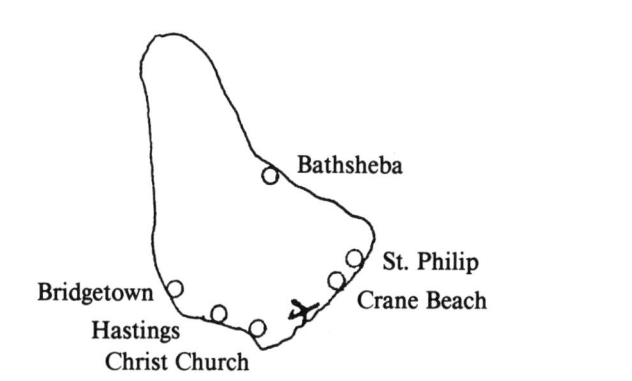

Caribbean Bed & Breakfast

While most Caribbean islands are volcanic, 166-square-mile Barbados is made of coral; the 60,000-year-old coral base of the island acts as a natural purification system, providing some of the purest water in the world. Its mainly flat and open topography also boasts gently rolling hills and has accounted for the island's history of prosperous sugar production. The influence of Dutch traders is present today in the abandoned windmills that grace the valleys, once used to power the first sugar factories.

The history of Barbados is drenched in British tradition, law and rule. The island was settled by the British in 1627 and soon after named "Little England." After some 300 years of British authority, Barbados became an independent nation in 1966, structured with an elected representative assembly.

Many airlines fly directly into Barbados, as well as connect with other islands in the Caribbean. The international airport there has the longest runway in the area and is capable of accommodating the largest of jets. United States citizens need only identification (passport, birth certificate or voter's registration card) and a return ticket for entry, and a small departure tax is collected upon leaving the island, unless the stay was for less than 24 hours.

The Barbados dollar is the currency. Many of the stores and restaurants will accept major credit cards and traveler's checks as well. Electricity on the island is fairly reliable and operates on North American standards. The language of Barbados is English, but with a distinctive Creole variation referred to as a Bajan dialect. The island is on Atlantic Standard Time all year and shares the same time as the East Coast during Eastern Daylight Saving months.

Barbados enjoys warm, sunny days, cooled by constant sea breezes year-round. The winter temperature ranges from 70 to 85 degrees; summer ranges from 76 to 87 degrees. Brief showers occur September through November. June through October is the hurricane season, but hurricanes are unusual on the island. The most recent was in August 1980, but before that the island had not been touched by a hurricane since September, 1955.

Getting around Barbados is easy via taxi, bus or rental car. Taxis, located at hotels, airport and important destinations, are not equipped with meters but can be hired by the hour (or any part of) or by the mile. Rental cars and scooters and bicycles are available by the day or week; driving is on the left side of the road. Those opting for rental car transportation should note that the airport rental car agencies often close in late evening. Also, the roads around the countryside tend to be bumpy and curvy, not always well marked and populated by fast, local drivers who do not adhere to the 20 to 30 mile per hour speed limits, so drive cautiously. Bus service on the island is comprehensive offering blue Transport Board buses as well as colorful mini-buses on scheduled routes, and fares are very reasonable. Local tour operators offering specialized island tours are well represented.

Barbados has a population of approximately 258,500 persons with around 97,600 in the capital, Bridgetown. Active Bridgetown jammed with small, crowded shopping streets is full of historic reminders; a suggested walking tour with map is available at any tourist information booth there. The Careenage, a river flowing through the city, is bustling with colorful fishing boats, and Trafalgar Square, not resembling the English landmark, has a statue of Lord Admiral Nelson and is near the Public Buildings which date back to 1748. Just outside the capital are many interesting sights. Pelican Village, on the road to Bridgetown Harbour, consists of huts that sell local handicrafts and is a favorite stop for the cruise line passengers docked nearby. The Hastings area near the city boasts a large array of old mansions and great houses, now businesses, inns and private homes.

Those interested in native flora will want to visit Welchman's Hall Gully, a botanical garden with exotic fruit and spice trees; Turner's Hall Woods, 45 acres of the only virgin forest on the island; and Andromeda Gardens with its terraced gardens of exotic and colorful plants.

Several old fishing villages set in natural beauty and displaying colonial period architecture can be found around the shoreline of Barbados. Reminders of sugar plantation days are at the Morgan Lewis Mill, a restored Dutch sugar cane planter windmill open to the public in St. Andrew. Other sights worth visiting include the Newcastle Coral Stone Gates from the movie *Island in the Sun* and commanding views of the magnificent east coast beaches. Spectacular views are also had from Cherry Tree Hill, flanked by casuarina and mahogany trees. The East Coast Road through St. Joseph to Bathsheba is a popular driving tour with a look at the dramatic surf, treacherous reefs and the charming seaside village of Bathsheba, reminiscent of England's rocky coastal towns.

Caribbean Bed & Breakfast

A special excursion to Harrison's Cave near Welchman's Hall Gully goes past historic homes, churches and fields of sugar cane. The tour of the caves begins with a slide show, then entails a guided tram ride into the cavern environs with its bubbling streams, waterfalls and deep pools. The public is also guided on a walk beside a 40-foot-high waterfall during the tour.

Historic sightseeing around Barbados includes visits to many old churches and institutions including St. John's Parish and Codrington College, which was built in 1702 and is the oldest institution of higher learning in the Western Hemisphere. Quite notable is the antique woodwork that graces the college's church. Historic touring should also include Holetown where the British first landed and Gun Hill, a 19th-century convalescent center for British West Indies troops and the location of a giant 1868 white coral-stone-carved lion.

Ample sporting facilities exist in Barbados. The coral reefs to the south and east offer beauty and a wide range of marine life for scuba, skin divers and spearfishermen. Two sunken wrecks are popular exploration spots. Deep-sea fishing in the north and south include catches of blue marlin, dolphin, wahoo, tuna and sailfish. Yachting, surfing, para-sailing and windsurfing are popular water activities as well.

The national sport of Barbados is cricket, but soccer, horse racing, polo, golf and tennis are well represented. Several riding stables are on the island.

Barbados' nightlife encompasses discos, pubs, beach picnics and boat party cruises. Five movie theaters and two drive-ins are also on the island. The Bajan Queen, a gingerbread-adorned boat that docks in Bridgetown's Careenage, offers a unique dining cruise. A wide range of cuisine is offered in Barbados; local dishes include *cou-cou*, flying fish and mauby, a bittersweet drink made from boiled bark extract.

Several annual festivals showcase the local color and history of the island. The Holetown Festival takes place in February, the Crop-Over Festival is in mid-summer, and the National Festival of Creative Arts spans the months of October through November.

For more information on Barbados contact:
  Barbados Board of Tourism Office
  800 Second Avenue

Barbados

New York, New York 10017
(212) 986-6516
or
3440 Wilshire Blvd., Suite 1215
Los Angeles, CA 90010
(213) 380-2198

Bagshot House
St. Lawrence
Christ Church, Barbados
West Indies
(809) 428-8125

Inn; 16 units; Expensive/Moderate MAP;
No credit cards; Children ok; Smoking ok.

Location: On beach; 2 mi. to town; 6 mi. to airport.

This small inn fronts the pink coral sands of the St. Lawrence coast and offers a natural lagoon for swimming. The Bagshot House was the first small modern hotel to be built in Barbados. It was constructed on the site of an old family home also called "Bagshot House" after the town of Bagshot in England.

The contemporary concrete structure with split-level roof has a spacious front courtyard, beach frontage and a relaxing garden patio. The dining area, guest lounge and entry are all decorated in pleasant pastel shades with handmade rush carpets, tropical decor and wrought-iron dining tables and chairs. The 16 guestrooms all feature private baths and twin beds, radios, telephone, and some boast ocean-view balconies. The guestrooms have pastel color schemes with floral curtains and wall-to-wall carpeting.

Both breakfast and dinner are included in the lodging at this b&b; breakfast may be American or European. Dinner is table d' hote, and sandwich and soup lunches are available.

Owner and manager of Bagshot House, in operation for over 29 years, is hospitable Mrs. Eileen Robinson. Mrs. Robinson takes pride in the repeat clientele who come back each year for a stay in this informal and unique setting.

Caribbean Bed & Breakfast

Berwyn Inn Guest House
Rockley
Barbados
West Indies
(no phone)

Guest house; 5 units; Inexpenive/ Inexpensive CP; No credit cards; Children on approval; No smoking.

Location: 1 mi. to beach; 2 mi. to town; 6½ mi. to airport.

This prim little 1935 residence is just like a visit to your favorite aunt's or grandmother's house. Mrs. Olivia Jones is the owner, manager and the cook of the Berwyn Inn, which keeps her busy. This "home away from home" is tidy, clean and full of homestyle memorabilia and quaint touches that make you feel as though you are visiting a relative.

The guest enters the quaint inn through the parlor, a small room with television, comfortable furniture, family portraits and mementos and a curio cabinet filled with antique china and glassware. The color scheme, like the exterior, is blue, but Olivia is contemplating a new paint job and colors very soon.

The cozy rooms have shared baths, except one with a private bath, double or twin beds, dressing tables, sinks in the rooms, wooden floors with rugs and lots of homey accessories that make each guestroom cheerful and warm.

The breakfast at this b&b is very generous and varies with Mrs. Jones' mood and the guests' desires. A typical breakfast might include bacon, eggs, bananas, toast with marmalade or guava jelly and slices of cucumber, sweet pepper and tomato, along with coffee, tea or hot chocolate and juice.

Mrs. Jones will provide lunch and dinner upon request and often finds herself cooking every meal on a regular basis when a guest discovers her cooking prowess. Her favorite meal involves an impromptu "tea party" on the front veranda when she might put out a delectable tray of sandwiches, pudding and sauces or even her homemade chow mein.

The Crane Beach Hotel
Crane Beach
St. Philip, Barbados
West Indies

Barbados

(809) 423-6220
Rep: Robert Reid Associates

Historic inn; 25 units; Moderate-Exp./ Moderate EP; VI,MC,AE; Children ok; Smoking ok.

Location: On beach; 12 mi. to town; 5 mi. to airport.

This prestigious inn was built in 1790 as a country mansion home, perched on a cliff 60 feet above the most beautiful beach in Barbados. Added onto as years went by, the historic abode was officially registered as a hotel in 1867. Today, guests may lodge in one of the two main areas of the inn: in the restored 18th-century structure or in a much later-built, two-story building a short, country-road stroll away and separated by an impressive grove of coconut trees. Though the original structure offers more charm and the more deluxe units, both buildings offer tranquil, awe-inspiring views of the blue-green sea and sugar-white sand below.

The manager of the Crane Beach Hotel, Mr. Peter McKeever, is a congenial host who, along with his pleasant staff, keeps the top-grade hotel running smoothly. He has supervised the fairly recent renovation of the original inn's interiors and is happy to talk about the hotel's plans for further enhancement.

At first glance Crane Beach might remind you of a Grecian palace with its sweeping drive, spacious lounge with life-size statuary, arches and columns and the bright blue-watered, large Roman pool with pillars that touches the edge of the cliff. The lounge and reception area here are decorated tastefully with comfortable rattan sofas and chairs and a color television. Guestrooms in the older section are located off of this area, and the dining pavilion and outdoor terrace bar are a few steps away on the opposite side of the pool.

The dining pavilion, open to the sea with spectacular

Caribbean Bed & Breakfast

views, has a canopied tent ceiling and rattan furnishings. Guests may dine here for all three meals as well as afternoon tea from 3:30 to 5:30 p.m. Breakfast may be continental or full English-style, and a special buffet luncheon is served on Sundays. The dinner cuisine is excellent, and local specialties include pumpkin soup, shrimp curry and fried flying fish. The pretty terrace bar is spacious with ample, comfortable seating. Guests may choose to have lunch here and survey the grandeur of the setting.

The guestrooms at the Crane Beach Hotel are all nicely appointed and vary dramatically in the historic section. The accommodations here include 1,200-square-foot, two-bedroom suites with beautiful contemporary furnishings and full kitchens as well as spacious, antique-filled suites with pedestal canopy beds draped in turn-of-the-century prints, armoires, old exposed-brick walls and French-doored terraces with views of the incredible sea. Each room in this higher-priced section offers unique beauty enhanced by its tasteful decor.

The newer section, probably built in the 1940's, is called the "Boxill" section and offers more reasonably priced accommodations, but the same wonderful views and high standards of cleanliness. Guestrooms here offer an even more secluded location, and there is a second pool in a tropical garden setting. The Boxill rooms are located in a pastel-pink building with white columns and shutters and a large veranda overlooking the ocean. Each room is named (St. John, St. Lucy, St. Philip, etc.), and all units are basically the same with louvered windows, built-in closets, dressing tables, rockers, indoor-outdoor carpeting, bathrooms with tubs and less modern fixtures, dark wood furnishings, white walls and air conditioners or fans. A downstairs lounge area has a Mediterranean feel with wrought-iron chandeliers, high-back chairs and arched entries. Guests may follow the country road, leading to the hotel's tennis courts, back to the main hotel or may take the "sandy" route down an unpolished path to the beach. A pleasant stroll through the fine, powdery sand leads to a steep coral path to the Roman pool of the Crane Beach.

In addition to solitude, guests at the Crane Beach are treated to entertainment by popular entertainers three nights per week during on-season. Guests may relax by the poolside and drink in the sounds of a ballad singer or a soothing duet with the background accompaniment of gentle waves caressing the shore below.

Barbados

Fairholme Hotel and Apartments
Maxwell
Christ Church, Barbados
West Indies
(809) 428-9425

Inn; 31 units; Inexpensive/ Inexpensive EP;
No credit cards; Children ok; Smoking ok.

Location: Across from beach; 6 mi. to town; 5 mi. to airport.

The Fairholme is actually a converted plantation house that was once a part of the Old Maxwell Plantation. The area around the hotel is so developed that you would not suspect a plantation had existed in that particular spot—that is, until you walk around the still-tranquil grounds of the hotel or peek inside the 1880 structure itself. The original sugar cane manager's residence with a Mediterranean influence and fancy wrought-iron grillwork has been altered somewhat but still has the hurricane shutters and 12-inch-thick walls that give away its age.

Accommodations at the Fairholme consist of 11 guestrooms in the old mansion and another 20 apartments that were built in 1974 in a similar Mediterranean-style architecture. The apartments have kitchenettes with all the necessities, private shower baths, twin beds, air conditioning, small private patios and simple decor with block walls. The mansion's offerings, on the other

Caribbean Bed & Breakfast

hand, are all very individual with rooms located both upstairs and down. All of these rooms have private baths, some with spacious tubs and others with showers; some have sinks in the room as well. Iron headboards, armoires, rattan and flowered curtains and bedspreads are used throughout to make the mansion guestrooms personally yet simply furnished. All of the 31 units at the Fairholme are immaculately maintained.

The guest lounge of the main house has blue commercial-type carpeting and a mixture of antique and 1950's contemporary furnishings. It's not out to win design awards, but does win out on hospitality and comfort. A piano here encourages guests to relax with music, and a small patio off the lounge is the site of romantic evening coffee-sipping.

The dining area of the mansion has red tile linoleum and black wrought-iron tables and chairs that blend well with the arches and thick stone walls. A few antique serving buffets add warmth to the room. The menu here includes reasonable breakfast, lunch and dinner fare.

The grounds, to the back, are far off the busy road and have a rural and hospitable charm as well. The spacious, grassy area has an abundance of colorful hibiscus in shades of orange, pink and red; lots of hanging planters and potted flowers and plants; fruit trees with lovely aromas, a medium-size pool; a bar and informal entertainment area; and a welcoming resident cat and dog. Across the street from the Fairholme are its sister apartments, the Sheringham Beach, which offer another 24 units and a nearly private, family-style beach that is used by both hotels.

The manager of the Fairholme Hotel is Joyce Noble, a very pleasant, congenial person who believes in giving her guests special attention. The result is that the establishment is not only charming, but gives very personal service. Not surprisingly, the Fairholme has many repeat visitors.

Kingsley Club
Bathsheba
Barbados
West Indies
(809) 433-9422/433-9558

Barbados

Historic inn; 8 units; Inexpensive/ Inexpensive EP;
Credit cards accepted; Children ok; Smoking ok.

Location: Across from beach; near town; 12 mi. to airport.

Located in the foothills of Bathsheba, on the north end of the island, the Kingsley Club offers picturesque views of the rugged Atlantic shoreline. This stretch of wide and rocky beach that meets with pastoral, green hills and trees is reminiscent of English coastal areas and brings a different kind of Caribbean charm to this historic inn.

Built as a plantation family's dwelling in 1800, the inn has a tranquil feel on its lawn-covered hilltop site surrounded by two acres of landscaped gardens and trees. The white structure with green, pitched roof and green awnings is neat and unassuming. A flight of stairs leads to the dining area and reception area. The dining room, offering an interior area and a sunporch section with beautiful ocean views, is very charming and renowned for its homemade cuisine. The white wicker chairs and loveseats are covered in quaint Laura Ashley prints of blue, and the white wicker tables boast pretty burgundy and white Laura Ashley print coverings with contrasting napkins and little bouquets of fresh flowers. The feeling is turn-of-the-century and relaxing, and the establishment's popularity is revealed in the busy luncheon trade that dines on four courses, homemade soup through pie.

An old-fashioned feeling of hospitality is also in the lodging end of the inn. The decor is a blend of simple, but clean, contemporary and rattan furnishings. The eight guestrooms, located along a long corridor, all have the same spectacular views of famous Cattlewash Beach and similar furnishings. Guest accommodations include four double-bed rooms with private baths, wooden floors with area rugs and tropical print fabrics, three "double-double rooms" with similar furnishings and one suite with a sitting area. All of the modest, but pleasant rooms are air cooled by the ever-present hilltop breezes.

The friendly staff and owners of the Kingsley Club, Loris and Sherry Arevian, make the inn a special place to stay where the guest may enjoy a peaceful getaway and some homestyle dining.

Caribbean Bed & Breakfast

The Ocean View
Hastings, Barbados
West Indies
(809) 427-7821

Historic inn; 40 units; Moderate-Exp./ Moderate EP; Credit cards accepted; Children ok; Smoking ok.

Location: On beach; 2 mi. to town; 8 mi. to airport.

The Ocean View is one of the oldest hotels in Barbados, founded in 1901, and is known for its old world charm and courteous service. The staff of 57 has an average length of service of 17 years; the two Bajan head cooks boast over 30 years of employment at the inn. The pink and white, gracious colonial house on the ocean transmits a traditional elegance throughout.

The 40 guestrooms at Ocean View are all different, some small and intimate, others spacious and airy. Some of the guest accommodations are furnished in the original mahogany antique beds and armoires, while others are decorated in rattan and island furnishings. All of the guestrooms have private baths, air conditioning and polished wooden floors. A few of the units offer views of the sea and quaint detailing such as petal design cut-outs over the doorways. The guest accommodations, on the second floor, are reached by a beautiful mahogany staircase off the parlor.

The main parlor offers an attractive assortment of antique furnishings, a stately grandfather clock, fresh floral arrangements and comfortable seating. The "Crystal Room," named so because of the impressive crystal chandelier hanging from the carved-beam ceiling, has more intimate seating with pastel print couches, antique tables and a large, formal antique dining room set. Tasteful oil paintings hang throughout the small hotel.

The dining room of the hotel has an almost boat-like feel as it reaches out to the dramatic sea. White tables and chairs, various antique tables and sideboards give the room a period feel, while the white lattice ceiling and arches offer an airy atmosphere. The hotel holds a Sunday Planters' Luncheon Buffet, a hotel tradition for many years, with Bajan specialties such as flying fish, pepperpot and callaloo soup. All three meals are offered at the hotel.

Guests here may enjoy the pretty white sand beach or a protected natural coral pool. A cocktail bar with piano offers a relaxing atmosphere adjacent to the restaurant.

To illustrate the personal attention offered by the staff at Ocean View, a few of the regular services include beds turned down at night, shoes shined while you sleep, room service and gracious table service such as vegetables passed in elegant silver dishes.

Sam Lord's Castle
St. Philip, Barbados
West Indies
(809) 423-7350
(800) 228-9290

Historic inn; 259 units; Expensive/ Moderate EP;
Credit cards accepted; Children ok; Smoking ok.

Location: On beach; 14 mi. to town; 7 mi. to airport.

At the core of this 72-acre resort is the well-known Sam Lord's Castle completed in 1833 and built by Sam Lord, a villainous pirate who lured ships to their destruction on a Bajan reef and then plundered their riches. The magnificent castle boasts a ceiling copied from Windsor Castle by English craftsmen, rooms full of Chippendale furniture and priceless antiques and paintings. The entire downstairs is kept museum-like and is a popular tourist destination in Barbados. Non-guest admission, which is refundable with a purchase at any of the gift shops or restaurants on the grounds, is charged.

After Sam Lord's death in 1844, the castle remained a residence until the 1900's when it was first used as a hotel. The Marriott Corporation bought Sam Lord's in 1972 and has since developed the then 30-unit inn to a 259-unit resort. Only 11 guestrooms are offered in the castle itself, all reflecting the

Caribbean Bed & Breakfast

charm of an 18th-century castle and decorated in canopies and antiques. The rest of the accommodations are located around the very lovely garden grounds in contemporary hotel structures with typical, modern furnishings. Also around the luscious acreage are three pools, game rooms, seven tennis courts, beauty shops, gift shops, five restaurants and more. A private sandy beach is just a few steps away.

18

Trinidad and Tobago

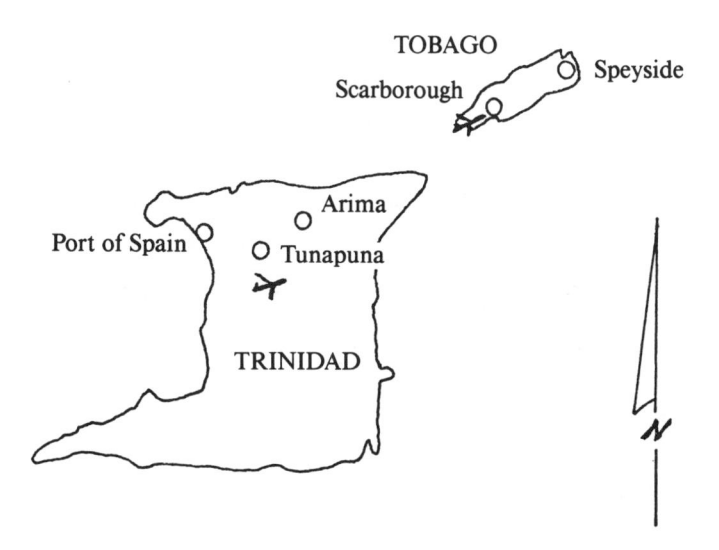

Caribbean Bed & Breakfast

The two-island country of Trinidad and Tobago in the southernmost portion of the Eastern Caribbean offers an incredible mixture of geography, cultures and abundant wildlife. A wide variety of daily airline flights arrive on the islands from North America, and plentiful inter-island flights connect the islands with other islands in the Caribbean and South America. Cruise ships call regularly here as well. Visitors to Trinidad and Tobago do need a valid passport and an on-going or return ticket for entry.

Getting around the two islands can be accomplished by buses which are inexpensive and by taxis which are plentiful and marked by an "H" on the license plate. Rental cars are also available, and U.S. visitors may drive up to 90 days on their license. Driving is on the left side of the road.

The monetary unit is the Trinidad and Tobago dollar, but larger hotels will honor credit cards and traveler's checks as well. The electrical current is 115 or 230 volts, so be sure to check before using American appliances. English is the main language of the two islands, but French, Spanish and even Chinese and Hindi can be heard. Trinidad and Tobago are on Atlantic Standard time all year, which gives them the same time as the East Coast during Daylight Savings months.

The tropical temperatures on Trinidad and Tobago average 74 degrees at night and 84 degrees during the day year-round. Trade winds keep even the warmest days comfortable.

For additional information on Trinidad and Tobago, contact:
Trinidad and Tobago Tourist Board
400 Madison Avenue, Suite 712-14
New York, New York 10017
(212) 838-7750

Trinidad

Roughly rectangular in shape, Trinidad is approximately 50 miles long and 37 miles wide. Its over one million inhabitants create an interesting international ambience with African, British, Spanish, Portuguese, Chinese, French and East Indian nationalities all represented on the island.

Christopher Columbus discovered the lush, green island with golden sands in 1498 on his third voyage and named it after the three prominent mountain peaks on the southeast coast and after

Trinidad and Tobago

the Holy Trinity. In 1523 the Spanish established their first settlement here as a base for gold expeditions, which also brought England's Sir Walter Raleigh to Trinidad. Raleigh did not find gold, but used the asphalt from Pitch Lake to caulk his ships. Angostura Bitters, Trinidad's contribution to the drinking world, was brought to Trinidad for commercial production, where it still is produced—its formula a guarded family secret.

Port of Spain is both the capital of the Republic of Trinidad and Tobago and the largest city in Trinidad. The city, whose population is a mixture of over 40 races, represents a blend of old and new structures—Victorian gingerbread houses nestled among modern skyscrapers. Frederick Street is the main shopping area with local handicrafts, boutiques and Oriental bazaars. At the north end of Frederick Street is the National Museum and Art Gallery with displays of the dazzling Carnival costumes, and nearby are the Botanic Gardens and Emperor Valley Zoo with tropical plants and local wild animals.

Historical sights around the island include the 1804 Fort George with its panoramic views; Fort Picton; Gasparee Caves, known for its interesting stalactites and stalagmites; and River Estate, one of the island's greatest sugar cane plantations, which later became a center for agricultural experimentation.

The Queen's Park Savannah, in the foothills of the Northern Range, comprises 200 acres of racecourse, football, hockey and cricket areas, along with magnificent tropical trees and plants. The African tulip tree found here is called the "flame of the forest." Near here are elaborate gingerbread-draped mansions, now official residences and offices, and the Queen's Hall, a modern cultural center.

Wildlife abounds in Trinidad; the continental origin from and proximity to South America has resulted in the unusually diverse fauna. The species list includes 108 mammals, 400 birds, 55 reptiles, 25 amphibians and 617 butterflies. The Asa Wright Nature Center at Spring Hill Estate was founded to provide a recreation and tropical wildlife study area. Spring Hill is a cocoa-coffee-citrus plantation surrounded by an impressive rain forest. A special Christmas tour of the Center is conducted each year and features an annual Audubon Society Bird Count.

The Caroni Bird Sanctuary with acres of marshland and mangroves also has flocks of Scarlet Ibis and is close to Pitch Lake, which produces asphalt for roadmaking exported all over the

Caribbean Bed & Breakfast

world. Horlis Reservoir and Cleaver Woods Park near Sangre Grande provide a scenic drive through lush, tropical jungle. Northeast from here is beautiful Balandra Bay; south from Sangre Grande is the spectacular Cocal with miles of coconut trees that canopy the road and granting views of the ocean to one side and dense, colorful tropical vegetation to the other side. The scenic drive leads to Mayaro Bay with palm trees, wide sandy beach and blue-green water.

Nightlife in Trinidad includes plenty of places to dine, drink and listen to steel band and calypso music and watch limbo dancing. Calypso began in Trinidad and the witty verses can be heard everywhere on the island. Steel bands also originated from Trinidad and Tobago and are capable of playing any style of music. The cuisine on the island is as international as its people—Chinese, Indian, creole, French, Italian, continental and local dishes. Local specialties include Callaloo soup (a mixture of crabmeat, okra and dasheen leaves), "pastelles of minced meat" (meat mixed with corn flour and wrapped in banana leaves) and exotic concoctions of rum, the national drink.

Carnival, held each New Year through Ash Wednesday, is called a way of life in Trinidad and Tobago; it combines spectacular colors, costumes and on-going gaiety. The costumes, music, parades and gala parties make the event a popular tourist attraction.

Monique's Guest House
114 Saddle Road
Maraval
Trinidad
West Indies
(809) 629-2233

Guest house; 7 units; Inexpensive EP year-round;
No credit cards; Children ok; Smoking ok.

Location: Near town; 15 mi. to beach; 19 mi. to airport.

Michael and Monica Charbonne have opened their quaint and tidy suburban family home to guests in the luxuriant Maraval Valley, just a few minutes away from Port-of-Spain. The Charbonnes are most hospitable hosts who make sure "the guest becomes a member of the family upon arrival." They offer seven

Trinidad and Tobago

simply furnished rooms, all with private bath, to guests. The guestrooms include some with carpeting, but all boast air conditioning, both hot and cold water and comfortable, clean surroundings.

Each guest at Monique's has full use of the house which includes television on the porch, a sitting room and a small gallery overlooking the lawn and roadway. One communal dining room has shared guest tables adding an "at home" feel. Homecooked breakfasts and dinners are provided at reasonable rates. Lunch is not available, but snacks are served on request.

The immaculate and informal guest house offers the use of a nearby swimming pool to its guests, and the innkeepers will happily assist in touring plans.

Also on the Island

Asa Wright Nature Centre and Lodge
Spring Hill Estate
Arima
Trinidad
West Indies
(no phone)

This former coffee, cocoa and citrus plantation is nestled in a rain forest within a wildlife trust. The conservancy area is also a study facility and refuge and boasts over 100 species of birds, including many rare inhabitants. The Centre is the locale of the annual Audubon Bird Count each Christmas. The lodge itself is a turn-of-the-century structure with rural warmth and simple accommodations with private baths. Guests here enjoy a homey living room and library appropriately decorated in bird illustrations and a dining room with ample, family-style meals. The rain forest surrounding the inn and reserve is lush with, not only wildlife, but also fruit and spice trees, ferns and tall bamboo. Rates with meals included are inexpensive.

Mount St. Benedict Guest House
Tunapuna
Trinidad
West Indies
(809) 662-3258

Eight hundred feet above sea level with views over the Caroni Plain and Piarco Savannah is a Benedictine monastery and right below it this peaceful guest house that once served as a religious retreat. The guest house is no longer a part of the monastery, but the hilltop lodging still offers the same solitude and natural beauty that made it an ideal retreat shortly after the turn of the century.

Mount St. Benedict Guest House lies less than ten miles out of Port-of-Spain on a Tunapuna promontory covered with hibiscus and oleander. The guest house is neat and clean and offers 11 rooms to guests. The rooms have comfortable yet spartan furnishings and sinks with cold water. The shared baths down the hall have hot water for bathing. Though not fancy, the guest accommodations are adequate and definitely restful.

The dining area has picture-window views of the valley and serves simple and ample local food, family style. A living room has comfortable seating. Guests may enjoy this tranquil spot with all meals included for inexpensive rates, which also include a homemade tea-time treat.

Tobago

Tobago, 116 square miles in area, is 20 miles to the northeast of Trinidad and can be reached by daily flights from its sister island. This tranquil island is known for its unspoiled beauty—its coconut tree groves, miles of uncrowded beaches and spectacular underwater reefs.

Tobago, also called the "Robinson Crusoe Island" as the legendary home of the famed character, changed hands repeatedly between the English, Spanish, Dutch and French and became a pirates' hide-out. In 1762 the British invaded and cleared out the pirates; Tobago later became prosperous as a sugar-producing island.

Scarborough is the chief port and capital of Tobago with a population of about 17,000. Homes cling to the hillsides and an exotic market takes place here. Fort King George, built in 1777, was constructed on half-hill and half-headland, which it shares with a lighthouse. The Powder Magazine of the fort still stands as well as the Bell Tank. Scarborough is also home to the Botanic Garden.

The hills of Tobago offer impressive views. Main Ridge runs almost the entire length of the island and reaches 1,800 feet at its highest point, giving dramatic views of bays, coves

Trinidad and Tobago

and beaches lined with palms, breadfruit, mango and banana trees. Of the many scenic beaches, Pigeon Point Store Bay, Turtle Beach and Mount Irvine Bay, which has an 18-hole championship golf course, are among the finest.

Nature-lovers may visit the crystal-clear Nylon Pool and Buccoo Reef in Buccoo Bay. Buccoo Reef comprises acres of breathtaking submarine gardens that display many different types of coral in all colors and shapes, various tropical fish and other creatures that create a haven for the scuba diver or snorkeler. Non-swimmers can enjoy the scenery through glass-bottom boats or by wading through the crystal-clear water.

Deep-sea fishing is also famous in Tobago. Kingfish, tarpon, crevalle, sailfish, marlin, wahoo and bonefish are popular catches.

A special visit from Tobago to the island of "Little Tobago," also known as Ingram's or the Bird of Paradise Island, is worthwhile. Off the northern tip of Tobago, it is the only place outside New Guinea where the birds of paradise exist in their wild state.

Arnos Vale
P.O. Box 208
Scarborough
Tobago
West Indies
(809) 639-2881

Inn; 28 units; Deluxe/Expensive MAP;
AE; Children ok; Smoking ok.

Location: On beach; 10 mi. to airport.

This small beach resort sits on a lush 400-acre estate filled with tropical gardens abloom with every possible local flower and quiet paths that lead to nowhere special, but everywhere serene and naturally beautiful. Once a sugar plantation, the inn, submerged in oleander and frangipani, has few remnants of those days intact. The complex on a hill now includes the main house with red roof and stone facade at the top of the hill, a few cottages nestled just above and the remaining rooms plus informal restaurant on the beach below at Arnos Vale Bay.

Caribbean Bed & Breakfast

The main house has attractive warm and comfortable furnishings in its guest lounge and lobby and contains the main dining area on the terrace with spectacular views of the bay. The English and local cuisine is excellent; all three meals are offered. Guests at Arnos Vale receive both breakfast and dinner as part of their stay. Occasional beach barbecues are held, and a more casual restaurant is located beach side.

Guestrooms at the inn vary in size and location: a few very nice accommodations are located in the main house, a few are nearby, and the rest are at beach level. All of the 25 guestrooms and 3 suites boast private baths and terraces and are decorated attractively in tropical prints and locally made furniture. Many of the guest accommodations offer superior views of the sea.

In addition to enjoying the picturesque swimming beach, guests may lounge by the swimming pool or use the inn's tennis court.

Blue Waters Inn
Batteaux Bay
Speyside
Tobago
West Indies
(809) 639-4341

Inn; 11 units; Inexpensive EP year-round;
No credit cards; Children ok; Smoking ok.

Location: On beach; 20 mi. to town; 29 mi. to airport.

The Blue Waters Inn received its name over 20 years ago in honor of the bright blue Atlantic waters that wash up to its sandy shoreline on pretty Batteaux Bay. The informal inn is located in a remote countryside setting on the northeast coast of the island, and its surroundings attract bird watchers from all over who find the property is also a sanctuary for Tobago's many species of rare birds.

Winding country roads through small, picturesque towns lead to the hilltop inn with views of the bay at its feet. The small hotel is formed of simple cabanas that were built in the 1950's as a teenage summer camp. Fred and Barbara Zollna run the

Trinidad and Tobago

hospitable and casual inn with 11 rooms and cabanas with simple decor and private baths.

The open dining room of the inn, with adjacent bar, serves fixed, daily menus, but with advance notice the Zollnas will provide for special dietary requirements. Blue Waters serves breakfast, lunch, dinner and light snacks.

Besides relaxing in the tranquil surroundings, guests may enjoy fishing, tennis, shuffleboard, scuba, skin diving and boat trips to Little Tobago arranged by the hospitable hosts.

Della Mira Guest House
P.O. Box 203
Scarborough
Tobago
(809) 639-2531

Guest house; 12 units; Inexpensive EP year-round;
No credit cards; Children ok; Smoking ok.

Location: ½ mi. to beach; ½ mi. to town; 8 mi. to airport.

The really special thing about this simple guest house overlooking the sea is its congenial hosts, Neville and Angela Miranda. The 1954-built West Indian home offers a pleasant staff and lots of personal attention to its guests who stay in the 12 guestrooms with private baths, hot and cold water and views of either the sea or the hills and historical Fort King George.

The Della Mira has provided family-style, budget accommodations to the staff of a few movies filmed on the picturesque island as well as accommodating the Prince of Hungary. The guestrooms and common areas are simply furnished but clean. The living room has a television and small bar for guests, and the guest house lobby is decorated with leafy plants and fresh flowers. The dining room with white wrought-iron seating and brightly painted walls has a lovely pool and garden view and serves all three meals as well as picnic lunches.

The grounds of the guest house are pleasant, the front area with a moon-shaped lawn and tall pine. To the right is the guest house's beauty salon run by Mrs. Miranda. A flowery hedge gives privacy to the guestrooms fronting the inn, and a rectangular-shaped lawn with flower garden makes up the rear of the grounds.

Caribbean Bed & Breakfast

A freshwater swimming pool is set within the garden, and an aviary with a wide variety of local birds is there as well.

Club La Tropicale is adjacent to the guest house; Della Mira's guests have automatic membership in the club with true West Indian ambience. The popular night spot provides dancing and the lively entertainment of steel bands and calypso on weekends. The guest house is situated conveniently 50 yards from the ocean and one-half mile from town.

Also on the Island

Coral Reef Guest House
Milford Road
Tobago
West Indies
(809) 639-2536

The Coral Reef is a simple, informal guest house about halfway between the airport and the steamer jetty. A short distance away is a pretty, coconut-lined beach. The 14 guestrooms of the modest guest house are air conditioned, have private baths with hot and cold water and are sparsely furnished but neat. The small dining room in green and white is airy and serves local dishes. An upstairs sun deck provides panoramic views and an occasional steel band for dancing. Double occupancy with breakfast included is inexpensive. Your gracious hostess is Cora Murray.

Mount Irvine Bay Hotel
P.O. Box 222
Tobago
West Indies
(809) 639-8871

On the site of a former sugar mill plantation, this sprawling, luxury resort still boasts the old sugar mill that is now an open bar and delightful dining terrace. The tropical landscaped grounds offer 64 guestrooms in a two-story building overlooking the sea and the professional golf course as well as

Trinidad and Tobago

23 cottages around the grounds. All of the accommodations are attractively decorated in contemporary furnishings and coordinating tropical prints. The carpeted rooms feature modern, private baths and relaxing terraces. The cottages offer two-bedroom suites with private patios. The hotel has a lovely pool with a swim-up bar alongside the Sugar Mill Restaurant, an adjoining 18-hole golf course (guests play at reduced fees), two tennis courts, a shopping arcade and a palm-shaded beach with bar. Rates are expensive during off-season and deluxe on-season on the MAP.

19

Netherlands Antilles

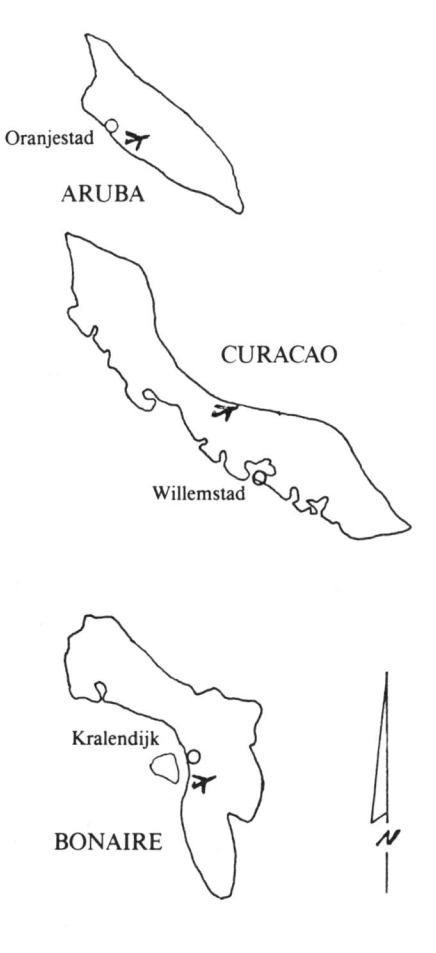

Caribbean Bed & Breakfast

Not far off the coast of Venezuela lie the three "ABC" islands—Aruba, Bonaire and Curacao—that constitute the southern complement of the Netherlands or Dutch Antilles Islands. The other Caribbean Dutch islands of Saba, St. Eustatius and St. Maarten form what is called the Dutch Windward Islands.

These three small islands reflect their Dutch heritage in the interesting 18th-century architecture and old-world charm that abounds, in contrast to the modern gambling casinos and popular international shopping also there. Dutch is the official language of the islands, but the local dialect of "Papiamento" is most prevalent in these islands. This dialect evolves primarily from Spanish, Dutch, Portuguese and some African, English and French. Most of the 232,000 population also speak English and Spanish.

The currency of the three islands is the Netherlands Antillean guilder or florin. U.S. dollars and credit cards are also accepted widely. The electrical voltage on the islands is the same or compatible with U.S. appliances. The Netherlands Antilles are on Atlantic Standard Time all year. When the East Coast is on Daylight Saving Time, the time is the same in both locations.

The government of these Netherlands Antilles is the same as the Dutch Windwards, the six islands collectively forming the Netherlands Antilles and being members of the Kingdom of the Netherlands. The Queen is the sovereign of the Kingdom and is represented by a Governor appointed by her.

Aruba

Aruba is the most western of the Leeward group of the Netherlands Antilles and measures 19.6 miles long and 6 miles wide. The dry climate, with only 20 inches of rain per year, and the always sunny skies yield only a slight change in the 83-degree weather from day to night. This dry, almost arid climate gives Aruba, as well as her two sister islands, unusual Caribbean scenery. A wide variety of cacti, rock formations and trade wind-sculpted Watapana trees create an Arizona-type landscape. The southwest coast of the island offers seven miles of pure white beach, lined with palms and bathed by calm, clear blue-green water. The northeast coast, on the other hand, is characterized by wild waves and a natural coral bridge carved by the sea's on-going rage.

Netherlands Antilles

After its discovery in 1499, Aruba was a part of the swashbuckling pirate era that followed. The Dutch ultimately took control of the island in 1816, and in 1824 gold was discovered, bringing riches to the island until about 1913. Evidence of the Gold Rush days is found in the abandoned mines that dot the sagebrushed countryside. Actually, it was "black gold" or oil that made Aruba prosperous. After the oil was discovered in 1924, Exxon soon established a refinery on the island.

Regular flights arrive daily in Aruba from the United States, and connections are available from South America, Puerto Rico and the Dominican Republic, among other destinations. United States citizens need to show proof of identity in the form of a birth certificate, passport or voter's registration card and must pay a nominal departure tax. Cruise ships serve the island regularly, and tourism is a large industry on Aruba. Getting around the island can be done by bus, taxi or rental car. Buses run daily between town and hotels, and taxis with fixed rates are available. Most American car rental agencies are represented, and only a valid U.S. license is required. Driving here is American-style, to the right.

Aruba's capital city, Oranjestad, offers some Dutch architecture, an active harbor and a few historic sights, such as Fort Zoutman and the William III Tower. But the capital town attracts most visitors because of its almost duty-free shopping. Merchandise imported from South America and all over the world as well as local handicrafts are for sale in the many shops with no sales tax charged and almost no duty. The Watapana Festival held here every Tuesday night is a colorful market place with local, reasonable island handicrafts and native foods for sale.

Exploring other parts of the island reveals that Aruba has some fine beaches, among those Eagle Beach and Palm Beach that are characterized by white sands and turquoise waters and the contrasting hotel-casinos that line the shore. Driving through the *cunucu* or countryside, the visitor will view modest, colorful homes with small, well-kept tropical gardens that are set against a background of windswept divi divi (or Watapana) trees, cacti and rocks.

Along with viewing the Natural Bridge on the windward coast, the visitor will see the unusual rock formations of Ayo and Casibari as well as the coves of Andicouri, Dos Playa, Boca Prins and Frenchman's Pass and the sand dunes of California and

Caribbean Bed & Breakfast

Prins. The cliff-perched Pirate's Castle at Bushiribana on the windward coast is a deserted gold mill, similar to the one found in the ghost town of Balashi. The village of Noord is known for St. Ann's Church with its hand-carved 17th-century Dutch alter.

The calm, clear waters of Aruba make all water sports inviting and popular. Palm Beach is one of the safest swimming spots around. Sailing trips are available on catamarans; deep-sea charter boats can be rented for the day or half of the day. Although Aruba has no professional golf courses, the Aruba Golf Club offers an unusual course with oiled sand greens.

Aruba's Las Vegas-type strip has five casinos with gambling and live entertainment, as well as several local nightclubs, discos and and dancing spots. Restaurants range from local Aruban establishments to fast food to fine eateries. The food choices are international with an emphasis on Chinese and French.

For additional information on Aruba contact:
Aruba Tourist Bureau
1270 Avenue of the Americas, Suite 2212
New York, New York 10020
(212) 246-3030

The Edge's
L.G. Smith Boulevard 458
Oranjestad, Aruba
Netherlands Antilles
(011-599) 8-21072

Guest house; 11 units; Moderate/ Inexpensive EP; AE,VI,MC; Children ok; Smoking ok.

Location: 50 yards to beach; 2 mi. to town; 10 mi. to airport.

The Edge's is one of Aruba's finest alternatives to the high-rise hotels that populate the shoreline. The small and secluded complex of intimate apartments offers the traveler a high degree of personal service given graciously by resident manager and owner Elizabeth "Betty" Johnson and her hand-picked staff who speak three languages. A good following of repeat clientele and an impressive guest book with comments acclaiming the hospitality of their hosts make the Edge's a special spot in the Netherlands Antilles.

The 11 apartments which face the ocean in the exclusive Malmok residential area are about a 10-minute walk from the Holiday Inn Hotel and Casino. The two 1969-built buildings with white stucco arches are separated by a pleasant courtyard "green" with lots of lounging area. A relaxing whirlpool spa with decking is adjacent and offers serene ocean views. Around the grounds are pretty little gardens and neat planters filled with tropical flora or cactus.

The current owners purchased the property in 1981 and completely refurbished with fresh paint, pretty white terrazzo floors, quality mattresses, air conditioners, new appliances and attractive outdoor furniture. All of the apartments at the Edge's are ground-floor level with private entrances, and all but one unit (the "Petite") have spacious, private tile or wood patios off sliding-glass doors and furnished attractively for outside dining. All of the units feature kitchenettes, many hidden cleverly behind folding French doors, with refrigerators, dishes, toaster, coffee pot and all the necessary utensils for cooking. The deluxe apartments offer king size beds and a separate sitting room with a double-bed sofa; standard apartments have twin beds.

The decor of the guest house, in attractive red and white or orange and white motifs, is pleasantly airy and immaculate. The modern baths are spacious and boast pretty tile and shower stalls. Clock radios are supplied in each unit, and color television may be had for a small additional fee per day. Complete maid service with linens is offered every day except Sunday and holidays.

A public telephone is located on the outdoor green between buildings as is an ice maker, laundry service and a bar with Dutch beer and soft drinks. Although no meals are offered on the premises, the thoughtful innkeepers at the Edge's make a habit of placing coffee, juice, beer, cheese and crackers in the refrigerator of all late-night arrivals.

Longer stays at the Edge's make the guest house even more reasonable than it already is with special rates for stays of a week or longer; monthly rates are available also. The Edge's also begins its off-season rates right after the Carnival in

Caribbean Bed & Breakfast

March, giving the traveler to Aruba a jump on the generous off-season.

Curacao

This island 35 miles off the coast of Venezuela is a miniature Holland, boasting the most interesting architecture in the West Indies. The Dutch influence on the 37-mile-long by 7-mile-wide Curacao goes back to the mid-1600's when the island was ruled by the Dutch Stuyvesant; the numerous forts and ramparts that protected the island are still evident. In 1915 one of the largest oil refineries was built here, turning the sleepy island into a teaming work and living place with Curacao becoming the most populated island of the Netherlands Antilles.

The countryside, reflecting the island's dry, sunny climate, offers desert scenery distinguished by three-pronged cactus, aloes and the divi divi trees molded by the trade winds. Dutch windmills, used for irrigation, are seen all over.

Daily flights from the United States arrive in Curacao, and connections are available to other parts of the Caribbean and South America. United States visitors need only proof of citizenship in the form of a passport, birth certificate or voter's registration card and must pay a small departure tax. Curacao is a popular cruise ship port; inter-island flights between Curacao, Aruba, Bonaire and St. Maarten are available on ALM. Also, a special ferry boat service departs each Tuesday from Curacao bound for Aruba.

Getting around the island can be achieved by taxis that carry official rate sheets according to destination, by bus, by sightseeing taxis and buses or by car rental. Good roads (with driving on the right side) and international signs make renting a car a good option here, and the major car rental agencies are represented.

The "storybook" village of Willemstad is not only the capital of Curacao, but also the government seat of the Netherlands Antilles. An unusual pedestrian bridge, Queen Emma, connects the two sides of the city that has grown on both sides of the picturesque canal. The bridge swings open for ships that pass more than 30 times a day. The immaculate streets of Willemstad are lined with 200-year-old houses in bright pastels with steep gables and red-tiled roofs. A walking tour of the old "European" city provides a remarkable selection of low-duty,

Netherlands Antilles

international shopping, as well as many reminders of its history. The Mikve Israel Synagogue with its fascinating Dutch Colonial architecture is located in the heart of town. Dating from 1732, it is the oldest synagogue in the Western Hemisphere. Fort Amsterdam, the site of the Governor's Palace and the 1769 Dutch Reformed Church, is also set in the Colonial town. Near the bridge is the Floating Market, a colorful display of docked boats from Venezuela and other Caribbean islands selling tropical fruits, vegetables and more. Fort Nassau on a hilltop offers great views of the town and houses an unusual restaurant built within the old ramparts.

The countryside or *cunucu* of Curacao displays towering cacti and rolling hills topped by historic plantation houses. Going east, the visitor can view the Amstel Brewery (the only beer in the world brewed from salt water) and the Curacao Liqueur Distillery as well as the botanical garden and zoo. Groot St. Joris is a coconut grove northeast of town where coconuts may be personally selected and then opened on the spot. Spanish Water, also to the east, is a popular water sport and yachting spot.

West of Willemstad is the bright yellow and white 1650 plantation house, Jan Kok Landhuis, now a restaurant. Boca Tabla has a dramatic grotto carved in the rocks and grants beautiful views of the north coast along this same route. The St. Christoffel Reserve Park here has beautiful flora and fauna with trails and contains the highest peak on the island at 1,213 feet, covered in wild orchids. Near here the Ascension Plantation, a typical restored landhuis (plantation house), is open to the public the first Sunday of each month.

The city of Willemstad becomes almost magical at night as soft lights illuminate the enchanting roof lines of the Dutch buildings and more dramatic lights overhang the main streets. Four casinos, several discos, international restaurants and some local "folkloric" shows are there for the enjoying. Many of the restaurants offer unique dining ambience, such as a historic landhuis with Dutch and colonial antiques or an ancient fort turned bistro with dark wood beams and stone walls. Popular dishes include "stuffed cheeses" and the Dutch adopted Indonesian delicacy, Rijsttafel, offered in some special dining establishments.

For more information on Curacao contact:
Curacao Tourist Board

Caribbean Bed & Breakfast

    400 Madison Ave., Suite 311
    New York, New York 10017
    (212) 751-8266

Avila Beach Hotel
Penstraat 130-134
P.O. Box 791
Willemstad, Curacao
Netherlands Antilles
(011-599) 9-614377
(800) 223-9868

Historic inn; 45 units; Moderate/ Inexpensive EP; AE,DC,VI; Children ok; Smoking ok.

Location: On beach; 1 mi. to town; 10 mi. to airport.

    This gracious, mustard-yellow colonial inn offers the best of what picturesque Curacao has to offer: architectural beauty, local charm and history, personal service, a secluded beachside location walking distance to town and ultra-modern facilties. In other words, the Avila Beach Hotel gives the traveler a very close look at the real Curacao without sacrificing comfort and does so at very reasonable prices.
    The Avila Beach consists of two buildings, both built in the colonial style. The older, two-story structure was built around 1780. This mansion was historically known as the Belle Alliance and served as a residence of Curacao governors between 1812 and 1828. It was converted to a hotel in 1949 and purchased by the present owner and director, Mr. F.N. Moller, in 1977. A gracious and enthusiastic host, Mr. Moller is a native of Denmark who has lived in the Netherlands Antilles since 1960. A five-year remodeling program has recently been completed at the Avila Beach under his direction.
    Driving up to the hotel, just a few minutes out of downtown Willemstad, you'll notice other mansions of similar vintage though not so well restored. The pretty Dutch colonial with white pillars and trim and small balconies under the upper windows is stately behind the circular drive bordered by well-manicured gardens.

Netherlands Antilles

The spacious lobby, used often for musical events and art exhibits, has attractive gold ceramic tile, rattan furnishings, a polished piano, wood-beamed ceilings and arched doorways. Lots of fresh flowers, overhead fans and brass lamp sconces filling the room with soft light, original Curacao watercolors and classical background music set the tone for this relaxing and charming spot. A small conference or banquet room (one of two offered) is located off the lobby area.

The lobby opens onto a quiet patio area that leads to the hotel's beach area and restaurant and bar. Miniature turn-of-the-century lampposts are scattered about here between the palms and planter-enclosed gardens. The bar, shaped like a schooner, overlooks the sea as does the Belle Terrace restaurant of the hotel with split-level dining. Tiny lights are hung from the pretty arbor above the restaurant's outside eating terrace. The Belle Terrace offers reasonable Scandinavian and local cuisine with an emphasis on fresh fish. Lunch and dinner are offered here along with a breakfast buffet served from 7 to 10 a.m. each morning.

Lounge chairs with tables for refreshments and thatched umbrellas for shade are positioned comfortably around the hotel's own small and protected beach that provides a pleasant and safe swimming or sunning spot. Large beach towels are provided at the front desk for guests' use. Also, a small sundry store is conveniently located on the back patio area.

While the Dutch and Curacao architecture has been carefully preserved on the exterior of the buildings, the guestrooms at the hotel have been totally refurbished and reflect a Scandinavian-modern decor. The contrasts are surprisingly pleasing and, as Mr. Moller explains, very practical. The sleek, neat look of the guestrooms includes polished tile floors, crisp white walls, built-ins hung off the floor for maximum cleanliness and air conditioning. The attractive decor has a different look in each of the individually designed rooms that are, likewise, all different in size and form. The windows are covered with a pretty striped canvas covering and original watercolors grace the walls of the rooms; some boast ocean views. All of the guestrooms have private, modern baths.

Despite the size of the Avila Beach Hotel it manages to convey the hospitality usually found in establishments much smaller. Its staff and management work hard to make it a relaxing, family-style hotel with a lot of repeat business.

Caribbean Bed & Breakfast

Bonaire

The coral-reef island of Bonaire, 5 miles wide and 24 miles long, offers an uncrowded alternative to touring the "ABC's." The desert-like landscape is notable for housing the beautiful flamingo, as well as 145 other species of birds in its southern area with a salt lake.

The island's brilliant blue-green water and sugar-white sand are matched by the brightly colored tropical fish that abound. This fact along with water visibility topping 100 feet makes it a haven for scuba and snorkeling aficionados. Note that the preservation-minded islanders do not allow spearfishing or coral collecting.

Bonaire was discovered in 1499 by the Spanish; the Dutch arrived in 1634. Salt mining eventually became a major industry on the island, and its production re-emerged in the 1960's along with tourism.

The island is a 15-minute airplane hop from Curacao, and a nominal departure tax is levied. Taxis with established rates are available as well as rental cars; driving is on the right side. No public bus system exists, but sightseeing bus and taxi tours are available.

Besides water sports and bird-viewing, visitors might opt for a cruise to the uninhabited island of Klein Bonaire for a picnic and beach excursion. Touring around Bonaire might include a visit to the capital, Kralendijk. This small Dutch town is bathed in pastel shades and offers some shopping bargains. The bay city has two churches worth viewing as well as the Instituto Folklore Bonaire with museum offerings. Fort Oranje here has an ancient cannon intact.

North and inland from the capital is Gotomeer, the location of a salt lake and some flamingos. Washington/Slagbaai National Park at the northern end of the island is a 13,500-acre game preserve with over 130 species of birds. Nestled in this cactus forest with coral rock formations are two lakes that are popular with flamingos and an excellent snorkeling beach, Playa Foenchi.

The southern section of Bonaire is made up of salt flats with the largest accessible flamingo nesting and breeding grounds in the world. Primitive stone huts once used by the salt workers/slaves have been rebuilt here by the government. The 1837-built lighthouse, Willemstoren, is on the way south from here to Lac Bay, an excellent reef-protected swimming and snorkeling spot.

Netherlands Antilles

One casino at the Hotel Bonaire supplies most of the nightlife on the island other than an occasional local show or beach barbecue, often held at the same location.

For more information on Bonaire contact:
Bonaire Tourist Board
1466 Broadway, Suite 903
New York, New York 10036
(212) 869-2004

Carib Inn
JA Abraham Boulevard 46
Bonaire
Netherlands Antilles
(011-599) 7-8819

Guest house; 7 units; Inexpensive/ Inexpensive EP; AE; Children ok; Smoking ok.

Location: On beach; near town; 1 mi. to airport.

Bonaire's attraction as a diving locale makes this small inn's appeal especially inviting to diving aficionados. Located on the premises of the Carib Inn is its own dive shop with a full selection of gear for sale and rental equipment. The inn's dive boats dock right at the private pier, and special reef trips to exclusive sites are offered. When weather permits, the inn takes guests with a lot of experience on "wreck" diving expeditions.

Built as a private house in 1968, the Carib Inn was converted in 1979 to an intimate dive resort by Bruce Bowker, the owner and personal host at Carib Inn. The economy-minded rooms have shared baths and overlook the swimming pool and patio. Two large upstairs rooms can form a suite and offer a balcony with ocean views. Maid service is offered Monday through Friday. Although no meals are offered at the inn, kitchenettes with refrigerators and electric kettles are available. Restaurants and shops are within walking distance.

Bruce Bowker personally runs the informal inn, giving each guest his attention and knowledge of the area, especially his diving expertise.

Reservation Representatives

American International Hotel Representatives
(800) 223-5695

American/Wolfe International
6 East 39th Street
New York, New York 10016
(212) 725-5880
(800) 223-5695

Anita MacShane (Fort Recovery)
302 West 12th Street
New York, New York 10014
(212) 924-7820
(212) 929-7929 (nights, weekends)

David B. Mitchell & Company
200 Madison Avenue
New York, New York 10016
(212) 696-1323

International Travel & Resorts
25 West 39th Street
New York, New York 10018
(212) 840-6636
(800) 223-9815

The Jane Condon Corporation
211 East 43rd Street
New York, New York 10017
(212) 986-4373

Nisbet Plantation Inn
613 Missabe Building
Duluth, Minnesota 55802
(218) 722-5059
(218) 722-5046

Rawlins Plantation
111 Charles Street
Boston, Massachusetts 02114
(617) 367-8959

Ray Morrow Associates
360 Main Street
Ridgefield, Connecticut 06877
(203) 438-3793
(212) 697-2340
(800) 243-9420

Reservation Systems, Incorporated
6 East 46th Street
New York, New York 10017
(212) 661-4540
(800) 223-1588

Resort Villas International
30 Spring Street
Stamford, Connecticut 06901
(203) 965-0260
(800) 638-4794 (CT)
(800) 243-2654, ext. 260

Robert Reid Associates, Inc.
845 Third Avenue
New York, New York 10022
(212) 832-2277
(800) 223-6510

Rockresorts Reservations
(800) 223-7637
(800) 442-8198 (NY)

Scott Calder International
152 Madison Avenue
New York, New York 10016
(212) 535-9530
(800) 223-5581

Sontheimer-Hazlett Ltd.
25 W. 39th Street, Suite 1003
New York, New York 10018
(212) 840-6655

Tryall Golf and Beach Club
P.O. Box 3492
Alexandria, Virginia 22302
(703) 370-8377
(800) 336-4571

Index

Admiral's Arms Inn, 32–33
Admiral's Inn, The, 135–137
air conditioning, 21
airlines, 12
American International Hotel
    Representatives, 263
American Plan (AP), 27
American/Wolfe International, 263
Anchorage Hotel, 219–220
Anchor Inn, 114
Anguilla, 158–159
Anguilla Department of Tourism, 159
Anita MacShane (Fort Recovery), 263
Anse Chastanet, 215–216
Antigua, 134–135
Antigua and Barbuda Department
    of Tourism, 135
Arcade Inn, 73–74
architecture, 15–16
Arcos Blancos, 74–75
Arima, 239
Arnos Vale, 245–246
Aruba, 252–254
Aruba Tourist Bureau, 254
Asa Wright Nature Centre
    and Lodge, 243
Avila Beach Hotel, 258–259

Bagshot House, 229
Barbados, 225–238
Barbados Board of Tourism
    Office, 228–229
Basse-Point, 175
Basseterre, 133
Bathsheba, 225, 227
Bequia, 195, 205
Berwyn Inn Guest House, 230
Biras Creek Hotel, 130–131
Bitter End Yacht Club, 131
Bluebeard's Castle, 90–91
Blue Heron Beach
    Hotel, The, 137–138

Blue Waters Inn, 246–247
Bonaire, 260–261
Bonaire Tourist Board, 261
Boot's Guest House, 217
Bottom, The, 161
breakfasts, 18
British Leeward Islands, 133–160
British Virgin Islands, 119–131
British Virgin Islands
    Tourist Board, 120
British Windward Islands, 195–223
Buccaneer Inn, 121–122
Bunkers' Hill View
    Guest House, 91–92

Calabash, 212–213
Canario Inn, El, 75–77
Cane Bay Plantation, 105–106
Caneel Bay, 115–117
Cap Haitien, 53–55
Captain's Quarters, 163–164
Caribbean Tourism Association, 219
Carib Inn, 261
car rentals, 20
Casa del Frances, 85–86
Castaways, 220–221
Castries, 195, 214–215
Cayman Islands, 35–39
Cayman Islands Department
    of Tourism, 37
Charela Inn, 44–45
Charlestown, 133
children, 20, 27
Christ Church, 225
Christiansted, 87, 107
clothing, 21
Club Comanche, 114
Cobblestone Inn, The, 197–198
Coconut Beach Hotel, 204
Coconut Hill Hotel, 157–158
Condesa Inn, La, 77–78
Continental Plan (CP), 26

Convento, El, 78–79
Copper and Lumber
    Store, The, 138–140
Coral Reef Guest House, 248
Cotton House Hotel, 207
Crane Beach Hotel, The, 230–232
Cranston's Antique Inn, 164–165
credit cards, 27
cruises, 12–13
Cruz Bay, 87
Curacao, 256–258
Curacao Tourist Board, 257–258

David B. Mitchell and Company, 263
Della Mira Guest House, 247–248
De Montevin Lodge Hotel, 50
Dieppe Bay, 133
Dominica, 218–219
Dominican Republic, The, 67–70
Dominican Tourist Information
    Center, 69
Doncella 109, 79–80
Dutch Windward Islands, 161–173

Eastern Caribbean Tourist
    Association, 142, 196
Eaton Hall Great House, 45–46
Eden Rock, 190
Edge's, The, 254–256
Erma Eldemire's Guest House, 37–38
European Plan (EP), 26

Fairholme Hotel and
    Apartments, 233–234
Fairview Inn, 143–145
Florencia Guest House, 159–160
Fort Burt Hotel, 127–128
Fort-de-France,175, 177
Fort Recovery, 122–123
Frederiksted, 104–105
French Government Tourist
    Office, 177
French West Indies, 175–193
French West Indies
    Tourist Board, 177
furnishings, 16–17

Galleon House, 92–94
Gingerland, 133
Golden Lemon, The, 145–146
Golden Rock Estate, 150–151
Gosier, 175

Grand Cayman, 36–37
Grand Hotel Oloffson, 56–58
Grand Turk, 29
Grand View Beach Hotel, 198–201
Green Parrot Inn, 216–217
Grenada, 207–209
Grenada Tourist Office, 209
Grenadines, The, 196, 204–205
Guadeloupe, 184–186
guest houses, 26
Gustavia, 175, 189

Haiti, 53–65
Haiti National Office
    of Tourism, 55-56
Hanover Parish, 48
Harbor View, 94–95
Hastings, 225
Heron Hotel, The, 201–202
Hibiscus Hotel, 190–191
historic inns, 26
Horny Toad, The, 170–171
Horse Shoe Bay, 209–210
Hostal Nicolas de Ovando, 69–70
Hosteria del Mar, 80–82
Hotel Astra, 46–47
Hotel Bois-Joli, 188–189
Hotel Bristol, 183–184
Hotel Castilla, 70
Hotel 1829, 95–97
Hotel Frangipani, 205–206
Hotel Mont Joli, 58–59
Hotel Roi Christophe, 59–60
Hotel Splendid, 61–63
Hotel Victoria, 184
Huldah Sewer's Guest House, 117

Inn at English Harbour, The, 141
Inn at Mandahl, The, 97–99
inns, 26
Inter-Island Hotel, 160
International Travel and Resorts, 263
island-hopping, 12
Island View Guest House, 99–100

Jacmel, 53–55
Jamaica, 41–51
Jamaica Tourist Board, 43–44
Jane Condon Corporation, The, 263

Kingsley Club, 234–235
Kingston, 41–43

Kingstown, 195, 197
Kingstown Park Guest
  House, 202-203
Le Manoir Alexandre, 64
Le Picardie, 60
Les Saintes, 175, 188
Little Dix Bay, 131
Lodge Hotel, The, 106-108
Long Bay Beach Resort, 123-124
Long Bay Hotel, 141
Luquillo Beach, 71-73

Maison Greaux Guest
  House, 100-101
Mandeville, 41-43
Manoir de Beauregard, 178-180
Maraval, 242
Mariner's Inn, 204
Martinique, 177-178
Mary's Boon, 166-167
Mary's Fancy Hotel, 168-169
meals, 26
medical concerns, 21
Miller Manor Guest House, 101-102
Modified American Plan (MAP), 27
Monique's Guest House, 242-243
Montego Bay, 41-43
Montpelier Plantation Inn, 151-153
Montserrat, 156-157
Montserrat Tourist Board, 157
Moorings-Mariner Inn, 128
Mooshay Bay Publick House, 172-173
Mount Irvine Bay Hotel, 248-249
Mount St. Benedict Guest
  House, 243-244
Muriel's Guest House, 156
Mustique, 195, 205

Negril Beach, 43
Netherlands Antilles, 251-261
Nevis, 142, 149-150
Nisbet Plantation Inn, 153-154, 263

Ocean Terrace Inn, 148-149
Ocean View, The, 236-237
Ocho Rios, 41-43
off-season, 19, 26
Olde Yard Inn, 129-130
Old Gin House, The, 172-173
Old Manor Estate, 154-155
on-season, 19, 26

On the Square, 149
Oranjestad, 251, 253
Orchid Hill Guest House, 50-51
Oyster Pond Yacht Club, 171
packing, 22
Papillote, 221-222
Parador Martorell, 82-83
Parador Oasis, 85
Pasanggrahan Royal Guest
  House, 169-170
Petionville, 53-55
Philipsburg, 161, 166
Pink Fancy, 108, 110
Plantation de Leyritz, 180-182
plantations, 26
Plymouth, 133, 157
Port Antonio, 41-43
Port-au-Prince, 53-55
Prince Hotel, 61
Puerto Plata, 53-55
Puerto Rico, 71-86
Puerto Rico Tourism Company Office
  (Government of), 73

rates, 26
Rawlins Plantation, 147-148, 263
Ray Morrow Associates, 263
Relais du Moulin, 186-187
reservation representatives, 263
reservations, 19-22
Reservation Systems, Inc., 263
Resort Villas International, 263
Richmond Hill Inn, 51
Road Town, 119-121
Robert Reid Associates, Inc., 263
Rockley, 230
Rockresorts Reservations, 264
Roseau, 195, 218
Ross Point Inn, 210-211
Royal Dane Hotel, 110-111
Runaway Bay, 41-43

Saba, 162-163
Saint Aubin Hotel, 182-183
St. Barthelemy (St. Barts), 189
St. Croix, 104-105
Sainte-Anne (Guadeloupe), 185
Sainte-Anne (Martinique), 178
St. Eustatius, 171-172
St. George's, 195, 208-209

St. Jean, 189
St. John, 115
St. John's, 133
St. Kitts, 142–143
St. Kitts and Nevis Tourist Board, 142
St. Lucia, 213–215
St. Lucia Tourist Board, 215
St. (Sint) Maarten, 166
St. Maarten, Saba and St. Eustatius Tourist Office, 162
St. Martin (French), 192–193
St. Philip, 225
St. Thomas, 89–90
St. Vincent, 196–197
Salt Raker Inn, 31
Sam Lord's Castle, 237–238
San German, 71–73
San Juan, 71–73
Santo Domingo, 53–55
Santos Guest House, 65
Scarborough, 239, 244
Scott Calder International, 264
Scout's Place, 165–166
Sebastian's on the Beach, 124–126
Secret Harbour Hotel, 211–212
Selene's, 117–118
Serge's Guest House, 188
service tax, 26
shared baths, 21
smoking, 27
Sontheimer-Hazlett Ltd., 264
Soufriere, 195, 214
South Caicos, 30–31
South Cove, 38
Spanish Main Inn, 140–141
Speyside, 239
Spice Island Inn, 213
Sprat Hall Plantation, 111–113
Springfield Plantation, 222–223
Sugar Mill Estate Hotel, 126–127

Terra Nova Hotel, 47–48
Terre-de-Haut, 188
Tobago, 239–249
Tortola, 121
Tortuga Club, 38–39
travel agents, 12, 20
Treasure Isle Hotel, 128
Tres Palmas, 83–84
Trinidad, 239–249

Trinidad and Tobago Tourist Board, 240
Trinite, 175
Tropical Hotel, 192
Tryall Golf and Beach Club, 48–50, 264
Tunapuna, 239
Turks and Caicos Islands, 29–33
Turks and Caicos Tourist Board, 31
Turks Head Inn, 33

U.S. Virgin Islands, 87–118
U.S. Virgin Islands Division of Tourism Office, 89

Valley, The, 133
Vieques Island, 71–73, 85–86
Villa Beach, 204
Villa Creole, 63–64
Villa Santana, 103–104
Virgin Gorda, 128–129

water, 21
Willemstad, 251, 256–257
Windwardside, 161

yachts, 12–13
Young Island, 195
Young Island Resort, 207

Zetland Plantation, 155–156

East Woods Press Books

American Bed & Breakfast Cookbook, The
America's Grand Resort Hotels
Backcountry Cooking
Berkshire Trails for Walking & Ski Touring
Best Bed & Breakfast in the World, The
Blue Ridge Mountain Pleasures
California Bed & Breakfast Book, The
Campfire Chillers
Campfire Songs
Canoeing the Jersey Pine Barrens
Caribbean Bed & Breakfast Book, The
Carolina Curiosities
Carolina Seashells
Carpentry: Some Tricks of the Trade from an Old-Style Carpenter
Catch-of-the-Day — Southern Seafood Secrets
Catfish Cookbook, The
Charlotte: A Touch of Gold
Coastal Ghosts
Complete Guide to Backpacking in Canada
Creative Gift Wrapping
Day Trips From Baltimore
Day Trips From Cincinnati
Day Trips From Houston
Day Trips From Phoenix/Tucson
Drafting: Tips and Tricks on Drawing and Designing House Plans
Exploring Nova Scotia
Fifty Years on the Fifty: The Orange Bowl Story
Fructose Cookbook, The
Grand Old Ladies
Grand Strand: An Uncommon Guide to Myrtle Beach, The
Healthy Trail Food Book, The
Hiking from Inn to Inn: Maine to Virginia
Hiking Virginia's National Forests
Historic Country House Hotels in the U.K.
Hosteling USA, Third Edition
How to Afford Your Own Log Home
How to Play With Your Baby
Indiana: Off the Beaten Path
Interior Finish: More Tricks of the Trade
Just Folks: Visitin' with Carolina People
Kays Gary, Columnist
Maine Coast: A Nature Lover's Guide, The
Making Food Beautiful
Melancholy Bay, An Odyssey
Mid-Atlantic Guest House Book, The
New England Guest House Book, The
New England: Off the Beaten Path
Ohio: Off the Beaten Path
Parent Power!
Parks of the Pacific Coast
Race, Rock and Religion
River Reflections
Rocky Mountain National Park Hiking Trails
Saturday Notebook, The
Sea Islands of the South
Separation and Divorce in North Carolina
South Carolina Hiking Trails
Southern Guest House Book, The
Southern Rock: A Climber's Guide to the South
Sweets Without Guilt
Tar Heel Sights: Guide to North Carolina's Heritage
Tennessee Trails
Toys That Teach Your Child
Train Trips: Exploring America by Rail
Trout Fishing the Southern Appalachians
Vacationer's Guide to Orlando and Central Florida, A
Walks in the Catskills
Walks in the Great Smokies
Walks with Nature in Rocky Mountain National Park
Whitewater Rafting in Eastern America
Wildflower Folklore
Woman's Journey, A
You Can't Live on Radishes

Order from . . . **The East Woods Press**
429 East Boulevard • Charlotte, NC 28203 • (704) 334-0897
For orders only, established accounts and charge card customers may call our toll-free answering service:
(800) 438-1242, ext. 102   In N.C. (800) 532-0476

Travel Books from
The East Woods Press

Please send me the travel books itemized below:

Quantity	Title	Each	Total
	America's Grand Resort Hotels, *Fensom*	$10.95	
	Best Bed & Breakfast in The World—U. K. Edition, *Welles*	$10.95	
	California Bed & Breakfast Book, *Strong*	$ 7.95	
	Caribbean Bed & Breakfast Book, *Strong*	$ 9.95	
	Mid-Atlantic Bed & Breakfast Book, *Ross*	$ 7.95	
	New England Bed & Breakfast Book, *Ross*	$ 7.95	
	Southern Bed & Breakfast Book, *Ross*	$ 7.95	
	Subtotal		$
	Shipping		$ 1.50
	Total Enclosed		$

Prices subject to change

Send order to:
The East Woods Press
429 East Boulevard
Charlotte, NC 28203

ALLOW 4 TO 6 WEEKS FOR DELIVERY

Please send my order to:
Name _____
Street _____
City _____ State _____ Zip _____

My check for $ _____ is enclosed.

Or charge my MasterCard or Visa
Account No. _____
Expiration Date _____

For charge orders only, call our **toll-free** number: (800) 438-1242, ext. 102. In North Carolina (800) 532-0476. We will refund your money, excluding shipping costs, if you are dissatisfied for any reason.

☐ Please send me your **Free** book catalog.